The

Concordia Pulpit

for 1985

CONTRIBUTORS

Gerhard Aho
Fort Wayne, IN

Steven H. Albers
Kirkwood, MO

Hubert F. Beck
College Station, TX

George H. Beiderwieden Jr.
Decatur, IL

Victor A. Constien
St. Louis, MO

Edwin H. Dubberke
St. Louis, MO

Richard A. Eissfeldt
Chesterfield, MO

C. George Fry
Fort Wayne, IN

Oscar A. Gerken
Eustis, FL

Ronald H. Goodsman
DeWitt, IA

Rudolph A. Haak
Cambridge, MN

Otto C. Hintze
Crestwood, MO

Waldemar F. Hischke
St. Louis, MO

Oswald C. J. Hoffmann
St. Louis, MO

Frederick W. Kemper
Stevensville, MD

Frederick G. Klein
Charlotte, NC

Theodore J. Kleinhans
Appleton, WI

William B. Knippa
Austin, TX

Allen P. Kolkman
Oceanside, CA

Eugene L. Krentz
River Forest, IL

Bruce J. Lieske
Fond du Lac, WI

Curtis R. Moermond
Wilton, IA

Daniel G. Mueller
San Antonio, TX

John F. Niermann
Wichita, KS

Rudolph F. Norden
St. Louis, MO

Norbert C. Oesch
Bakersfield, CA

Theodore W. Schroeder
Mehlville, MO

Rex D. Spicer
Fenton, IA

Frank D. Starr
Lufkin, TX

Walter W. Stuenkel
Frankenmuth, MI

B. Dale Thomas
Utica, MI

Oswald F. Wagner
Portland, OR

Ronald W. Weidler
Tampa, FL

Dean O. Wenthe
Fort Wayne, IN

The
Concordia Pulpit
for 1985

Series B Gospel Readings

Publishing House
St. Louis

ACKNOWLEDGMENTS

Biblical references, unless otherwise marked, are from the Revised Standard Version of the Bible, copyrighted 1946, 1952, © 1971, 1973. Used by permission.

Scripture quotations marked TEV are from the Good News Bible, the Bible in TODAY'S ENGLISH VERSION. Copyright © American Bible Society 1966, 1971, 1976. Used by permission.

Excerpts marked JB are from THE JERUSALEM BIBLE, copyright © 1966 by Darton, Longman & Todd, Ltd., and Doubleday & Company, Inc. Used by permission of the publisher.

Hymn quotations from *Lutheran Worship (LW)*, copyright © 1982 by Concordia Publishing House, are used by permission.

Hymn quotations marked *TLH* are from *The Lutheran Hymnal*.

The quotation in "Personalizing Life" (The Nativity of Our Lord) is from *The Martin Luther Christmas Book*, translated and arranged by Roland H. Bainton. Copyright 1948 by W. L. Jenkins. Used by permission of The Westminster Press.

Quotations (2 Epiphany) from A. M. Hunter, *The Gospel According to John*, The Cambridge Bible Commentary, copyright 1965 by Cambridge University Press, are used by permission.

The quotation (2 Epiphany) from WHEN BAD THINGS HAPPEN TO GOOD PEOPLE by Harold S. Kushner is reprinted by permission of Schocken Books Inc. Copyright © 1981 by Harold S. Kushner.

Excerpts (3 Epiphany) from "The Hollowing of America" are copyright 1982 Time Inc. All rights reserved. Reprinted by permission from TIME.

INDEX

CONTENTS

How to Reach Through Preaching

Oswald C.J. Hoffmann

Reaching Through Preaching

George Gobel once closed his weekly telecast with the statement: "This program is being broadcast throughout the world to the armed forces— of our enemies!"

This unusual twist on a familiar stereotype might offer a serious reminder to the Christian church regarding its preaching. The purpose of Christian preaching— if it is really preaching in the New Testament sense of the term— is always a conscious reaching into the camp of the enemy.

Over the years it has been my privilege to preach occasional sermons in almost every kind of parish, to occupy the pulpit in a small rural parish in Minnesota and in an active urban congregation in New York City, and to speak to large audiences over the radio and at mass rallies. The nature of my work has given me many opportunities to observe preachers at work in various settings. Analysis of my own preaching habits, together with observation of the preaching habits of others, leads me to believe that the real struggle of preaching does not consist, primarily, in planning the preaching program, in finding time to prepare the sermon, or in developing more effective delivery, important as all of these considerations may be. Finding the point of closest contact with the enemy constitutes the real problem. Whether in the preparation of a series of sermons or of an individual sermon, all the rest seems to fall into a pattern once this problem has been solved.

The problem exists, whether one is preaching to a congregation that consists mostly of professing Christians or is delivering an evangelistic sermon to an audience of unbelievers. It is with the preacher whether he is preaching on the pericopes or on a series of free texts.

The preacher has to know who the enemy is and where he is to be found. He cannot be in the position of an American church body so aptly described by a distinguished visitor from abroad: "They fear the devil very much, but they do not know where he is."

The people sitting in front of the pulpit are not the enemy. In a theology that recognizes, as ours does, the basic depravity of human nature and the inability— the complete inability— of man in his natural state to please God, there lies a subtle trap for the unwary. The temptation is great for the preacher to identify the enemy and the camp he occupies. Yielding to this temptation, inevitably and often unconsciously, the preacher begins to develop an association between his attitude toward sin and his attitude toward the sinner— in other words, toward people. The result, if it cannot actually be described as hatred, turns out to be a real contempt for people that seems to be based on a theological fact. The fact— in this case, sin— is real. The mental construct is not based on the reality on which it appears to be built.

No theological truth that we espouse justifies contempt for people. It is impermissible to despise people, no matter how perverse their ways of thought and action, for whom, when they were yet enemies of God, Christ died. The death of Christ and His resurrection are the controlling factors in our approach to people.

Great is the preacher who on Sunday morning can reach out into the heart of a young woman who has borne a child out of wedlock because of her involvement with a young man who had no intention of marrying her, and of the young man, whose parents have provided a sorry home for him to grow up in, with the result that every now and then he goes on a drunk and occasionally winds up in the snare of a girl he has picked up in his drunken stupor. Great is the man who can reach out to such people with a hand that exposes the hatefulness of sin — their sin — and still conveys the warm touch of a man who loves them as people. A reach like that is the reach of Christ Himself.

Lutherans of America have become enthusiastic about missions. Our thinking appears to run something like this: "Think how we have developed since the days of Martin Luther! Of course, Luther's lack of mission-consciousness was directly traceable to the necessity of reestablishing the old but new faith, to frame planks for the building of future houses. Now, however, we have the time and opportunity to put Luther's doctrines to work in a New Testament outreach for souls."

With our growing enthusiasm for missions has come the development of a concept that has gripped the hearts of many in our church with a mighty grip. It can be described as a "love for souls."

"Love for souls" often gives every appearance, however, of being an abstract love. In the name of "love for souls" men can rant in the pulpit against people, in some cases even against individual people in their congregations who happen to have crossed their paths or their swords, as the case may be. All this, experience has shown, can become a part of the ministry of a man who is fully convinced that he is engaged in the great, universal, God-pleasing work of bringing in the sheaves. As much as any man, he is sure he is a lover of men's souls.

How does this conception of the ministry and of preaching square with that of St. Paul?

> For though I am no man's slave, yet I have made myself everyone's slave, that I might win more men to Christ. To the Jews I was Jew that I might win the Jews. To those who were under the Law I put myself in the position of being under the Law (although in fact I stand free of it), that I might win those who are under the Law. ... To the weak I became a weak man, that I might win the weak. I have, in short, been all things to all sorts of men that by every possible means I might win some to God. I do all this for the sake of the Gospel; I want to play my part properly (1 Cor. 9:19-23 Phillips).

Is this not the complete description of a reaching ministry? one that reaches for *people*? where the pastor is willing to put himself in the place of the people to whom he is preaching even as Jesus Christ, in a larger and higher sense that evokes our devotion, put Himself in the place of us all?

Yet there is the ever-present temptation for the ministry to assume the character of a professional career rather than of a personal mission. The symbol of the purely professional ministry is that impersonal "love for souls" that can so easily be the expression, with reverse English, of the preacher's contempt for, or his indifference toward, people.

People are not "souls." They are *people*. Because he was dealing with people, Paul was willing to put himself under the Law, though he was actually free of it. If he had not been weak — if he had never heard of a thorn in the flesh, and if he had been another Goliath — he would still have committed himself to the proposition: "To the weak I became a weak man, that I might win the weak." He would have become a slave, too, "that I might win more men to Christ." He had been a Gentile, he would still have become that Jew.

Can we say that we have a reaching ministry if our preaching gives no positive evidence of this same empathy this willingness to identify ourselves with the people — the sinful people — into whose lives we are trying to reach?

We are not in a handkerchief-war of diplomacy with the enemy. The mere fact that our preaching is meant to be a divine handshake with the people before us is sufficient indication that we do not regard them as the real enemy. Indeed, many of our Christians in the pew, I am convinced, are just as eager to communicate with the preacher as he is to communicate with them. Battling the enemy in his own life and badgered by the enemy's allies, the world and his own sinful nature (specifically that lower nature termed by Luther the "Old Adam," always a present possession alongside that new nature that is the Christian's real self by virtue of his being in Christ), the average Christian would love nothing more than to have God put a figurative arm around his shoulder through the words of the preacher.

The Enemy

The preacher who looks on the people in the pew as his enemies will often find them to be his enemies. We must recognize the real enemy if we are going to reach into his camp and make effective contact. What is it that has twisted people into a misshapen caricature of what God wants them to be?

You know the categories of evil as well as I do. I do not think that anyone has improved on the systematization of Luther that labeled the enemy as "the devil, the world, and our flesh." Yet I should like to submit that the real enemy is the devil.

In seminary days it may be possible to argue about the devil as if he were a theological abstraction cooked up by some theologian to explain the presence of evil. However, when you take up your pastorate in a congregation, you soon become convinced that the devil is not holed up somewhere in a dogmatics course. You see the devil at work, making use of the tendency of the world to follow the leader. When everybody else hangs up pictures, you are supposed to hang them up, too. When everybody else is giving way to the appeal of immorality, you find the young people of your community — and the older ones as well — giving way, too. The drift that characterizes a world that is all too ready to listen to the Prince of Darkness becomes a real problem for you. For no one ever yet drifted toward God, and the purposeful planning of an intelligent mind behind it all soon becomes apparent to you.

At the most unexpected times you discover that the devil has been hard at work in your congregation. Right under your nose jealousy and quarreling arise in your women's society just when you thought everything was going wonderfully. The voters' assembly erupts suddenly in a violent explosion that obviously has been building up for some time in a way of which you were quite unaware. The young people's group evaporates under your watchful eye at the very moment when you were planning a vigorous program of winning the lapsed from the confirmation classes of the last five years.

The devil's activity in the personal lives of your people constitutes one of the most vexing difficulties of pastoral ministry. Some of the greatest disappointments of your ministry result, not from the failure of a prominent member to support your fond dream of a new church building, but rather from the spiritual obtuseness and moral lapses of people from whom you had been led to expect greater things. The nastiness that underlies a pietism based on self-righteousness; the capabilities of the human tongue when it is realeased from its obligations to Christ; the lust of the flesh, the lust of the eyes, and the pride of life as they are exhibited in the lives of "good" church members — all these bring forcefully to your attention the reality recognized so graphically by St. Peter: "Your adversary the devil prowls around like a roaring lion, seeking someone to devour. Resist him, firm in your faith" (1 Peter 5:8-9).

What have you to offer people that will enable them to get rid of the tyranny occupying their lives and making a shambles of their existence? You really have nothing of your own that could do that. But you are the messenger of God, who most certainly can do it for them. You have come to proclaim — REVOLUTION AND VICTORY — in the name of Christ.

There will always be those in every community who will stand aside and complain, as they did at Thessalonica: "These men who have turned the world upside down have come here also" (Acts 17:6). Well and good! The world is upside down, and there is nothing to set it right side up but the Gospel that has been entrusted to us — the Good News of freedom through forgiveness in Christ.

Knowing the enemy and the country he has occupied, we have no alternative. Our work is cut out for us. We cannot be afraid of crossing people's prejudices. No apologies are necessary. No compromise is possible. We must — and shall — proclaim the will of the Lord whose ambassadors we are.

Men speak of religion today as if it were refined imbecility, as though it were a spiritual chloroform that people have to take until the sharp surgery of life is over. Far from that, the doctrine you and I preach is robust and brawny, shattering and upsetting ten thousand things that now seem to be settled on firm foundations. We proclaim, in short, the cross of our Lord Jesus Christ.

When we reach out to the camp of the enemy, it must be appparent to everyone in that camp for whom we speak. We do not speak for Him if we proclaim the kind of religion that is described by C. S. Lewis as "Christianity and water." He pays his respect to that kind of religion in *The Case for Christianity:*

> Very well, then, atheism is too simple. And I'll tell you another view that is also too simple. It's the view I call Christianity and water, the view that just says there's a good God in heaven and everything is all right — leaving out all the difficult and terrible doctrines about sin and hell and the devil, and the redemption. Both these are boys' philosophies.
> It's no good asking for a simple religion. After all, real things aren't simple. They look simple, but they're not.

The facts of our faith are deceptively simple. They are the crucifixion, the resurrection, and the ascension of our Lord Jesus Christ. When it preached these facts, if we read the Book of the Acts aright, the early church was extremely conscious of the activity of the Holy Spirit, molding and remolding the hearts of people through the power of the Gospel.

To relate these facts to the sin in the lives of his hearers — not to the sin in the lives of the hearers of John the Baptist, but to the sin in the lives of *his* hearers — is the task of the Christian preacher. You will notice the response in your hearers — indeed, you will see it on their faces — every time you relate the cross to sin as *they know it* in their own lives.

Relevancy, in this case, will take you every time to the atonement. You will not be able to avoid it. Herman Gockel told me that on the Hollywood set where "This Is the Life" was being produced, one of our actresses came to him with a question. She said, "Pastor Gockel, you always say that Christ died for our sins, and our sins are forgiven. What's the connection?"

That's the question you will forever be answering in your preaching: What's the connection? The connection in every case will be the atonement of Christ for sin and for sins. It is precisely the *hyper hemon* of the atonement, this "in our behalf," that provides release from that tight constriction around the hearts of the people, causing them personal anguish and keeping them from opening their hearts to God.

Has our preaching this New Testament emphasis? I do not ask this question in a spirit of suspicion toward my brethren in the ministry. I believe that our ministerium is exceedingly close to the realities of the faith. But even though we are agreed on the principle, it is always in place to question the reality of the practice.

Wherever in the Scriptures a preacher had to proclaim the necessity of duty, he always found its roots near the cross. Even the commonplace duties of the home drew power from the cross: "Husbands, love your wives, *as Christ loved the church and gave Himself up for her*" (Eph. 5:25). If St. Paul was talking about the solution of differences of opinions about nonessential matters, he went to the cross: "Do not let what you eat cause the ruin of one *for whom Christ died*" (Rom. 14:15). All of life is linked to the cross, to the crucified Christ. Every problem is attacked with the power of the Gospel. That was Paul's tool, and it is ours.

In one of his evening sermons, delivered on July 8, 1888, Spurgeon said that it "proved the divinity of our holy religion that it survived ministers." We can feel the condescension of God that makes us His messengers. We feel it even more when we refuse to be borne on the hands of angels like invalids and are not so worried about dashing our feet against a stone as about dashing against the enemy.

"Preach the Word," said a man of that stamp to a young man undertaking the ministry of the Gospel. "Be on the job in season and out of season." Preach the Word of God in the kind of style that you would expect from a man who is bought with the precious blood of Jesus and is reaching for Christian understanding and belief on the part of his contemporaries as well as for Christian attitudes and action based on that belief.

Reaching into the Hearts of People

In front of the preacher sits a congregation variously disposed to receive the message he is about to deliver. Here is an older woman, whose ruddy cheeks and pleasant manner tell you nothing of the drunkard whom she watches over day by day like a child, although he is supposed to be the head of the household. The preacher knows that she is going to tell him at the close of the service it was an excellent sermon, no matter what he has said or how he has said it.

On the other side of the aisle sits a girl whose pretty face is visibly strained with a desperate hope that this sermon will succeed. Next to her sits a young man who casts a knowing smile her way, as the congregation is seated after the reading of the text. The young man, a typical specimen of American manhood, faces the preacher with a certain air of wondering skepticism that amounts to a dare to reach across the gulf that seems almost to divide the pulpit from the pew.

The preacher, we have stated in the former part of this discourse, is attempting to reach into the camp of the enemy. These people sitting before him are not the enemy. Whether they are good Christians, or professing believers whose lives seldom seem to have been touched by the faith they profess, or even unbelievers who may have been drawn by what we might have to describe as curiosity but which in the language of the Holy Spirit might actually be something entirely different — the enemy is still the same.

The preacher knows the enemy, too. He has known him personally, because the preacher, too, is human. He is no angel nor, thanks to the Spirit of Christ that lives in him, is he a devil. That is why he has been called as a preacher, to reach forth what is in his heart to the hearts and lives of others.

Christian preaching—wherever it still reflects the spirit of the New Testament—comes from the heart of a man who has been touched personally by the compassion of God. He knows the reaching quality of divine compassion in Jesus Christ. He trusts Christ himself for personal salvation, with everything that it implies. He hasn't reached out for Christ. Christ has reached out for him. As the preacher mounts the pulpit, Christ is reaching out to him again for his heart and his hands in the Word He has given Him to preach to others.

I cannot imagine a Christian preacher whose inner being is not wrung to its core every time he proclaims that Jesus Christ "bore our sins in His body on the tree, that we might die to sin and live to righteousness" (1 Peter 2:24). More than any other thing, this has made him a preacher—that his own heart has been touched by the loving and compassionate appeal of the Gospel.

The church needs men today whose preaching makes it evident that they have been touched by this selfsame Gospel, regardless of how it is received. St. Paul did not mind having people point their fingers at him in ridicule. In fact, he was willing to take the same kind of judgment from his own congregation, as long as he had to take it *for Christ*. It appeared to him, you will recall, that the apostles had been ordained by God to bring up the rear of the procession, as men who were appointed to die in the arena.

> We are made a public spectacle before the angels of heaven and the eyes of men. We are looked upon as fools, for Christ's sake, ... You [the members of his congregation] have found honor, we little but contempt. Up to this very hour we are hungry and thirsty, ill-clad, knocked about and practically homeless.... Men curse us, but we return a blessing; they make our lives miserable, but we take it patiently. They ruin our reputations but we go on trying to win them for God (1 Cor. 4:9-13 Phillips).

It takes real men, who are willing to be known as the "world's rubbish," to keep on trying to win people for God in the kind of world in which we live. Thank God, there are men like this throughout our church body—and in other church bodies as well—whose ministry is more than the natural expression of an outgoing personality and whose preaching has a much greater purpose than to keep their hearers from getting restless for 20 minutes of a Sunday morning—men who love the Lord.

Men like that have a story to tell. They tell it as *news*, reaching for understanding and for faith on the part of the people to whom they preach. It is not wrong for the preacher to want his people to understand and believe. As a matter of fact, this yearning is a necessary ingredient of preaching, if it is to be effective.

Understand that the earnest intent of the preacher takes nothing at all away from the Holy Spirit of God, who must be at work if the human heart is to enjoy an enlightened understanding and is to be the repository of a vital faith in Christ. We certainly cannot tie the operation of the Spirit of God to good preaching or to the passion of the preacher. We cannot limit the work of the Spirit in the hearts of people even to the practice of preaching in the conventional sense of the term.

We can report, however, on the basis of a great deal of observation, that effective preaching is a powerful factor in effective congregational work. Effective preaching can help a pastor overcome the bad effects of other omissions and weaknesses in his pastoral work. I do not say that these failures may not catch up with him in time or that good preaching will excuse them. It is simply a fact, demonstrable by observation, that effective preaching is a vital part of an effective ministry.

Conversely, as the director of missions for one of our Districts pointed out to me, ineffective preaching can vitiate the results of a fine personal ministry. Pastoral work, bringing the pastor into personal contact with people, must be regarded as an important part of an effective ministry. "Still," said my mission friend, "the missionaries under my supervision can run their heads off canvassing their neighborhoods. They can make a good impression on the community through their personal witness to the Christian faith and through the expression of a pleasant Christian personality. They can be wizards at organization and reorganization. But if they can't preach, it never seems to amount to anything."

Effective preaching presupposes a conscious reaching on the part of the preacher for understanding. If this means anything at all, it certainly must mean that he wants people to understand what he is trying to tell them. What is even more important, he wants them to understand what God wants to tell them.

An intense desire to foster understanding on the part of the people of today is going to force the preacher to use the language of today. He needs to be aware of the various translations available today, and of their relative strengths and weaknesses. This is a routine prerequisite to understanding for the preacher who understands the original language of the text and is able to weigh confidently the relative merits of various versions.

The real problem of understanding arises when the preacher attempts to make clear to his congregation the great truths of our faith in the kind of language that will convey real meaning. Put yourself for a moment in the place of the man in the pew, who throughout the week may have had little contact with things spiritual (I am just describing his situation, not passing judgment on it). In the midst of an impassioned sermon, words like "grace," "sin," and "righteousness" whistle past his ears. He thinks he knows what the preacher is talking about, but he is not quite sure. Then, all of a sudden, the word, "justification" whips by. Now he knows for sure. He *doesn't* know what the preacher is saying.

There are some few inquirers who will insist on discovering the meaning of what they do not understand. Others will respond the way Leo Durocher did the first time he faced the youthful Bob Feller in spring training. After watching two fast balls split the middle of the plate without offering to strike, Durocher shouldered his bat and started for the dugout. The umpire called out to him that he had another strike coming. Durocher called back, "That's all right. I'm not interested any more."

Newsmen tell a story in such a way that people, ordinary people, will be interested and will try to understand it. Great newspapers like the *New York Times* have demonstrated that seeking understanding necessitates no loss of dignity in language or accuracy in reporting. It simply requires telling the story with a will to be understood.

However, the early church did not just tell its story to be understood. If we read the New Testament correctly, the first preachers told it as the *Good News*. They had a personal interest in the telling and in the way the story was received. They wanted people to believe, and that fact alone made all the difference in the world for their preaching. For them, preaching took the form of a conscious reaching for the understanding and belief of people, whatever other form it may have had.

In this connection, the revered teacher of homiletics, Dr. E. J. Friedrich, once shared an important truth about faith that we dare not forget in our preaching. If we think of faith too rigidly, he said, with our theological definition in terms of of knowledge, assent, and confidence, we are in danger of missing the most important point of all. "After all," said Dr. Friedrich, "the very essence of faith is that we find comfort in Jesus and everything that He has done for us and still does for us. The moment a sinner finds even a little comfort in Jesus, he has been converted and is a child of God. This may sound commonplace to you, but I had to learn it the hard way through my ministry to the sick and to persons who were spiritually disturbed and in their own opinion unable to believe."

Faith is the end goal of preaching. The final purpose of preaching is not to impress people with the histrionic attainments of the preacher, or to entertain people with lively stories that will hold their interest, or to build a large church that might give our church body a certain prestige in the community. The purpose of preaching is to bring people to faith — a warm, living, vital faith in Jesus Christ that will be translated into their lives and their characters.

That's why we preach the Gospel of forgiveness in Christ. Only the Gospel can accomplish what we hope to accomplish — and must passionately want to accomplish — through preaching: kindling and stoking the fire of faith in the hearts of people.

A pastor just out of the seminary for a year or two wrote to me:

The outstanding discovery I have personally made about preaching is this: The Gospel is the attraction, not the man the surroundings, the time. Of course, I realized this in seminary days, but now I know it for myself, that people knowingly or secretly long for good news from God. If we just let God say it...

Attitudes and Actions

Christians are not expected to act as blotters, continually sopping up and then drying up. Preaching does not fulfill its function if it does not recognize the obligation to point out this fact and to suggest practical

measures that will help Christians to acknowledge and fulfill their responsibilities as believers in Christ.

It is in this area that I hear the most criticism by the laity of preaching.
They are a loyal body of Christians not generally critical of our theology or
even of the quality of sermonizing to which they are subjected. They are
inclined, however, to voice the somewhat wistful wish that sermons were
"more practical." When you press them for an explanation of what they
mean by "more practical," it usually develops that they want to know how
the truth enunciated by the preacher affects them *personally*.

The question most lay people silently ask of the preacher is, What does
it mean to me? That question, if it is consistently unanswered, betrays the
fact that the preacher either is himself unaware of how Christian faith
works in the life of a believer, or has failed to reach in his preaching for the
attitudes and actions that ought to be the natural concomitant of a living
faith.

Advertising men say that an advertisement is not worth very much
unless it has a "hook" in it, that is, unless the reader, the hearer, or the viewer
thinks differently about the product being advertised and is willing to do
something about it. There is no pat formula for putting the "hook" into sermonizing any more than there is in advertising. But the preacher should be conscious of the fact that his sermon is more or less a failure unless it is there.

Anyone who has ever preached a sermon will have to feel somewhat
humble in discussing this aspect of preaching. All of us have had our
failures, and we might as well confess the fact. The mere confession is the
recognition of a problem and a promise to work at doing something about it.

A distinguished layman (one, incidentally, who does not make it a
practice to criticize his pastor) said to me, "I don't care to be told in
generalities of the joy and happiness of Christianity. I want to know what
joy and happiness it brings to me." This man is a receptive hearer, possessed
of a great deal of authentic Christian experience. All that is required on the
part of the preacher in instances like this is some authentic Christian
experience of his own and some Christian imagination to make the Gospel
relevant for the development of Christian attitudes and actions of the kind
that will be worthy of the faith we profess. This is no light task and demands
the best that is in a man who acts as a messenger of God.

What about the indifferent hearer? and the hearer who might just as
well be classed as indifferent, the one who thinks he knows it all? A friend of
mine, who retired from the ministry after long years of service, once put it
this way: "Our church has two problems, the people who have not been
Lutherans long enough, and those who have been Lutherans too long."
What he meant to say was that every preacher has the difficulty of "getting
through" to some people, and they are not all newcomers to the faith.

A young pastor in the Midwest, who has made the ministry his avoca-
tion as well as his vocation, was not minimizing proper Christian indoctrination when he stated to me that people who have learned the catechism
in their youth often prove to be "tough customers" in the matter of develop-

ment of good Christian attitudes that will result in proper Christian action. When the preacher, on the basis of God's Word, calls for attitudes and action for which their youthful instruction may not have prepared them, such people are often inclined to reason that he must be saying, in a different way, what they already know. When this reasoning fails, they feel compelled to disagree with the preacher. "This is not to say that they do not 'enjoy' fresh preaching," said my young friend. "They do. But they insulated themselves against it by assuming that all they can do is to 'enjoy' it, since they have been fully indoctrinated. Indoctrination is conceived of as the filling up of a jar of a given size. When the indoctrination is through, the jar is full, and all the preacher can possibly do is to stir up the contents a bit."

Another young man, just graduated from the seminary and serving a parish in an older Lutheran community in the Midwest, provided me with a typically Lutheran example of how he attacked the problem of the inured hearer. (I call it typically "Lutheran," because it is the way Luther handled the problem in so many of his sermons.)

> If I tell my people that they must "do all things to the glory of God," they snore on. But if I tell them they can slop their hogs and change baby's diapers and milk cows to the glory of God, not only are their eyelids raised but their eyebrows, too.

In his own way, this young man has pointed up the suggestion of J. B. Phillips:

> The preacher and the writer may seem to have an apparently easy task. At first sight it may seem that they have only to proclaim and declare, but in fact, if their words are to enter men's hearts and bear fruit, they must be right words shaped cunningly to pass men's defenses and explode silently and effectually within their minds. This means in practice turning a face of flint toward the easy cliche, the well-worn religious cant and phraseology, dear no doubt [I seriously question whether they are dear] to the faithful but utterly meaningless to those outside the fold (*Making Men Whole* [New York: Macmillan Company, 1956], p. 44).

In all likelihood, reaching the indifferent or hardened hearer constitutes one of the knottiest problems the Spirit of God faces within the church. We preachers can do our assigned share as God's ambassadors by remembering that our task is not only to comfort the afflicted, but also to afflict the comfortable. We can do our utmost to cut through the tough skin of habit and indifference in order to reach the Christian heart pulsating beneath — reach it with the compelling power of the Gospel for the shaping of attitudes and actions growing out of a new affection for Christ.

Someone has said that as soon as the preacher gives the impression of being clever, he is no longer the tool of the Holy Spirit. The other side of that coin bears a statement by Spurgeon:

> My brethren, there is more eloquence in love than in all the words that the most clever rhetorician can ever put together. We win upon men not so much by poetry and by artistic working of sentences, as by the puring out of a heart's love that makes them feel that we would save them, that we would

bless them, that we would, because we belong to them, regard them as brethren, and play a brother's part, and lay ourselves out to benefit them.

Of all the attitudes that Christians need to display today, I can think of none greater or more necessary than compassion. Actions originating in Christian compassion are bound to be right actions, whether they have to do with family life, congregational affairs, or the relationship between races. Compassion is the burden of our preaching—the everlasting compassion of God in Jesus Christ. Compassion is a goal of our preaching—compassionate attitudes and actions on the part of our people.

How is a great Gospel like ours to be preached if not in the spirit of compassion? If there is one thing we preachers need, it is the grace of compassion. We want to have the compassion to feel instinctively the need of people, and the compassion to understand their downfalling and their backsliding. If our doctrine is of the holiness of God, the horribleness of sin, the reality of grace, and the divine resources for regeneration and restoration —how ought we to preach it?

"A Gospel of infinite compassion," said J. H. Jowett in his sermon on the power of the cross, "must be preached in the spirit of compassion in which it was born. My brethren in the ministry, we need to pray, and to pray long and to pray fervently, that we may never become hard."

When John Wesley visited Newcastle-on-Tyne for the first time, he reports in his *Journal*, he encountered such blasphemy and such cursing, even from the mouths of little children, as he had never heard before. He had only one thing to say about it, "Surely this place is ripe for the Master."

Seeking a text to reach these people, Wesley picked the tenderest one he could find: "He was wounded for our transgressions; He was bruised for our iniquities." In the next paragraph he tells how, when he had finished, the people clung to his clothes and to his hands. He had brought them to the cross.

If we are to reach into the hearts of people, we must share with them this spirit of divine compassion. We shall be able to share it only if we ourselves live near the cross.

Sermons on the Gospel Readings, Series B
Three-Year Lectionary

Watch with Joy

FIRST SUNDAY IN ADVENT
MARK 13:33-37

Frederick G. Klein

"The universe we live in is dying." That is the rather startling word from the scientific community whose duty it is to watch the stars and planets of our universe.

A study published by American astronomers has caused quite a sensation among scientists worldwide. The report contradicts the widely held view of astronomy, the study of stars and planets, that our universe is constantly expanding.

This is not so according to the study. Instead, there is evidence to suggest that the pull of the sun is becoming stronger. In time the force of gravity will begin pulling celestial bodies together. It is believed that the sun will grow larger as it pulls the planets and other bodies of the solar system ever closer and closer. According to this scientific theory, our solar system is on a collision course with a fiery, explosive death! The study goes on to inform us that the shift from sailing away from the sun to sailing into the sun is even now taking place.

Now, before you greet this new theory by selling all your stocks and cashing in all your savings for one last fling before the end, hear the report through as it concludes that the coming fiery death of mother earth is predicted to be some nine million years in the future! Although that is not much time as astronomers see it, you and I need not feel compelled to spend this afternoon working up escape routes!

Watch

The report does, however, alert us to the truth of Jesus' words in Mark's gospel. "Take heed, watch; for you do not know when the time will come." In five short verses Jesus signals us to "watch" no less than four times. He wants to remind us that the earth will also die.

We, along with all living things, are destined to meet God in eternity. A day is coming when everything you see, everything you hold near and dear, will be no more. At that time all people will stand face to face with God.

Watch with Gloom

When we hear that the end of all things is near, our human nature becomes gloomy, doesn't it? A certain melancholy sets in. We can become depressed, fearful, apprehensive, even downright scared!

Visions of prophets of doom parade themselves before our eyes. We perhaps have the urge either to run away or to dismiss the whole subject with a fatalistic shrug of the shoulders.

Scripture explains the gloom or seasoned indifference we experience each time we hear that we are dying people in a dying world. It is caused by the fact of sin in human life. We are in rebellion against God and the way He wants us to live.

Confronted with the choice of living either in obedience to the commandments or by our own rules, we always make the wrong decision. And so we live with the ugly sense of guilt day in and day out. With Paul we confess, "I do not do the good I want, but the evil I do not want is what I do" (Rom. 7:19). "The wages of sin is death" is the Bible's verdict on our rebellion (Rom. 6:23).

We all feel the weight of that death sentence in our lives. Whether we choose to acknowledge it or not really doesn't matter. All too easily our lust and our greed show that we are paralyzed by sin. Like spoiled children, we want our own way, or we will throw a temper tantrum at God. Gossip or a spiteful nature that refuses to forgive is evidence enough that we do not live up to God's expectations for the human race. So we watch for the approaching end like a naughty child watching for his father's car to pull into the driveway — watching and waiting for the punishment that is sure to come.

The fear is only increased when we realize that by ourselves we are powerless to please our Father in heaven. Our rebellion has become second nature to us. As much as we would like to pass the blame for not measuring up to God's standards to others, we can't. Excuses that blame family, friends, background, or education for the trouble in which we find ourselves won't hold water. The problem with us is US! The problem is here — in the heart, in the mind, deeply embedded in our personality. Confronted with temptation, we yield to it more times than we would like to admit.

Watch! For what? Watch for the coming verdict of guilty? Watch for the approaching punishment, the coming exposure of our true selves before everybody? Watch for the coming gloom, the fiery destruction? No wonder we don't want to know when that time will come.

Watch with Joy

But wait a minute. Jesus Christ calls us to watch with joy, not with a foreboding dread. The intention of His instruction to watch is not to cast us down, but to lift us up. In the season of Advent we watch for Christmas and the joy of the announcement of the Savior's birth. Our Lord calls us to watch with the joy of children who watch for Grandmother to come for a Christmas visit laden down with gifts!

If we are to watch with joy as the end time approaches, we need to remember who is speaking in Mark's gospel. We need to remember what gifts He has given to us who believe in Him.

Jesus Christ is speaking in Mark 13 — the one who left the glory of heaven as God's Son and became a human being in Bethlehem's manger. He is the one who came to us as the son of a human mother to redeem us who were under the guilty verdict of the Law. He is the one who has made us sons and daughters of God.

Suffering and dying on the cross of Calvary. Jesus Christ has freed us from the verdict of death. He has ended the power of death over us and opened the gates of eternal life to all who by the Spirit's power bend the knee to His Lordship.

His Gospel is the good news of peace and wholeness, not a threat to bring dread and terror. As St. Paul writes, "Christ is the end of the Law, that everyone who has faith may be justified" (Rom. 10:4). As we confess our sin, God is faithful and forgives everyone of them in Jesus Christ. We stand in a close, harmonious relationship with God through the blood of Jesus Christ. Yes, "the wages of sin is death, but the free gift of God is eternal life in Christ Jesus our Lord" (Rom. 6:23).

Watch with Expectation

When we have abiding faith in Jesus Christ and rely on His promises, the end is not only the end. The end of time is really a whole new beginning in an eternity with God in heaven. We who watch for the end of this world with faith "wait for new heavens and a new earth" (2 Peter 3:13). In that new creation there will be no more death, no more grief, crying, or pain.

That is why we watch with joy and expectation and not as those who have no hope. We are citizens of the Kingdom which that day will bring — brothers and sisters in God's own family. In Holy Baptism God puts His claim of ownership on us. We are His now and through eternity. In Holy Communion He comes to us to renew and restore us so that we are able to watch with joy. His Word to us is true, and we can rely on it.

Watch with Work

The joy of that kind of watching moves us out to do God's work while there is still time. We are an army under orders from our Commander-in-Chief: "Go therefore and make disciples of all nations, baptizing them in the name of the Father and of the Son and of the Holy Spirit, teaching them to observe all that I have commanded you" (Matt. 28:19-20).

Watch with joy as you and I eagerly fulfill that command with the Spirit's help. Watch with joy as our words and actions bring others from death to life. Watch with joy as our talents and skills put to work in the Kingdom make that Kingdom a reality at home and around the world. Watch with joy as our money invested in the spread of the Gospel yields rich dividends, bringing many from the gloom of despair to the radiant joy of life.

As we begin the season of Advent today, we hear the voice of Jesus saying, "Take heed, watch; for you do not know when the time will come." Faith already now begins to hear the distant voice of the angel on the horizon also say, "Be not afraid; for behold, I bring you good news of a great joy which will come to all the people; for to you is born this day in the city of

David a Savior, who is Christ the Lord" (Luke 2:10-11). And so we watch
with joy.

Begin at the Beginning

SECOND SUNDAY IN ADVENT
MARK 1:1-8

Edwin H. Dubberke

Almost 2,000 years have passed since Christ first came to our world. Thus
the faith and church founded on Him is getting pretty old. In the minds of
many people it definitely shows its age. To them Christianity is like a totter-
ing old man — quite weak and ineffective and definitely out of tune with
the times. For the most part it seems to be a far cry from the fresh vitality of
faith, witness, and life in the early church described in Acts. Over the years
the Christian faith has become "established." It has its "traditional" way of
saying and doing things. Many charge that the dynamic faith proclaimed
by the apostles has been buried under a musty, boring religiosity that
excites few people — and changes even fewer. In many respects the
evidence is hard to deny.

This raises a challenge to us who have just entered a new church year.
As we look forward with anticipation and yearning for spiritual growth in the
weeks ahead, we will profit by first going back to the roots of that vibrant
faith that once was an observable mark of Christ's followers. With a prayer
for the Spirit's renewing light and power, we simply need to go back
and

Begin at the Beginning
The Gospel Is a Person

Perhaps one of the biggest mistakes people make when they try to
evaluate or even talk about the Christian faith is that they think of it in
terms of historical facts, formulas, and rules. That is why they tend to see
Christianity as something out of the distant past — as ancient history. But
in today's Gospel St. Mark expressly states that the Good News on which
our faith is founded centers in a person: "Jesus Christ, the Son of God." He
is not only the beginning but also the middle and the end of the message
about our salvation. It is significant that Mark does not take time to give
information about Jesus' birth and childhood as Matthew and Luke do.
His one goal is to present this unique person — who He is and what He
has done.

Distinctive Name

Mark is very precise in naming the object of his attention. His name is
Jesus, a rather common name among the Jewish people of that time. It

means "God helps" or "saves." For Jesus, however, it was descriptive of His very purpose in life. "You shall call His name Jesus, for He shall save His people from their sins" (Matt. 1:21).

Mark also calls Him Christ or Messiah, a name that identifies Him as the fulfillment of countless Old Testament prophecies about the coming of the Lord to save His people.

Finally, Mark states Jesus' divine origin. He is the very Son of the eternal God who came to dwell with mankind in order to reveal the Father's love as it had never been revealed before.

More Than a Name

Because the Gospel proclaims the person Jesus Christ, not just facts or philosophies about Him, it is always as lively and vibrant, powerful and active as He is — and He is very much alive. While it is true that He died the sacrificial death of the cross, He has risen from the dead. "I am ... the living one," says Jesus; "I died, and behold I am alive forevermore" (Rev. 1:18). Everything that Jesus was during His brief visible stay on our planet He still is — loving, merciful, kind, powerful, deeply concerned about the welfare of every human being. "Jesus Christ is the same yesterday and today and forever" (Heb.13:8).

True and meaningful faith in Jesus Christ is therefore a matter of knowing Him as the person He is, accepting all that He has done for our salvation, and trusting that He now bestows all the blessings of eternal life on us personally. Our Lord Himself declared, "This is eternal life, that they know Thee the only true God, and Jesus Christ Whom Thou has sent" (John 17:3). The apostle Paul spoke of his faith as a personal experience with Christ. He writes to the Philippians, "All I want is to know Christ and to experience the power of His resurrection" (Phil. 3:10 TEV). His life was so entwined with his Lord that he could say, "For to me to live is Christ" (Phil. 1:21). The more we get to know Jesus as a living person and not just a teaching of the church, the more of an impact He will have on our faith in Him and our life with Him.

How do you get to know someone better? You obviously do it by being around them, seeing what they do, and listening to what they say. It is as you get to know a person's inner feelings that you really know them. Since the person Jesus is at the heart of the Gospel, which is the heart of the Bible, the more we drink in that holy Word, the more we get to know Him. Expanding and dynamic faith always must begin there.

Preparation for Receiving Him

The coming of the Lord into our lives is a great event and calls for preparation. This preparation is so important that at Jesus' first coming God sent a special messenger in the person of John the Baptizer to "prepare the way of the Lord." John was that voice in the wilderness, foretold in prophecy, who would announce comfort to God's people. His message proclaimed "a baptism of repentance for the forgiveness of sins."

People from all walks of life flocked out of the cities and villages into the Jordanian wilderness to hear John and be baptized after confessing their sins. All the while he kept telling the crowds that he was really nothing compared to the one who would follow him, the long-promised Messiah. John's task was only to prepare the crowds for the coming Savior-King.

To Dried-up Lives

People today — people like you and me — still need much preparation if the coming of Jesus is going to bring any permanent blessings and changes in their lives. In many ways our lives can be compared to the dry and lonely wilderness of John's time. "All flesh is grass," says Isaiah in today's Old Testament Reading. "The grass withers, the flower fades" (Is. 40:6-7).

The beauty and joy of life can so easily and quickly dry up. It happens when romance and marital bliss turn into fighting or unfaithfulness, and divorce divides again those made one by God, even forcing separation of children from one of their parents. It happens when alcohol or some other drug gains control of a mind only to eventually becloud and destroy it. It happens in a Christian home when a beloved child turns from the faith and spurns the loving concern of the heartbroken parents. Although loud voices in our society proclaim that we have moved beyond the confines of "old-fashioned" moral standards, there are countless men, women, and young people who are haunted by a guilty conscience because of sexual sins. Fear and loneliness are the constant companions of many who populate nursing homes and inner-city ghettos — and are by no means uncommon to suburbanites either.

A man was visited by his neighbor whom he had known for a long time. The neighbor was intelligent, made lots of money, and had just about everything he could want. The visitor sat in his friend's kitchen, buried his face in his hands, and said, "God, but I'm bored!" Two weeks later he took his own life. Such is the wilderness where people live — and die! And it is to such people, even to us, that the way must be opened for Christ to come with healing and life.

Turnabout Needed

Well, if people are caught in such miserable situations of life and so desperately need help, what is the obstacle to the Savior's coming? The answer is sin — not just the individual sins of thought, word, or act, but the deep-seated alienation from God that causes us to go our own way, break His commandments, and disregard his glory. Consciously or unconsciously we all want to be our own master. We want to control the little area of the world in which we live and everyone in it. We want to satisfy the desires of our own hearts, even at the expense of others. We are in love with ourselves, and yet we constantly make ourselves miserable by what we are and do.

Now if you set out from Chicago intending to go to New York and suddenly found yourself in South Dakota, what would you have to do? Obviously, you would turn around and go in the opposite direction. So if you realize that the way you are living is an offense to the holy God and is taking you away from Him to your eternal ruin, what do you have to do? In our text John the Baptizer told such people to repent. That literally means to "change your direction," beginning with a change in your very heart and attitude. As God's law more and more pierces us like spiritual X rays, exposing the deadly sin that permeates the depths of our being, we need to confess it openly and turn away from it.

Many people who are already Christians ask why they need to confess their sins since God surely knows what they are. The important question is, do we? Because of the residue of sin within us, we daily stumble over temptation. More often than we care to admit, we begin to slide away from our commitment to our Lord because what we want is in a different direction. Thus Luther urged that we should, in connection with the ongoing significance of our baptism, "by daily contrition and repentance" die to sin and lust. Thus "the way of the Lord" is open into our hearts.

Forgiveness Flows In

Then, just as those who went out to the Baptizer with repentant confession received forgiveness of their sins, we receive forgiveness from God. The apostle John so clearly stated it: "If we confess our sins, He is faithful and just, and will forgive our sins and cleanse us from all unrighteousness" (1 John 1:9). But note carefully now: Forgiveness does not come to us because we have repented as if we have somehow met a qualification and therefore deserve a reward. This is not at all the case. Forgiveness is always based on the sacrifice of Jesus Christ on the cross by which He made full and advance payment of our debt of sin.

In Christ God's grace has won forgiveness for all the world. That is why Christ is the Good News of the Gospel. Without Him there is no good news for sinful mankind. Repentance knocks down the obstacles to receiving Him. By faith in Him and His cross forgiveness flows to us, forgiveness so complete that God no longer even remembers our sins (Jer. 31:34).

The Gift He Bestows

The forgiveness of which John the Baptizer spoke to the people was the same as the forgiveness we receive in Christ. At the same time John called the One who was coming a much greater person that he, who would bestow a much greater gift. "He will baptize you with the Holy Spirit." John could only point people to the Savior, but the gift of the Spirit that Christ bestows enables us to live an energetic life for and with our Lord.

More Than Forgiveness

Right here a key truth surfaces that may very well help to explain the difference between the vitality of the early church and the church as we know it today. Many who profess faith in Christ are only seeking forgiveness for their sins from Him. They are like the college student who admitted to his pastor, "I'm a Christian because I don't want to go to hell." The Gospel speaks not only of a rescue but also of a restoring. Jesus told Nicodemus he must be "born anew. . .of water and the Spirit" (John 3:3,5). Another time He said, "I came that they may have life, and have it abundantely" (John 10:10). Jesus comes to those lost in spiritual death and surrounded by spiritual darkness and says, "I am the light of the world; he who follows Me . . . will have the light of life." (John 8:12). Even though we were "dead through the trespasses and sins" in which we were once caught, God has "made us alive together with Christ" (Eph. 2:1,5).

Normally we buy an appliance or other equipment so that we can use it, not for storage. God purchases us by the death of Christ for living now, not for storage until we are called to glory. "He died for all, that those who live might live no longer for themselves but for Him who for their sake died and was raised" (2 Cor. 5:15). This is the unique character of Christian living. Life from Christ is life lived for Christ.

Spirit Power

The power for a life that is markedly different from the world around us is the Holy Spirit, whom Christ poured out on His church at Pentecost and whom He continues to send to His people. Jesus called the Spirit "Comforter," one who, having brought us to faith, would keep us close and alive in our Savior. It is the Spirit who can make our life fruitful in "love, joy, peace, patience kindness, goodness, faithfulness, gentleness, self-control" (Gal. 5:22-23). Since every believer in Christ has received the Holy Spirit through His Word and sacraments, the encouragement of the apostle Paul is more appropriate for us: "If we live by the Spirit, let us also walk by the Spirit" (Gal. 5:25).

Do you desire to live a life that truly demonstrates your faith? Do you feel there are wilderness areas in your spiritual life that need rejuvenation? Go back again to the basics of the Christian faith — Jesus Christ, the Son of God; repentance and forgiveness; the power of the Spirit of Christ. By God's grace the difference will soon be obvious.

Sent to Bear Witness to Jesus

THIRD SUNDAY IN ADVENT
JOHN 1:6-8, 19-28

Rudolph A. Haak

All traffic makes room as an ambulance speeds down a busy street with siren screaming. Obviously the driver knows where he is going. He travels much faster than the regular speed limit because he is given special privilege and authority by community officials. He feels the responsibility of being sent on an important mission. As he arrives at his destination, he moves speedily and skillfully into action so that the lifesaving rescue operation may not fail.

To some degree this illustrates what the life of a child of God is meant to be. I think of the busyness of the pre-Christmas season (about what?), the hurry and the rush (for what goal or destination?). The Lord would like to direct the whole life of every Christian in such a way that our goal is to bring light and new life to people. He would teach us, who are often so eager to develop new skills, the skills of using the Gospel and the sacraments.

Our Christmas preparation will be dull and unproductive unless we get a renewed grip on this basic truth: We are

Sent to Bear Witness to Jesus
Remembering the Great Commission

John was sent by God (v. 6), and his purpose was to bear witness to Jesus that all might believe through Him (v. 7). On the first Christmas the angels were chosen to be God's messengers to tell about Jesus' birth. Now, as Jesus began His public ministry, He sent His chosen messenger, John.

John had a special focus in life. Every move that he made and every word that he spoke flowed from the basic conviction that Jesus Christ should be exalted. Even all questions about his own identity and person were answered primarily in terms of his relationship to the Lord Jesus. For the benefit of the people around him he pointed to Jesus and said, "Behold, the Lamb of God, who takes away the sin of the world!" (v. 29). John was God's special messenger sent at a special time.

The Lord has His special messengers for every time. For today He has you and me! Surely you remember His commission to His disciples, "Go therefore and make disciples of all nations, baptizing them in the name of the Father and of the Son and of the Holy Spirit" (Matt. 28:19). In John's gospel Jesus tells His disciples, "As the Father has sent Me, even so send I you" (20:21).

God sent Jesus to deliver people from the slavery of their sin. He sent Him to take the punishment for the sins of every person on Himself and to provide righteousness for all. In Jesus' resurrection all this was accomplished. His victory over sin is our victory by faith. And God means to give this victory to every single person in the world. Therefore it is said of John (John 1:7) that God sent him so that all might believe.

He sends us for the same reason. He looks to us to bear witness to Jesus so that all people might believe in Him and have life. Those who believe in Him are restored to a right relationship to God (spiritual life) and receive the gift of eternal life. What an exciting mission! As we look around us at people today we must add, What a great *need* for such a lifesaving rescue operation!

Law and Gospel in the Witness

In order to bear witness we need some equipment. We have it in God's Word—in the Law and in the Gospel.

John identified himself to the priests and the Levites as the voice crying, "Make straight the way of the Lord" (v. 23). Elsewhere he is described as preaching a baptism of repentance for the forgiveness of sins (Luke 3:3). He urged every person to remove all obstacles that might stand in the way of Jesus' entry into the heart. All things that hinder faith and prevent a person from believing in Jesus must be removed.

This is also an essential part of our witness to Jesus today. If He is to enter our hearts, He needs to climb around and over many obstacles. Our love for the glare and glitter of the things of Christmas must move over and give way. The desire to receive must be turned into a desire to give. The effort to build Christmas around food, money, fun, and unrestrained satisfying of fleshly appetites must be replaced by a settled focus on the Christ whom God sent to be our Savior. The subtle, almost hidden passions that enslave us — some of which we hardly acknowledge — must be recognized as sin and pushed out of the way. The striving for worldly, fleshly pleasure must be dethroned and the way opened for Jesus to be King and Lord of our lives.

God makes the path straight in us through the message of His love and the working of the Holy Spirit. The way is cleared as the Holy Spirit shows us the the meaning and effect of Jesus' love. In love He provides righteousness — for you. In love He pays the penalty for your sins and suffers and dies in your place. He wins the victory over sin, death, and the devil through His resurrection, and your faith in Him makes that victory yours. In all this He gives you eternal life.

You wouldn't let the "junk" of this world block the path of His coming, would you? Make the path straight and say with the hymn writer:

> Ah, dearest Jesus, holy Child,
> Make Thee a bed, soft, undefiled,
> Within my heart, that it may be
> A quiet chamber kept for Thee. (*TLH* 85:13)

The Holy Spirit has brought us to repentance and enabled us to receive the Lord Jesus by faith. So our message to those around us and to all who are not members of God's family provides the straight path for His coming. Therefore the cry needs to go out, "Make straight the way of the Lord!" Clear away the junk and the debris that make Jesus' entry difficult or even impossible. With one sweep of the mind and heart push away the heaps of packaged hopes and dreams, when opened and examined, prove to contain only disappointment, hurt, despair, and death. Don't fix your eyes on what the world is doing in this pre-Christmas season. Look carefully at what God is doing. He sent Jesus again today, through the proclaimed Gospel, to take over a wasted life, to give it direction and meaning, to give it peace and joy, and to bring it into a beautiful relationship with the heavenly Father. Make the path straight!

The changed life of the "sent one" is a powerful witness to those who are blinded by the worldly glitter that surrounds them. The message of repentance and the great love of God in Jesus Christ provide the straight path through us to those whom God would reach with His forgiving love in Christ Jesus. Proclaim it with vigor and with joy! Proclaim it to those who have not heard it and to those who have. This is a great task of those who are sent.

Christian Baptism — A Part of Christian Witness

The text suggests a special road that Jesus travels to take over the hearts of those whom He loves. This is the road of the sacrament of Baptism.

John baptized sinners who repented. This caused the Pharisees to question his action and to ask him for credentials for performing such baptisms. John's baptizing was an offense to many. But his authority came from God, and in his baptizing God was at work forgiving sins, making entry into hearts, and gathering people into His family. John's baptism differed from Jesus' baptism in that it pointed ahead to what Jesus would do in His life, death, and resurrection. However, it was identical in that it provided the forgiveness of sins and a means through which God brought people into His kingdom.

Again today we recall that among the last words Jesus spoke to His followers was His command to make disciples, "baptizing them in the name of the Father and of the Son and of the Holy Spirit" (Matt. 28:19). This is a road (means) through which the Lord makes entry. To the extent that we fail to administer it according to His will, we block His chosen path. In Baptism God is at work. He enters the heart, throws down the idols that are there, and casts out all foreign spirits that have no right to be there. In Baptism He initiates the action of love, which begs for acceptance and a corresponding response of love for God. In Baptism God forgives our sins and declares that He is our beloved Friend. He enables us to believe and accept Jesus as Savior and Lord.

We, like John, are "sent. . . that all might believe through Him" (v. 7). The power of this simple act that we are asked to *do* lies in the person of Jesus. He provides the righteousness that Baptism bestows. He does the suffering and dying from which Baptism delivers us. He rises victoriously from death to life and gives us that victory in Baptism. He broke the hold (slavery) of Satan from which Baptism delivers us. All that God does for us in Baptism He does because of what Jesus has already done.

This lifesaving rescue equipment is simple to operate but is so very mysterious in its working and power. It's simple so that none may presume to be sent on a lifesaving mission without it or without knowing how to use it. With simple trust in the words and promises of God we apply water in the name of the Father and of the Son and of the Holy Spirit. No person need ever be without it — or the gift that it brings.

It is mysterious in what it does because God is at work in it with His power, with His cleansing grace, and with His love. In Baptism He works a miracle, the miracle of faith. Surely it doesn't surprise us that we do not understand God when He works His miracles. As a Christian congregation we are sent to baptize in the name of Jesus. The doing of it is an important part of our witness to Jesus.

I can (just now) think of one (many) to whom He surely has sent me — that they might believe. I must hurry. A life is at stake. His equipment must not be idle. What a shame if I am too slow — or should even miss going — and that life be lost.

Jesus Is Coming

FOURTH SUNDAY IN ADVENT
LUKE 1:26-38

Rudolph A. Haak

Are you just a little excited about Christmas? It's only two days away, you know. Christmas cards, Christmas music, special odors from the kitchen, packages of various colors and sizes appearing under the tree — all these seem to do something to all of us to get us just a little excited about Christmas.

We may be a little excited about gift giving — the surprise and the joy anticipated on faces — or about receiving gifts. We may be a bit excited about special vacation plans — doing some of those things we've always wanted to do. We may be a bit excited about family members coming, some of whom we haven't seen for a long time. We love those special friends whom we never really see often enough; how great to have a time to really enjoy them! We invited them. They said yes and we are almost ready. Exciting!

But did we forget that Jesus is coming? We haven't really invited Him, nor did we really plan our Christmas around His presence, but this morning we remember that He is the most important part of Christmas — and it's really true that

Jesus Is Coming

Who He Is

We have heard that before. Remembering some of the past Christmases, the thought doesn't really excite us — until we remember *who* He is.

Son of Mary

Today's Gospel tells us that He is the Son of Mary. We have always known this, but we haven't always considered what it means — that He was truly a human being. It means that God's law, given to us and to all human beings, applied to Him also. Since He was sent by God, it means that His special mission on earth was to live under that law without a single violation of it. And as the years went by, He fulfilled that purpose so that throughout His earthly life He was without sin. This is important for me to remember because He can only be my Savior if He is truly human, living under the law of God and keeping it perfectly.

Furthermore, He can be my Savior only if He dies as a human being. The one who takes my place must be a man (human being). "The wages of sin is death" (Rom. 6:23). "The soul that sins shall die" (Ezek. 18:4). In this God was talking to human beings, to people like you and me who sin against Him daily. But now when this judgment of God falls on me, Jesus stands in the way to receive the full force of it — to let me go free. What a special guest to receive!

"And you shall call His name Jesus (Savior)" (Luke 1:31). He can be this to me only if He is truly Mary's perfect Son. That's who is coming to us again this Christmas.

Son of God

But St. Luke also tells us that He is the Son of God (v. 32). As Mary was tossing around in her mind how it could be possible that she could be the mother of God's Son, the angel said, "The Holy Spirit will come upon you, and the power of the Most High will overshadow you; therefore the Child to be born will be called holy, the Son of God" (v. 35).

I don't understand how this could be — that Jesus could be the Son of God in the womb of Mary and be born of her. The only part that I understand is that God worked a miracle of love for me on the first Christmas so I might enjoy the miracle of salvation on every Christmas. You see, at one and the same time, even today, Jesus is Mary's Son, a true human, and God's Son, true God. Mysterious! But true! Praise Him!

For Jesus also needed to be true God in order that His perfect keeping of the Law might count for all men. That's why Jeremiah said of Him, "This is the name by which it [the righteous Branch to spring forth for David] will be called: 'The Lord is our righteousness'" (Jer. 33:16). Jesus' righteousness counts for me as I stand in God's presence. Where will you get yours? Unless you have it, you cannot stand in God's presence nor enter His heaven. Because Jesus is God's Son, true God, His righteousness is enough to count for you, too, and for every human being who lives on this earth. What an exciting gift! It came on the first Christmas and comes again and again, even today.

But there is more. Jesus' suffering and dying was not just that of another man. It was God's Son who died, and because He was true God, His dying counted for every person. St. Paul writes to the Corinthians, "He died for all" (2 Cor. 5:15). Being loaded with your sin, my sin, and the sin of the whole world, His suffering and death had infinite value. Because He was true God, conceived by the Holy Spirit, "the Son of the most High," His death satisfied the wrath and judgment of a God who justly punishes sin.

That tells us very much about who He is. He is your Savior and mine. Looking at us this morning, He says of us, "Not guilt. You are clean. You are free from the punishment of your sins, for I have borne them all on the tree of the cross."

That's surely the most exciting person who could come. Christmas is the anniversary of His birth. Let's be ready!

Great

But there is more. The angel said to Mary, "He will be great" (Luke 1:32). He was great in the sight of God, for He carried out His Father's will perfectly. He was great in the sight of God because through His perfect obedience and death He opened the way for God's lost children to return to Him again. God rejoices in this.

He is great in the sight of those who accept Him as Savior because He has overcome for us every enemy. The devil is overpowered. He has won the victory over the guilt, the punishment, and the slavery of sin and makes that victory ours through faith. He victoriously left the grave on the first Easter morning and for us has changed temporal death into the doorway to eternal life. We don't see much greatness in the Bethlehem infant, nor as He flees before the angry Herod, nor as He seems to be altogether hopelessly destroyed in death on the cross. But all of this was part of the path to victory and serves to demonstrate His greatness. He is the One who is coming! Exciting!

A King

And still more is told us about Him: "Of His kingdom there will be no end" v. 33). The King is coming! That's not just an exciting thought but a fact. His is a rule with truth in the power of His grace and love. He knows no geographical boundaries. He rules by His grace and love wherever people respond to Him in faith and love. The power of His reign is seen as His love reaches out to every person. "The King of love my Shepherd is," writes the hymnist (*LW* 412). With longing heart He reaches out to you and me with His love — so very eager for our acceptance of Him, so very eager to hear us say, "I love you, too." And everyone who confesses this He makes, not a subject, but a ruler with Him in His kingdom of grace. What a person! What an exciting guest! He is coming today!

How He Comes

Of course, we want to know how He comes so that we don't miss Him or treat Him rudely. For Mary He came through the power of the Holy Spirit, as God's servant, the angel Gabriel, anounced. He came in a way that to us is mysterious and miraculous.

In Word and Sacrament

In a way equally miraculous He comes to you and me through God's Word and Sacraments. Jesus, our Savior, is not necessarily to be found where we think He ought to be, but where He chooses to be. His means of coming are not controlled by how we might think He should come. He comes in ways of His own choosing. Where His Gospel is proclaimed, where His great love for us is made known, that's where He will be in this season and every season. That's where He will meet you in fulfillment of His promise. Of course, that will be the most important part of your Christmas — to be sure that Jesus has made entry into your heart through the Gospel.

To Hearts He Has Prepared

He won't tolerate the presence of sin. He will not stay with other unholy company in your heart. However, He will perform the cleansing as He takes over His place there. He is eager to do it as you ask Him to cleanse you, and the impact of His love and presence will make your Christmas the most exciting and blessed ever.

Mary didn't understand it all perfectly, but she accepted the message, the servant role, and the Child in her womb with ecstatic joy and gratitude. It was not long before she broke out in song with the words, "My soul magnifies the Lord, and my spirit rejoices in God my Savior" (vv. 46-47). She had an exciting blessed Christmas. Jesus was there.

Through Us to Others

A note of sadness mars the beauty of it all. Even at this moment I can think of many who have never responded positively to the touch of the Savior's love. I can think of some who are so caught up in worldly pursuits that they have no regard for the person of Christ and only use His name in cursing. I can think of some who surely have heard, but have not understood or believed it. I can think of many who have never heard. What an awful Christmas for them!

Once God used His special angel to announce His Good News. Today He uses messengers just as special—you and me. Of course, He could use an angel again or the stones on the hillside to shout His message, but He doesn't. He has made no other provision than that those who reign with Him should share in the joy of bringing His love to all.

After God showed Mary her servant role through the angel, she said, "I am the handmaid of the Lord; let it be to me according to your word" (v. 38).

The people who have not responded to Jesus in faith and love are not out there to mar your Christmas with a note of sadness. They are there to add to the excitement and joy of Christmas. Think of the exciting miraculous things that will happen when, in the most winsome way, you tell them of Jesus' coming and His love. Jesus is not only coming. He is here, promising that as you bring the message of the Gospel to people so they may become His disciples, He commits Himself, "Lo, I am with you always, to the close of the age" (Matt. 28:20). Yes, Lord, since You're going with me, I'll go! How exciting! What a blessed Christmas!

Personalizing Life

THE NATIVITY OF OUR LORD
CHRISTMAS DAY
LUKE 2:1-20

Ronald W. Weidler

Every time it happens, I feel like screaming. It's enough to make even an easygoing person angry. I'm talking about how people are often treated like mere numbers.

People Are Often Treated Like Numbers

Our Common Experience

I know my experience isn't unique. We all know how that feels. It's totally frustrating, isn't it? Have you ever lost your wallet or had it stolen? Losing whatever money you had in it is sad enough. But am I not right that the worst part of the ordeal comes in losing all your numbers? You're forced to notify your creditors that your cards are missing. The folks at the Social Security office have to be told so you can get a new card. The bank needs to know your 24-hour plastic money card is gone so payment can be stopped should a thief discover your "personal identification number" and try to use it. You're even afraid to drive without a license. Solving all these problems takes precious time. It's a terribly frustrating job.

Being treated like a number is downright degrading, too. Assigning numbers to people is a well-intended idea; I don't doubt that. It is supposed to make life go more smoothly and fairly for all. Our computerized world has many great advantages. But *having* a number shouldn't mean we get *treated like* a number! Sometimes it seems our life is purely at the mercy of chance. Who is it that assigns us our numbers anyway? Sometimes when I'm shopping, all I want to do is ask the cashier a simple little question (like "Where's the boy's room? My son has this urgency"). But to have him or her scowl back with a terse "You'll have to take a number and stand in line!" seems cold and humiliating.

Being treated like a number can also make us victims. Before we left for vacation last summer, I sent for our renewal auto tags. (Cars need numbers too, you know!) But when we returned, the tags still hadn't arrived in the mail. I waited. then I started to worry, feeling a bit guilty about driving with expired plates. A phone call to the county courthouse revealed that my application and fee was never received. So I had to use my time to go down and straighten out the mess. My bank informed me it would cost me $10 to stop payment on my check. Then a month later I got a letter from the county treasurer. In it was my original check and an apology. It seems the courthouse had misplaced one whole day's worth of mail, only to rediscover their error later on. I was miffed. Then the thought occured to me, Just think! An errant push of a button might erase my line of credit! Could it erase my bank account? What if it erased ME? The thought is rather frightening—but guess who'd pay the penalty for that?

Nobody likes being treated like a number. But maybe the worst time of the year for this to happen is at Christmas. Business is brisk, schedules are packed, and store clerks are so busy that people are treated like something far less than persons. And here is where one of the facts of the Christmas story really hits home.

Jesus' Experience Too

Jesus Himself knows how it feels to be treated like a mere number, too. Remember that Mary and Joseph were in Bethlehem as part of a worldwide census. People had to be counted lest anyone slip through the cracks and not get taxed. Can't you imagine Mary and Joseph feeling frustrated, degraded, and victimized by Caesar's orders?

The experience in Bethlehem went the same way. The inn said "No Vacancy." You see, they were late in taking a number for that establishment. The fact that Mary was obviously pregnant meant little in our cold world. But don't get the idea Jesus' birth was not marked by the Roman Empire. We can rest assured Jesus was recorded by the census taker as another digit—just another number, a faceless Jewish peasant boy born in Bethlehem. And we recall how the puppet ruler, King Herod, also tried to find the number called "Jesus." He developed an inordinate, mad, hate-filled interest in the list of boys aged 0-2 born in Bethlehem. What a sad tale that was!

Our experience of being treated like numbers is not unique or simply modern. It's quite typical, painfully common and age-old. Just ask our Lord. Yet right here this same old wonderful story of Christmas has good news for us.

God Treats Us Like Persons

The Shepherds

Christmas underscores the welcome fact that God treats us like persons. Consider the place of those nameless, faceless shepherds in the account. As far as most were concerned, shepherds were real nobodies. They were a dime a dozen, a rough, tough class of unlearned men who smelled of their trade. You could list dozens of occupations that ranked higher than shepherd.

But through these men God tells all the world's nobodies, "You're somebody to Me!" "To YOU," the angel said, "is born this day in the city of David a Savior, who is Christ the Lord." God sent His heavenly host to treat *them*, mere shepherds, with His Christmas concert. He gave *them* the sign of where to find the promised Messiah. Christmas is the story of how our God always goes about personalizing life. And this welcome fact didn't apply only back there and then.

Personal for Us

Consider again the Good News of how each of us fits into this account. Christmas, of course, is the celebration of one Man's birthday. Each one of us has a birthday of his or her own. While our birth wasn't miraculous like Jesus' was, and while none of us can ever dream of saying we are very God of very God, yet the same God, who formed Jesus in Mary's womb, gave each of us life as well! That's the amazing truth we profess in our creeds: "I believe in God the Father Almighty, Maker of heaven and earth." Even more to the point are the words of Luther's explanation of the First Article: "I believe that God has made *me*... that He has given *me* my body and soul, eyes, ears, and all *my* members, *my* reason and all *my* senses, and still preserves them." You see, we believe God to be the intimate and personal Creator of us all. And at Christmas we recall that God's eternal Son became one of us and one with us.

But let's never forget, not even on Christmas Day, that this unique Son above all came *for* us! He came so He could live for us under God's law. He came so He could die for us under that law—the holy, immutable law that said, "The wages of sin is death," and "The soul that sins shall die." Jesus was the only Man ever born for the express purpose of dying. In His death He paid for the guilt of our sin, and He did that personally for each one of us! When He rose on Easter morning, He in effect promised each of us our own personal resurrection and our own eternal life with God.

Toward that end God's Holy Spirit, the same One who gave Jesus physical life in Mary's womb, gave each of us spiritual life in the waters of Holy Baptism. On that day God called each of us by name to receive His personal love and forgiveness pledged to us for Christ's sake. That's what Baptism is: God's miracle of personalized love for *you*. In a world so often given to cold callousness, God assures us again and again that He treats us quite differently. He treats us like persons, not like numbers.

So We Treat Others As Persons

Because that is true, through this Word of God the Holy Spirit moves us in turn to treat others in God's personalizing way. Don't you feel God's love stirring in your heart to make room for those who, like Jesus, are given no room in life's inn? In one of his many sermons on the Nativity, Luther hit this point in a very personal way:

> There are many in this congregation who think to yourselves, If only I had been there! How quick I would have been to help the Baby! I would have washed His linen. How happy I would have been to go with the shepherds to see the Lord lying in the manger! Yes, you would! You say that because you know how great Christ is, but if you had been there at that time, you would have done no better than the people of Bethlehem. Childish and silly thoughts are these! Why don't you do it now? You have Christ in your neighbor. You ought to serve him, for what you do to your neighbor in need, you do to the Lord Christ Himself!

That quote may be over 400 years old, but we know how contemporary Luther still sounds.

What are we doing throughout the year to personalize God's love for others? How desperately this sin-racked world of ours needs God's love from us! Consider just one illustration: Today Herod's senseless slaughter goes on. In the United States alone more than one million living but unborn persons, created by God, are snuffed out each year by abortion. These tender lives are thought of only as numbers and statistics. Our impersonal world is still the hardest on the defenseless. What shall we do to make room for them in life's inn?

We Christians today also have the privilege of personalizing the Gospel love of Christ to our neighbor. The Gospel says that the shepherds went and told others about the child in Bethlehem. That's how we too can work for peace — the peace of which the angels sang. It happens every time we tell others about the Prince of Peace whose birth we celebrate today.

What joy we have this day, and it's so very personal! Why? Because Jesus was born long ago for everyone here. May you and yours receive much joy in this ever Good News. Merry Christmas to each one of you — in Jesus' name.

A Matter of Life and Death

FIRST SUNDAY AFTER CHRISTMAS
LUKE 2:25-40

Ronald W. Weidler

There is a certain cartoon scene printed each year about this time. It depicts the present year as a tired figure of a very old man trudging to the end of his course where he greets the new year portrayed as an impish baby with a top hat. It's a somber moment as well as a light one. It is an end and a beginning — something both sad and joyous — a consummation as well as the hope for tomorrow. That's what I think of when I read today's Gospel — the meeting of the very old and very young, an end and a beginning, the fulfillment of a long-awaited hope. However, it is more than that. The way we view Mary's babe in arms is really

A Matter of Life and Death

The Fulfillment of Hopes

Certainly that was the way Simeon and Anna looked upon the Christ Child. The scene is the temple in Jerusalem when Jesus was only 40 days old. Joseph and Mary had come to perform two Old Testament rites — purification (which was for women after giving birth) and the sacrifice required for all firstborn sons. No doubt there were others in the Court of Women that day to do the same thing. Yet it was to this family that the old man named Simeon, of whom we know precious little, walked, asking to hold the baby. I suppose if I had been the parent, I would have been at least slightly cautious. Yet the old man seemed so harmless. What a touching scene followed — this old, old man cradling the newborn in his frail arms. How like the picture of Old Man Time and Baby New Year!

But there is more to the picture. To the parents amazement, the old fellow broke forth in a song. It was a heartfelt hymn of thanks for this Child. Simeon was overcome with joy and tearful jubilation. Why? Because his eyes beheld God's "salvation," that is, God's "saving thing," this baby in his arms.

Then there was the other old figure, a widow named Anna who was 84 years old (Could we possibly call her the figure of "Old Woman Time"?) Like most widows, Anna was quite poor. She depended on the alms and generosity of the temple precinct (her "home") for her livelihood. She chanced to come by at that moment and overheard Simeon's song. Like a flash and with a newfound spring in her step she hurried to "gossip" the Gospel about the child. Why all the fuss? What excited these two senior citizens so? It was really quite simple.

The hope and prospect of meeting this babe had been the focus of their entire life. Simeon is described simply as a pious, God-fearing man. But he was an oddity for his day. Simeon was one of the few left who had read, rightly understood, and believed the Old Testament promises concerning the coming Messiah. The majority of people had twisted the sacred record to fit their own hope for a coming political and military hero. Simeon knew better. He trusted the promises of a spiritual Hero who would come to conquer sin, death, and Satan. That day marked the zenith of his aged life. In some unknown way the Holy Spirit told him he would see the Messiah before his death. And the Spirit had tugged at him that day to go to the temple at the right moment. There Simeon saw the glorious fulfillment of his hopes. Likewise, the aged prophetess Anna was numbered with those still looking for "the redemption of Jerusalem."

Now it had all come true. Simeon and Anna were old, yes, but their future beamed brightly indeed. God had kept His precious Word, so this ancient pair stood on death's threshold fearless and confident.

Simeon's song, familiar to us all, is a triumph of faith and hope. "Lord, now lettest Thou Thy servant depart in peace." In effect, Simeon prayed, "Master, You may now release Your slave. I'm ready, dear Lord, for whatever may come. You've shown even me how much my life is in Your hands. So what can disturb me now? Life is good, but the best is yet to come." Simeon and Anna had as much happiness and joy as anyone could hope for — and more. I wonder how many today, at the end of the year, the week after Christmas, can say that.

The Beginning of Life

The mood of these post-Christmas days is always a bit depressing for many people. Many are depressed simply because Christmas is over, and as a pastor I get depressed because they're depressed! Cynically perhaps, I wonder how many wouldn't be totally depressed about now if not for the coming New Year's parties. By now vacations are about over. The Christmas toys are beginning to break, and the decorations are coming down. Another Christmas has come and gone, and for most people that means farewell to the joy of the season.

The reason for all this is simple: Most people celebrate Christmas only like a *birthday party*. Birthdays come once a year, a time for brief happiness tempered by the fact we are another year older. There is no real lasting significance to the average birthday celebration.

In contrast to that is the importance God places on Christmas, which to Him is like a *day of birth*. A couple looks forward with great anticipation to the coming of their child, much like Simeon and Anna were looking forward to the fulfillment of God's promise. Parents who feel depressed after that big day has come and gone, simply because it has come and gone, are in trouble. The day of the birth of their child is only the beginning of a whole lifetime in which love and joy can and will grow.

That's true despite the fact that no child's life is ever all sugarcoated sweetness, where junior never does wrong, never gets sick, and grows up to be president of the United States. A sign of maturity that I look for as I counsel wedding couples is their realization that being married and being parents takes a lot of hard work. Parents need a firm commitment to love each other and their family and to work ever so hard for it despite the times they will hurt each other. Mature parents realize that. But that never diminishes the joy that the birth of their child brings, does it?

Yet year after year people treat Christmas like a once-a-year festival where, for a while, the past is forgotten and the future ignored. The big attractions are the presents yet to be opened and the feast yet to be devoured. A few, perhaps, are touched by the quaint, old "legend" about a cuddly baby laid in a manger. But one week later the thrill is gone, the baby is forgotten, and the only interest and prospect now is the bottle of champagne to be opened at the New Year's Eve bash. Let's face it: People treat God and His Son with little more than harmless, sweet affection and passing interest at Christmas. Afterwards they pack them away just like the figures in the nativity scene.

But Christmas is not the story of innocuous sweetness that has no bearing on "real life." Actually, when you get right down to it, Christmas is a matter of life and death. Even in the midst of all his joy, Simeon realized that all too keenly. He prophesied that this baby would split the world, separating the people of God from all the rest, including the phony pretenders. Surely when King Herod sent his troops to slaughter the babes of Bethlehem, Simeon's words were painfully evident. He also said Mary's own heart would be pierced with sorrow over her Son and His mission. Surely as she watched Jesus die on Good Friday, Simeon's words came back, seemingly with a vengeance.

It's nice and joyful to sing a song of Christmas, to hold a candle in church on Christmas Eve, to exchange gifts, and to eat the feast. But if that's all the place Christmas has in your year, you've missed the point! But then, by virtue of the fact you are here today, it seems apparent you already know that. What remains for us is to learn anew the lesson of Simeon and Anna.

Building on the New Life

What we do with Jesus, the *entire* Jesus, is truly a matter of life and death. Simeon teaches us how vital it is to build life on the Rock of Christ. When our life's foundation is built on Him, no storm or sorrow can rob us of our true joy. Both testaments speak of Christ as a Rock. He is a Rock that will either save or destroy us. His death on Calvary and His resurrection on Easter will either cause life for all who trust in Him and His promises, or they will cause the death of those who reject Him and His Word of life. To keep Him as a tiny babe with no real claim on life is a sure way to get crushed. How tragic! For Jesus died to save us from our sins, paying the enormous debt of sin we all owe God. He came, not to condemn us, but that we might have life in all its abundance.

With Simeon we are to learn that having Christ in our heart brings lasting freedom. What a fitting motto for us, too: "Lord, now lettest Thou Thy servant depart in peace." It's not that we're planning on dying soon. Rather, we mean "Here, God, is my whole life. You gave it. You saved it. Now use it! Free me to be Your servant — free from spiritual shallowness and guilt, and from past and future fears."

From Anna we learn the lasting joy of rendering service to God, of living in God's temple and worshiping regularly. Here we feast on the Bread of Life in our life with God — His Word and Sacrament. From them we receive the motivation to join Anna in spreading the news of the Christmas Baby to others. We Christians need to tell and show others, perhaps especially our children, that Jesus is for the entire year.

Simeon and Anna preach a powerful sermon to us today. Knowing, believing, loving, and serving Jesus as Savior is a matter of life and death. Maybe it would be better to say, Jesus is a matter *for* life — every day of every year of life — and *for* death, One who was born to die so we can have confidence of eternal life even in the face of physical death.

Soon that bouncing, top-hatted, sashed baby boy named "1985" will crawl into our lives. Once again it will be the passing away of the old and the beginning of the new — a moment of sorrow and of joy — the consummation of one year and the hope of another tomorrow. My prayer for all of us is that we, like Simeon and Anna, greet the future with the joy and hope of Christmas fixed in our hearts. Then let us love and live with abandon for God, for surely that will make this a "Happy New Year," regardless of what may come.

A Most Unusual King

THE EPIPHANY OF OUR LORD
MATTHEW 2:1-12

Richard A. Eissfeldt

> For this his glad epiphany
> All glory unto Jesus be,
> Whom with the Father we adore,
> And Holy Ghost forevermore. (*LW* 81:5)

This story from the Gospel according to St. Matthew is familiar all over the Christian world. For many years most of us have heard how the Wise Men came from the East following that magnificent star, visited briefly with King Herod, and continued their journey until they came to Bethlehem, where their galactic guide stopped. And there they saw, for the first time, the baby, the Christ, the King, and they worshiped him, giving gifts of substantial value.

There are a number of unanswered questions in this portion of Scripture. Who were these Wise Men, these Magi, and where did they live? Why did Herod not go with them when he discovered from the scribes that the King was to be born in Bethlehem? Was this a tactical error on his part? What indeed was the star that brought the Magi a great distance to Bethlehem? We can, of course, propose answers to these questions, and certainly all manner of legend has been developed around them. But an element of mystery still shrouds the story.

Gifts Fit for a King

Yet one point of the story is very clear. These travelers were bringing gifts fit for a King. This is to be the focus on this Epiphany Sunday: The Wise Men, through the gifts they gave, acknowledged this baby's lordship, His right to be King, His inherited responsibility to establish His kingdom. (See the genealogy of Jesus according to Matthew 1:1-16.) The visit of the Wise Men to a rather unpretentious setting in Bethlehem one evening many years ago was not unlike a coronation, in which the visitors presented Him with gold, frankincense, and myrrh.

The commentaries on this text suggest a reading of Psalm 72:10-14 as an important cross reference. The verses describe two things: (1) that the promised King would be afforded great tribute and (2) that He would demonstrate great concern and care for the poor and dispossessed.

> The kings of Tarshish and of the islands
>   will pay him tribute.
> The kings of Sheba and Seba
>   will offer gifts;

all kings will do him homage,
    all nations become his servants.
He will free the poor man who calls to him,
    and those who need help,
he will have pity on the poor and feeble,
    and save the lives of those in need;
he will redeem their lives from exploitation and outrage,
    their lives will be precious in his sight (Ps. 72:10-14 JB).

The psalmist's words very naturally fit with this Epiphany text. Both Scriptures announce the arrival of a most unusual King. The psalmist describes a most unusual kingdom. The text from Matthew and the words from Psalm 72 declare for us that the birth of Jesus and the subsequent visit of the Wise Men are both points at which His ministry is forecast.

A King for the Poor

Yet this text and the psalm seem to have a contradiction. A King— regal, worshiped, sought after by Magi, the recipient of expensive gifts — to establish His kingdom by helping the poor, the needy, the exploited, and the outraged? The apparent contradiction turns out not to be one after all. For the Scriptures reveal time and time again that, in God's scheme of things, those in power have a responsibility to be on the side of the poor, the dispossessed, and the hopeless.

This Jesus — the King and also the Servant — was unmistakably on the side of the poor. Recall the great "woes" of Jesus against those who were in authority and were not taking care of dependent people. Jesus made it unmistakably plain that widows and homeless children were to be cared for, not neglected; that the sojourner within their gates was to be welcomed; that the naked were to be clothed, not ignored; that those in prison were to be visited, not forgotten; that the hungry were to be fed, not left to starve; that women were to be treated as human beings, not as property; that children were important; and that adults ought to emulate the faith of little children. He left very little doubt that His was a most unusual kingdom.

Can it be any different for the King's 20th-century followers. There is a story in the Gospel according to St. Matthew in which Jesus allows a woman to anoint Him with an expensive ointment. The disciples become critical of this, indicating that the ointment could have been sold for a good price and the money given to the poor. Jesus says to the disciples, "You have the poor with you always, but you will not always have Me" (Matt. 26:11 JB). Jesus was not suggesting that the poor *should* always be with us. He was forecasting that they *would* be. He acknowledged a sad fact of our local and national and global human condition — that there will be poor people. But for Jesus it did not end there. He acknowledged the condition of poverty by living His life as a response to suffering, poverty, oppression, and corruption in low and high places.

There are countless opportunities for us, the Kings' subjects, to ackowledge Him as King. We pay Him homage in our worship, in our speaking the Good News to others, and in our giving to local and larger ministries that are dedicated to serving the poor. Our witnessing in this world involves a two-pronged thrust: Proclaiming the Gospel of salvation through our Lord Jesus Christ and providing for the needs of those who encounter problems that seem to overwhelm them.

A King to Save All People

He was a most unusual King right from the beginning, when the strangers from the East followed a star to Bethlehem, all the way to the end when the King was crowned with a most unusual crown — not of gold, jewels, or any other valuable, but with a crown made of thorny vines designed to penetrate the skin of His scalp, to cut into His head so that blood would flow down His face. The King endured this for those of us who are too spiritually poor to meet His expectations. That includes us all. For all of us have sinned. We are all found wanting in God's sight. But the pain of that crown was not the end for Him; it was only the beginning. He was marched to Skull Hill, attached to a cross in a most vicious manner, left to hang in the heat of the day, pierced with a spear, and finally pronounced dead.

Why? is the great question. His followers did not know at the time. Hindsight is always better, and we are more fortunate from our vantage point than were the early disciples. The great why is answered: He was a most unusual king with a most unusual kingdom. He established His kingdom for us because we could not establish it for ourselves. The great light of Epiphany highlights the Good News that Jesus did it for us. And to make sure it was sealed by God, He rose on Easter morning.

It all started with His coronation in Bethlehem; it was lived out in ministry to people; and it ended (or so it appeared) on Skull Hill. But it did not end there, for the baby of Bethlehem and the Servant of people is our risen Lord and Savior who now reigns in glory.

He it is whom we worship — as did the early Wise Men. We worship Him with our psalms and hymns and spiritual songs, and we worship Him when we help our brothers and sisters in need.

The Epiphany light has shined on us. Let our light shine on others.

Hail to the Lord's anointed, Great David's greater son!
Hail, in the time appointed, His reign on earth begun!
He comes to break oppression To set the captive free,
To take away transgression And rule in equity.

He comes with rescue speedy To those who suffer wrong,
To help the poor and needy And bid the weak be strong;
To give them songs for sighing, Their darkness turn to light,
Whose souls, condemned and dying, Were precious in his sight.

Kings shall fall down before him And gold and incense bring;
All nations shall adore him, His praise all people sing.
To him shall prayer unceasing And daily vows ascend;
His kingdom still increasing, A kingdom without end (LW 82).

Baptism Proclaims Relationships

THE BAPTISM OF OUR LORD
FIRST SUNDAY AFTER THE EPIPHANY
MARK 1:4-11

Richard A. Eissfeldt

> The ancient teachers ordained three sorts of baptizing: of water, of the Spirit, and of blood; these were observed in the church. The catechumens were baptized in water; others, that could not get such water-bathing, and nevertheless believed, were saved in and through the Holy Spirit, as Cornelius was saved, before he was baptized. The third sort was baptized in blood, that is, in martyrdom (Martin Luther, *The Table Talk of Martin Luther*, tr. by William Hazlitt [Philadelphia: United Lutheran Publication House, n.d.], p. 197).

The Gospel for today focuses squarely on the first two baptisms referred to by Martin Luther. The baptism of blood, which Luther calls martyrdom, may be implied in this text but is not stated explicitly. This reading helps us understand that neither the baptism of water nor the baptism of the Holy Spirit can be separated from the relationships they create. We note two sections in the Gospel:

1. The baptism of water by John and its implications for relationship.
2. The baptism of the Holy Spirit by Jesus and its implications for relationship.

The Baptism of John

We look first at John and the baptism of water. Who was this John the Baptizer? His mother, Elizabeth, was related to Mary, the mother of Jesus. Recall the occasion when Mary visited Elizabeth prior to the deliveries of their children.

> Now as soon as Elizabeth heard Mary's greeting, the child leapt in her womb and Elizabeth was filled with the Holy Spirit. She gave a loud cry and said, "Of all women you are the most blessed, and blessed is the fruit of your womb. Why should I be honored with a visit from the mother of my Lord? For the moment your greeting reached my ears, the child in my womb leapt for joy" (Luke 1:41-44 JB).

This baby who "leapt in her womb" was to become known as John the Baptizer. He lived in Judea and apparently had close contact with the wilderness. It was in this wilderness that he began his public ministry "proclaiming a baptism of repentance for the forgiveness of sins" (Mark 1:4 JB). This Gospel may be focusing initially on John in an attempt to tie together the wanderings of the children of Israel in the wilderness with John. For John also lived a nomadic existence with his camel-hair garment and his sparse diet. Although "all Judea and all the people of Jerusalem made their way to him, and as they were baptized by him in the river Jordan they confessed their sins" (v. 5 JB), his life was to be interrupted by Herod, who had him arrested, imprisoned, and later executed.

The baptism of John was about a relationship. It was first of all a baptism of repentance for the forgiveness of sins. It was an opportunity for people who had apparently abandoned God to come back into relationship with Him. John the Baptizer was the instrument God used to effect that change in relationship. The tool God gave John was the simple act of baptism. It is still a simple act today. To say "simple" is not to imply that it is something to be taken lightly. It is rather to emphasize its availability to all of us. As the Judeans were brought into a relationship with God through the action of John's baptism, so we, at whatever age, entered the family of God when that pastor or chaplain or whoever took water and spoke the words "I baptize you in the name of the Father and of the Son and of the Holy Spirit." It is amazing that something as simple as water, connected with the Word, ties us 20th-century Christians together with John who lived so long ago. That's the historical perspective we need to keep in mind. There is a linkage between the early Christians and us. The water that brought the Jerusalem folk into a relationship with God is the same water that brings us into a relationship with Him.

Today's Gospel also suggests that we look at John's relationship with Jesus. It is here that the text seems slightly incongruous. "Jesus came from Nazareth in Galilee and was baptized in the Jordan by John" (v. 9 JB). If the purpose of Baptism is for repentance and forgiveness, then why would Jesus be baptized? According to Hebrews 4:15 Jesus was without sin! John certainly senses his inadequacy here, because earlier we hear him say, "Someone is following me, someone who is more powerful than I am, and I am not fit to kneel down and undo the strap of his sandals" (Mark 1:7 JB). John is not bestowing forgiveness on a Christ who does not need it. He is rather fulfilling his role as servant. His relationship to God was one of servant, and his relationship to Christ was one of servant. We have the same kind of a relationship with God.

The Baptism of Jesus

We now look at Jesus and the baptism of the Holy Spirit. Again we ask the question, why was Jesus baptized? We are not asking why He was baptized by John, but why He was baptized at all. It appears that Jesus, like John, was living out a role that had been given to Him, the role of servant. As previously stated, Jesus did not need to be baptized for forgiveness. But He did come into this world to serve, to be a servant. In fact He made it unmistakably plain that His mission in life was not to be served but to serve and to give His life as a ransom for many.

There is a message in that for us. Not only did Jesus give up His life in order to bestow on us everlasting life, but His serving nature is now also to be a model for how we live in relationship to other people — in our families, in our jobs, wherever our respective lives take us. A servant is not a person who is lowly, who grovels, who is someone people generally walk on. A servant can be viewed in that way, but to do so is an injustice. In the context of the Christian faith, being a servant means being in support of someone else or something else. If we are not supportive of one another in our relationships, we are missing the point of our baptism, and we are missing the point of our Christian faith. For being faithful to Christ means living not just for ourselves but also for those with whom we are in a relationship. Jesus proved Himself a servant by being baptized, and His Father was pleased. After Jesus was baptized, God spoke from heaven and said, "You are My Son, the Beloved; My favor rests on You" (v. 11 JB).

John said that Jesus would baptize with the Holy Spirit. Apparently this marked a significant difference between the ministry of John, who baptized with water, and that of Jesus. What does it mean to be baptized with the Holy Spirit? Does it mean to be able to speak in tongues? Does it mean to have the ability to heal the sick?

The clearest Scriptural statement of what it means to be baptized by the Holy Spirit comes from the apostle Paul who speaks of the fruits of the Spirit. These are some characteristics that will be evident in the life of a person who has been baptized by the Holy Spirit. They are "love, joy, peace, patience, kindness, goodness, trustfulness, gentleness, and self-control" (Gal. 5:22-23 JB). Paul lists these characteristics in vivid contrast to the person who lives a life of self-indulgence (see Gal. 5:16-21).

The fruits of the Spirit that result from the activity of the Holy Spirit in a person's life do not exist in a vacuum. In fact they can only exist, stay alive, and thrive in relationship. This does not mean that every day we live, we will be able to be totally loving, joyful, full of peace and patience, and all those other good virtues. We do slip. We all fall short of the glory of God. But since we are baptized by the Holy Spirit, we also know that Christ died for us, and because He did, we will worry less about our own goodness. It has been taken care of by Him.

And since we need worry less about that, we will have more time and energy to get about the business of demonstrating the fruits of the Spirit in our relationships with each other. That is what the Bible seems to mean when it speaks of "newness of life." This newness is like fresh bread, not stale bread. The old skeptic and philosopher Nietsche once said, "If you want me to believe in your Redeemer you are going to have to look a little more redeemed." He is referring to the sad fact that too often we Christians do not reveal the fruits of the Spirit of which Paul speaks.

We have been redeemed by Jesus' death and resurrection; we have been sanctified by the Holy Spirit. But being redeemed and being sanctified does not mean that we are sinners emeritus — that we once sinned but do not do it anymore. It does mean that we live in a relationship with God in which we are secure in His love and forgiveness, so secure that we are able, with His power, to live out the fruits of the Spirit in our relationships — in order to nurture those relationships. For that which is not nurtured dies.

On vacations my family traveled from the middle part of the United

States to the Rocky Mountains in Colorado. When one is coming from the east, it is necessary to drive through western Kansas and eastern Colorado. We have also made the trip from eastern Canada to the Rocky Mountains of Alberta. To do so one must obviously drive through eastern Alberta. A person who has not been to those sections of both Canada and the United States might assume some similarity in land conditions. But that is not so. Eastern Colorado is arid, parched, and dry. Eastern Alberta is green, lush, and alive. The reason for this dramatic difference? The land in Alberta is being nurtured by consistent summer rainfall, whereas the land in Eastern Colorado experiences very erratic and limited rain, giving life to little. So it is in relationships—whether that be human relationships or our relationship with God. You cannot ignore a relationship and assume it will continue. It must be nurtured with the power of the Word which the Spirit uses to produce those fruits that are part of our lives because we have been baptized by the Holy Spirit.

John baptized with water for repentance and forgiveness. Christ baptized with water and the Holy Spirit. Neither of the activities existed in a vacuum. You and I are the continuing recipients of the blessings of our baptism. We have forgiveness, and we have the fruits of the Spirit. They are ours by faith. Faith is more than the acceptance of certain tenets or doctrines. It is a relational thing. It involves trust in God, giving oneself to Him, putting one's life into His hands. It is from our baptism that trust blossoms, and allows us to live the full life God intends.

How Christ Deals with Doubt

SECOND SUNDAY AFTER THE EPIPHANY
JOHN 1:43-51

John F. Niermann

All of us wrestle with doubt. We doubt our ability, the promises of politicians, rosy economic forecasts, new and untried ideas. We don't hesitate to express these doubts either: "I'm not sure I can do that." "I don't think things are going to get better." "I don't believe it'll work. We've never done it that way before."

The doubt that causes the most anguish, however, is the uncertainty that God exists and that He loves. It's not necessary to rehearse all the reasons for this doubt. You know them well. Their depressing presence is familiar to you—the silence of God in response to tortured pleas for His help and His seeming indifference to evil that strikes indiscriminately, claiming innocent victims.

But we have difficulty admitting our doubts about God. To say what's actually on our mind would tread shudderingly close to blasphemy. We recall the words of Christ that unless we become like little children (which we understand to mean totally trusting and completely free from doubt), we cannot enter the kingdom of God. Warnings about the dangers of too much education were not uncommon in pious circles. The payoff could well be doubt, unbelief, and exclusion from the kingdom. Doubt, however, cannot be denied or avoided. It is painfully real, and it will therefore be helpful to observe how Christ deals with doubt.

Christ Accepts Doubt

In the first place, Christ accepts doubt. Jesus was recruiting His disciples. He had just found Philip and said to him, "Follow Me." Like one torch lighting another, "Philip found Nathanael and said to him, 'We have found Him of whom Moses in the Law and also the prophets worte, Jesus of Nazareth, the son of Joseph'" (John 1:43-45).

But Nathanael wasn't so easily convinced. He was from Cana, a short distance from Nazareth. Nazareth was an undistinguished place, and, as is typical of towns situated close to one another, rivalry had no doubt developed between the two villages. Nathanael was familiar with Nazareth. This wasn't the kind of town from which one would expect a king—from Cana, maybe, but hardly from Nazareth.

Furthermore, Nathanael wasn't unfamiliar with Messianic prophecy. Christ saw him sitting under a fig tree. "The rabbis recommended that men study the law 'under their own vine and fig tree'" (A. M. Hunter, *The Gospel According to John*, Cambridge Bible Commentary on the New English Bible, New Testament Series [New York: Cambridge University Press, 1965], p. 27). Nathanael, then, was a student of the Old Testament and would know there was no clear prophecy that the Messiah would come from Nazareth. Therefore, with more than a hint of contemptuous arrogance Nathanael bluntly challenged, "Can anything good come out of Nazareth?" (v. 46). Jesus of Nazareth didn't fit the mental image Nathanael had for God's Chosen One.

Isn't Nathanael's attitude a familiar one? We are knowledgeable people. We've spent time under our own "vine and fig tree." From our study of the Bible we know about the spectacular signs and wonders God performed— the destruction of the evil world by a flood, the deliverance of the Children of Israel through the Red Sea, the assaults on sickness by Christ, His tender regard for children, His compassion for the poor, and His triumph over death. This is the way a good God should act, and when we're confronted with His silence in the face of evil that randomly victimizes innocent people, our faith hesitates. God isn't conforming to the picture we have of Deity.

Jesus' reaction to Nathanael's doubt is startling. He didn't scold Nathanael for his arrogant put-down. He didn't lambaste him for his learning and say, "Nathanael, if you didn't rely so much on your own mind and reason, you'd have no difficulty believing Philip." There is not even a hint of a verbal slap on the wrist. Instead, Jesus complimented him. When he approached, Jesus said, "Behold, an Israelite indeed, in whom is no guile!" (v. 47).

Jesus was recognizing that there is honesty in doubt. Doubt doesn't want to be taken in. It probes and examines. It rejects what is false. It isn't satisfied with what it wishes were so, out is willing to wait for what is genuine and true. Nathanael was anxious for the coming of the Messiah, but he wasn't eager to accept just anyone who claimed the title.

This aspect of doubt is good and useful. As one preacher put it,

> It is a good thing that Paul doubted that anybody can be saved by the law. It is a good thing that Augustine doubted that he could find a full life in the red-light districts of Alexandria. It is a good thing that Luther doubted that works righteousness could bring inner peace. It is a good thing that Copernicus doubted that the world is flat Dr. Wallace Fisher, "The Anatomy of Doubt," *Catalyst*, 13, 4 [1981], p. 4).

The apostle John had this function of doubt in mind when he wrote, "Beloved, do not believe every spirit, but test the spirits to see whether they are of God" (1 John 4:1).

Don't, therefore, deny your doubt or repress it as an unthinkable act of impiety. Don't be afraid to face the truth that you sometimes have trouble with what you've been taught about God. Christ recognizes the useful role doubt plays and would applaud your honesty.

Christ Offers Proof

However, merely to accept doubt would be an inadequate remedy. Christ does more. He supports faith with proof. His description of Nathanael as an "Israelite indeed, in whom is no guile" drew the surprised response from Nathanael, "How do you know me?" When Jesus answered, "Before Philip called you, when you were under the fig tree, I saw you" (John 1:48), Nathanael knew that such a brief view from a distance would not have given any ordinary person an accurate picture of another's moral character. Jesus had to be more than ordinary. "Rabbi," exclaimed an excited Nathanael, "You are the Son of God! You are the King of Israel!" (v. 49).

But what kind of proof does God offer *us* that He exists and that He loves? Could it be that the signs of God's presence are so plentiful that we don't recognize them as footprints of the Divine but see them only as part of the ordinary? We normally think of the suspension of the laws of nature, such as the parting of the Red Sea, as a miracle offering proof of God's existence and care. But isn't there more proof in the predictability and precision with which the laws of nature work? Rabbi Harold S. Kushner in his book, *When Bad Things Happen to Good People*, observed,

> Our human bodies are miracles, not because they defy laws of nature, but precisely because they obey them. Our digestive systems extract nutrients from food. Our skins help to regulate body temperature by perspiring. The pupils of our eyes expand and contract in response to light. Even when we get sick, our bodies have built-in defense mechanisms to fight the illness. All these wonderful things happen, usually without our being aware of them, in accordance with the most precise laws of nature. That, not the... splitting of the Red Sea, is the real miracle (Harold S. Kushner, *When Bad Things Happen to Good People* [New York: Schocken Books, Inc., 1981], pp. 57-58).

Human senses can become so dulled to the miraculous that complaining can actually smother excitement over God's goodness and power. What a miracle it was for the Children of Israel to have manna supplied every day! It wasn't long, however, before they began to cry, "O that we had meat to eat! We remember the fish we ate in Egypt for nothing, the cucumbers, the melons, the leeks, the onions, and the garlic; but now our strength is dried up, and there is nothing at all but this manna to look at" (Num. 11:4-6).

Christ Gives Love

As important as proof can be to us, Christ doesn't want us to be obsessed with it. When Nathanael, impressed by Christ's miraculous knowledge, exclaimed with complete conviction, "You are the Son of God! You are the King of Israel!" (John 1:49), Jesus made a surprising response. Instead of expressing joy over Nathanael's faith, Jesus seemed to belittle the basis for that faith. He asked,

> "Because I said to you, I saw you under the fig tree, do you believe? You shall see greater things than these." And he said to him, "Truly, truly, I say to you, you will see heaven opened and the angels of God ascending and descending upon the Son of Man" (vv. 50-51).

One might suppose that it would have been better for Jesus to proceed slowly with Nathanael's natural skepticism and offer a whole series of proofs so that there would be adequate support to bolster his faith against future doubt. Jesus rather makes an increased demand on Nathanael's faith. He invites Nathanael to go beyond the correct appraisal of Christ's nature as Son of God and King of Israel and believe that he will see the glory of paradise and god's angels converging on the central figure, Christ.

Jesus' reaction to Nathanael's excitement over His Messiahship, for which Nathanael at that point had adequate proof, suggests that if we don't have the kind and amount of proof we think we need, it is by God's design. Proof has a way of calling attention to itself. For every proof there is contrary evidence, a "Yes, but have you considered this possibility?" Christ wants to call us away from a preoccupation with proofs to a faith that has its focus on Him and the unimaginable glories that God has prepared for those who love Him.

When Jesus speaks of the opened heaven and the angels surrounding the Son of Man, He prefaces His description with "Truly, truly, I say to you" (v. 51). This is the translation for *amen, amen*. The pious Jew concluded his prayers with *amen* (so be it), expressing his trust that God would answer. Jesus doubled the *amen* and placed it at the beginning of His significant sayings to express their absolute trustworthiness (Hunter, *Gospel According to John*, pp. 27-28).

Why should we believe Him? because there are proofs? No, rather because He loves us. When we make important decisions, whose advice do we rely on most? Isn't it the counsel of those who know us and love us rather than that of experts? To whom do we go with problems first, those who have the answers or those who will listen with sympathy and understanding? Love, more than expertise, begets trust. We trust in Christ, not because He has eliminated all the intellectual problems we encounter when we try to sort out our faith rationally, but because He suffered, died, and rose again to give us what our sin and mortality scream we need — forgiveness and life. That's love, and that love wins trust and banishes doubt. We don't say as Nathanael, "You are the Son of God! You are the King of Israel!" (v. 49). That's a head response to proof. Instead, we say with another famous doubter turned believer, "My Lord and my God!" (John 20:28). That's a heart response of those who have felt the nail prints in Christ's hands and the spear wound in His side and know that His suffering was for them.

It's Time for Everyone to Go Fishing

THIRD SUNDAY AFTER THE EPIPHANY
MARK 1:14-20

John F. Niermann

Make disciples of all nations. Preach the Gospel to every creature. We know that's our task. Epiphany reminds us again. Yet we find it easier to talk about it than do it. Why?

I'm not sure of all the reasons, but I believe our hesitancy results from the evil that works against the Gospel and from our own feelings of inadequacy. We look at the task and at ourselves and ask, Why try?

There's no denying it. The world isn't an inviting sight. In spite of diplomats' best efforts, war is a chronic disease of our globe. Iran, the Falkland Islands, Lebanon, Ireland, Afghanistan, Guatemala — the mere mention of these countries evokes scenes of carnage. Crime has turned countries at peace into paranoid societies barricaded behind dead-bolt locks, alarm systems, Doberman pinschers, and German shepherds.

Unabashed selfishness is the new ethic. Pick up any magazine with an article on interpersonal relations, and prominent in the discussion will be tips on how to initiate and develop a satisfying relationship with a lover. Lovers are discussed along with friends and spouses as part of a normal person's legitimate circle of significant people. Sociologist Amitai Etzioni in his book, *An Immodest Agenda: Rebuilding America Before the 21st Century*, has identified self-centeredness as the major threat to the American social fabric. John Leo in a review of Etzioni's book in *Time* says,

> Etzioni cited Pollster Daniel Yankelovich, who found that 17% of Americans are deeply committed to a philosophy of self-fulfillment — a feeling that ego needs, sensation and excitement take priority over work and the needs of others, including spouse and children. Another 63%, whom Etzioni calls "the ambivalent majority," embrace the self-centered philosophy in varying degrees. "That they also hold on to old beliefs is important." he says, "but it does not belie the fact that 80% of Americans have been affected by the new mentality" (John Leo, "The Hollowing of America," *Time*, Dec. 20, 1982, p. 85).

Leo further comments,

> Among Etzioni's other salient points: Emphasis on the "quality of life"...
> has wrought a retreat from work.... Romantic attitudes toward schooling...
> produce passive, unstructured classrooms filled with children who lack
> self-discipline.... In the age of ego, marriage is often less an emotional
> bonding than a breakable alliance between self-seeking individuals (ibid.).

It's easy to understand why we have little heart for the witnessing task.

The Wrong Time Is the Right Time

In explaining the "fullness of time" when "God sent forth His Son, born of a woman," preachers have been accustomed to cite the *pax Romana*, the network of Roman roads, and *koine* Greek, which was the universal language of the empire. These factors would pave the way for the spread of the Gospel. The stage was set; the time was right.

Today's Gospel, however, has a different understanding of the fullness of time. "Now after John was arrested," Mark writes, "Jesus came into Galilee, preaching the gospel of God and saying, 'The time is fulfilled, and the kingdom of God is at hand; repent, and believe in the gospel'" (1:14-15). It was after John was arrested that Jesus announced the fullness of time. The right time for Christ's ministry was at the wrong time — not when things were good but when they were bad.

And things really were bad. Not only was John arrested, but he would soon be killed, the victim of a lust-crazed king's reckless promise. There was no welcome for Christ either. He was born in a cattle stall. "He came to His own home, and His own people received Him not" (John 1:11). The leaders weren't about to jeopardize their cozy relationship with Rome by allowing a popular healer and teacher go unchallenged, and so from the very beginning they opposed Him and eventually put Him to death. The established religion was a shell of meaningless ritual. The scribes and Pharisees would pray and give alms on the street corners but neglect what Jesus called "the weightier matters of the Law, justice and mercy and faith" (Matt. 23:23). Herod, the name borne by several Palestinian kings during and after the time of Christ, has become synonymous with savage cruelty — the murder of the innocents and the beheading of John the Baptist.

The moral climate in Rome, the capital of the empire, was no better. Intrigue and murder were commonplace. Paul catalogs the corruption of Gentile society in the first chapter of Romans. "They were filled with all manner of wickedness, evil, covetousness, malice. Full of envy, murder, strife, deceit, malignity, they are gossips, slanderers, haters of God, insolent, haughty, boastful, inventors of evil, disobedient to parents, foolish, faithless, heartless, ruthless" (Rom. 1:29-31).

The modern world's transportation and communication systems far surpass anything that anyone in the first century would have dared dream of. Supersonic jets have cut travel time between continents from months to weeks to hours. Satellites make possible live interviews with people simultaneously in London, Paris, Washington, and Moscow. These satellites beam to our living rooms events as they happen in any spot of the world where it's possible to carry a video camera.

Yet it's not the magic that science has worked in shrinking our globe that makes our time especially the right time for the Gospel. It's the right time because it's more than ever the wrong time. The evil that discourages us makes the proclamation of the Gospel even more necessary. The world needs to hear that the kingdom of God is here. The world needs to know that the God who created the universe and everything in it is a gracious God who forgives sins because of the suffering and death of Jesus Christ. The world needs to repent, that is, make a 180-degree turn away from its willful disregard of God's claims, turn to God, and believe the Gospel.

The world needs to understand that there are alternatives to selfishness, greed, rapacity, violence, and revenge and that these alternatives are generosity, gentleness, and forgiveness. The world needs to believe that life can be better, that it can serve nobler ends. "Now after John was arrested, Jesus came into Galilee, preaching the gospel of God, and saying, 'The time is fulfilled ...'" (Mark 1:14-15). Now after the riots in Ireland, the rape and robberies in our cities, the fighting in the Middle East, the rampant selfishness in modern society we come "preaching the gospel of God, and saying, 'The time is fulfilled, and the kingdom of God is at hand; repent, and believe in the Gospel.'"

Everyone a Fisherman

The second factor that makes us hesitant to witness is that we're unsure of our knowledge and communication skills. In our age of specialization we're content to leave a task to one who has had training and experience. In the case of sharing the Gospel this means letting the pastors and missionaries who've had years of seminary training to do it. They'll be able to meet the objections of unbelievers and make a more polished presentation of the Gospel, we feel.

When Christ, however, was looking for recruits to catch people, He didn't look among the teachers of the Law, those who would be able to make a brilliant and polished defense of the new faith. Instead, He went out where men were working with their backs and hands to make a living. As He passed along the Sea of Galilee, He saw Simon and his brother Andrew, two fisherman, casting their net into the sea and said to them, "Follow Me and I will make you become fishers of men" (v. 17). Then He went on a little farther and found James and his brother John in their boat mending their nets and issued them the same summons.

Their vocation as fishermen would give them an understanding of the nature of their task as Christ's disciples. They were to be fishers of men with the same perseverance they used battling the rough waters of the Sea of Galilee to catch fish. They were to show the same inclusiveness as when they threw out their nets to enclose as many fish as possible. Christ wanted men who knew how to mend nets, who wouldn't let a tear that allowed some big ones to get away break their resolve as fishermen, but who would repair the tear and try again.

God has called us without exception — each one of us — with the variety and richness of our differing backgrounds to be fishers of men. "Wait a minute," someone objects. "Weren't the disciples, even though uneducated, a select group? Didn't Christ pick them and leave Zebedee, the father of James and John, and the hired servants in the boat? Didn't they continue to be fishers of fish? Isn't this really an argument for specialization?"

The best reply comes from Peter, one of those originally called as fishers of men. He didn't believe that this title applied only to the Twelve. To Christians in Pontus, Galatia, Cappadocia, Asia, and Bithynia — and to us — he writes, "But you are a chosen race, a royal priesthood, a holy nation, God's own people, that you may declare the wonderful deeds of Him who called you out of darkness into His marvelous light" (1 Peter 2:9). We can assume that Zebedee and the hired men heard the Good News of the Kingdom repeatedly from James and John, that they responded, and that they, too, in their own way became fishers of men.

It isn't ordination that God uses to call people to be His priests, His fishers of men, but Baptism. In Baptism God washes away our sins and gives us a rebirth into His family to become His "own people" in order to "declare the wonderful deeds of Him who called" us "out of darkness into His marvelous light." Baptism provides the power for mission and the heart of our message. In Baptism God makes real to us the forgiveness and life Christ won for us through His suffering, death, and resurrection, and these are "the wonderful deeds" we declare.

The world to which we witness is evil and we are inadequate. But evil makes this the fullness of time for the announcement of the presence of the Kingdom and for the call to repent believe the Gospel. And Christ's call makes us adequate for the task. "Follow Me," He says, "and *I* will make you become fishers of men."

Beyond Amazement to Faith

FOURTH SUNDAY AFTER THE EPIPHANY
MARK 1:21-28

Norbert C. Oesch

It could have been just another long leg of a journey — uneventful and unfulfilling. Instead it turned out to be exceptionally stimulating, enlightening, and thought-provoking. The gentleman I sat next to was Japanese — distinguished looking, well-dressed, and, as I was soon to find out, articulate. He was manager of the department of governmental affairs for a very large international firm. Mr. Kenji had a global mind; he understood events in history as they affected not just a single country, but the whole world.

As we talked, he quickly stated how blessed the United States was, what potential, what enviable resources and influence it had. But with sadness he shared how its position in the world was deteriorating. It had been passed by in many areas of technology and influence. Then he said, "But you know, you have every ingredient necessary to make your nation the utopia of the world, primarily because you have Christianity. If only all who claim to be Christians would live like Jesus, you would solve every social, political, and even economic problem in your country. He lived as every human ought to live. His life is the solution to your country's problems. And I say this not being a Christian myself."

What a powerful testimony, I thought, and yet how sad. Here is a man who highly admires Jesus and His teachings but has not yet known Him as his Lord.

How like the people of Capernaum! How like millions of people in our present world. How like many who call themselves Christian. Are you like this, too?

We are given this story in the life of Jesus in order that we might be called from merely admiring His power, authority, and life to being confronted with Him as He is, the God-Man. We are called to accept Him as God's provision for your life and mine, the One who is to be our Lord. Only if we allow Him to affect our lives as He affected the man with an evil spirit can we be cured of what possesses us. Only then can we be freed to live a fulfilled life in harmony with God's purpose for us.

Amazement Is Not Enough

Mark's Gospel gives us an account of Jesus' preaching and doing a miracle in Capernaum. He went to a synagogue and taught. People were amazed at what He said and the way He said it. Then He backed up His words with a miracle that clearly demonstrated His authority over evil. Again the people were amazed.

I suppose we shouldn't be amazed that the people of Capernaum were amazed. Amazement is one's first reaction to someone who does extraordinary things, whether in word or deed. After listening for ages to rabbis who hemmed and hawed about the Law, suddenly the people were confronted with a Man whose words had a ring of truth to them — yes, more than a ring. Things happened when He spoke. "Be quiet," He could say to a man whom no one else could silence, for a power more than human possessed him. But when Jesus spoke, the demon was silent. And when Jesus said, "Come out," the demon obeyed. Surely this Man spoke with authority. No wonder the people were amazed! You and I would have been amazed, too. Who wouldn't? It's one thing to talk; it's another to back up talk with actions.

When young Cassius Clay first entered the ring as a contender for the world heavyweight boxing title and boasted and bragged in pathetic poetry how he would stop his opponents, people laughed and scoffed. After he performed and became the Mohammed Ali who held the title four times, amazement replaced the laughter and scoffing. His deeds backed up his words. They gave his words authority.

However, amazement was not what Jesus was after. He was not just trying to make people drop their jaws; He wanted them to believe in Him. And this is precisely where we are in danger of coming up short, too. The people of Capernaum asked, "What is this?" not "*Who* is this?" They noticed only the new kind of teaching instead of the Lord, the Messiah, who delivered it. They marveled at the authority He used to speak to demons. They were especially impressed by the obedience of the demons since Jesus did not resort to the kind of magical formulas that others tried. But the crowd's reaction did not come near the real issue that was fearfully voiced by the demon: "What have You to do with us, Jesus of Nazareth?" They missed that more basic issue.

Jesus Is Either Life or Death

"What have You to do with me?" That's the question that every heart must ask of Jesus. It's a personal confrontation with Jesus — a call to know Him as more than an amazing man or a fine teacher (or, as in the case of Mr. Kenji, the one who demonstrated the way all people should live). It's a challenge to take the person of Jesus seriously as God and Lord. The demon saw it as a life-or-death matter: "Have You come to destroy us? I know who You are." Yes, the demon knew this was not merely an amazing man. He knew God incarnate was standing before him.

Jesus confronts each of us in life-or-death terms. He will either be life for us, or He will become our death. He will either be the One who gives life in a full relationship of peace with God, or else He will be our death, the stone of stumbling that will lead to destruction. The choice before us is utterly serious.

"I am the resurrection and the life," He says. "Whoever lives and believes in Me shall never die" (John 11:25, 26). "I came that they may have life, and have it abundantly" (John 10:10). Jesus confronts us so that the life He offers can become ours. Life is a truly reconciled and peaceful relationship with God. It means having His breath, His Spirit, actively living and breathing within us. It means having the righteousness of Jesus put over us so that God now accepts us as He accepts His Son. It means living with faith in Him as Lord. The life Jesus offers becomes ours not by standing back and being amazed at His authority and His deeds, but by coming to Him like the man possessed by an evil spirit and letting Jesus replace the sin that possesses us with faith in Him.

Failure to do so leads ultimately to death — separation forever from the love and forgiveness of God — final judgment. "He who does not believe is condemned already, because he has not believed in the name of the only Son of God" (John 3:18). God forbid that would be the lot of any of us.

But when we allow God's Spirit to bring us face-to-face with Jesus as Lord, when we seek to have Him cast out everything that holds us in its possession and away from Him, our lives can be healed. When God's Spirit casts out unbelief and replaces it with faith, then we are truly healed indeed.

That's not to imply that instantly every thought and word, action and reaction becomes pure and holy. What possesses us, especially unbelief, won't go without kicking and screaming. Indeed, all that is contrary to God won't be completely gone until the new age, when we live with the Lord in eternity. Despite the screaming and kicking of our old human nature, however, everything that separates us from God will have to go. We must submit to the greater authority that seeks to take over our lives, Jesus Himself.

The result will be the possibility of a life that reflects the purpose for which we were created — a life that reflects our God in the world of our relationships. Such a life will offer forgiveness to those who offend us, because Jesus and His work of forgiveness have become ours. Such a life will reflect a concern for the welfare of others and offer support, for example, for our fellow workers and employers.

This new life will work for the establishment of peace and justice in every arena of life, including race relationships and human rights. It will even move us to work for the common economic good of our nation and world, rather than merely for our own personal economic advantage at the moment. Such a life, established in more and more people, would even move our world toward the fulfillment of what Mr. Kenji envisioned, a world of placing one's neighbor's need above one's own. But such a utopia, impossible to be completed yet on this earth, cannot even begin to function by merely admiring Jesus as man. The new life begins by receiving Him as Lord. Then it's not a matter of imitating a noble person, but of being transformed through God's cleansing process.

Mr. Kenji confronted me with a Jesus to be admired. But before he left the plane, he was confronted anew with the person of Jesus as Lord. He was left asking the crucial life-or-death question, What, Lord, do You want with me? If he lets Jesus cast out all unbelief and replace it with faith, Mr. Kenji will have life, life in all its fullness. What a joyous day that will be! Like the man from whom the evil spirit was cast out, he will then be healed, made new in the person and work of Jesus.

It's the same for you and me. If we permit God's Spirit to move us beyond amazement to faith in Jesus as Lord, we too will be healed, made new in the person and work of Jesus.

Staying on Course

FIFTH SUNDAY AFTER THE EPIPHANY
MARK 1:29-39

Norbert C. Oesch

Jesus would have made a great corporate president. He had those two priceless characteristics that would have made Him great: He could handle the pressing needs of the moment, and He could keep long-range needs in perspective. He would have known where He was going, and although He wouldn't have neglected the work at hand, neither would He have permitted the work at hand to so distract or consume Him that He would lose sight or control of the long-range movement of the company. He had the balance to maintain the course.

Because Jesus could handle the immediate situation and still not lose sight of the long-range goal, He would have made a great farmer, too — nice, neat furrows and rows. Or He would have made a great sailor — staying right on course. Or He would even have made a fine congregational president — a problem solver and long-range developer. But He was not a corporate president, a farmer, a sailor, or a congregational president. He was a Savior — no, *the* Savior. And that made His ability to handle situations most important. He could deal with the immediate concerns of His people and yet not be deflected from His goal of bringing them eternal salvation. And the good news for us is that He has remained on course, and that He allows us to go with Him.

The Press of the Immediate

Most of us understand the press of immediate concerns. If your toe is bleeding, you don't stop to eat lunch first before you stop the flow of blood and wrap the toe. Immediate concerns demand immediate attention. The squeaky door gets oiled first, it is said.

A person's got to make a living, we say. You can't do much if there's no bread on the table. You can't teach people the Gospel if their stomachs are empty, we hear. First feed the belly, then tell them about God.

"I can't spend all day in prayer and Bible study. Who'll get the work done around here? Someone's got to cook, vacuum, and run to the store. Not everyone can be a Mary; someone's got to be a Martha."

"I've never had such a hectic day at the office! The boss was unreasonable. Who in the world could get all that work done?"

We know the press of the immediate. We live with it all the time. So did Jesus. In the Gospel for today He doesn't even have time to prop up His feet and relax after a big day of debate in the synagog and wrestling with evil spirits. When He finally gets to Simon and Andrew's home, He is immediately told about the need of Simon's mother-in-law. And after He has cured her, He is not finished. Dinner dishes are hardly cleared before Simon and Andrew set up a clinic n their home. One after another they come — the fevered, the infected, the insane, the possessed, the crippled, the hemorrhaging. The press of the immediate confronted the Lord.

Yes, He, like us, knew the pressures of immediate needs. The concerns He faced may not have been the same. He didn't have the same problems with bills, rising utility costs, taxes, health care, insurance, car and house payments, or rent. He may not have needed a calendar in order to keep all kinds of engagements and activities n order. But the immediate needs of His day were just as urgent for Him as ours are for us. After all, He knew He only had a few short years to accomplish His ministry. Three years later He would go to the cross. He had to show the people who He was — the Epiphany theme — and accomplish the act of redemption — the theme of the approaching Lenten season — in such a short time. The press of the immediate was real.

The Danger in the Immediate

The immediate needs must receive attention. This is affirmed by Jesus' unhesitating commitment to the sick, whether Peter's mother-in-law or the nameless throng at the door. The danger, however, is that the immediate can become so all-consuming that one loses one's perspective, indeed one's course.

A football team can start with a game plan, but if the opponent strikes with two touchdowns and a field goal in the first quarter, the game plan will be deserted; the immediate need takes over and consumes everything.

It's that way in a business, too. A corporate president needs to be concerned and involved to some degree with the daily operations, but if he becomes too caught up in them he'll lose his ability to plan, to manage, and to set policy.

Spiritually, the loss of perspective can happen to a church body, a congregation, or an individual. If a church body gets too engrossed in internal strife or problems, it can lose sight of its mission to send laborers into the whole world. If a congregation is concerned only about its own building program, it can become self-entrenched and fail to serve its community. Its very purpose goes unfulfilled. If an individual gets so wrapped up in personal problems, health, pain, or fears, there is a real danger of losing all perspective on what life is all about.

Ellen had an auto accident 16 years ago. Six years ago she had one leg amputated below the knee. Although she could have learned to walk with the aid of a prosthesis and perhaps a cane, she has become so engrossed in her handicap that she remains in a wheelchair, a bitter and angry woman. She has lost the perspective of herself as a daughter of the heavenly Father. She cannot see any purpose for her existence because she is so caught up in the immediate problems of her physical condition.

The Corrections to Stay on Course

Jesus easily could have lost His perspective. The situation was so urgent He could have been so consumed by the need to heal the sick that He forsook His preaching. And He could have failed to complete His mission as the Messiah, God's Redeemer in human flesh. But He did not. He used two simple but powerful corrections to keep Him on course. They were prayer and meditation — means of communion with His Father.

Long before it was dawn, He was up and off to a lonely place to pray and meditate on His Father's will. In the quiet and the solitude He was renewed. He was able to maintain the course of His mission. While the sunrise was barely lighting up the eastern sky, His prayers had already ascended beyond the rose horizon to the throne of His Father. Before the warm rays of the sun gave heat to His tunic, meditation on the priceless Word of God had warmed His heart. He was kept on course by prayer and meditation.

And thus He could say to the disciples, who had been dragged off course by their concentration on immediate problems, and who sought to drag Him off course as well by making Him focus only on their makeshift clinic to heal the gathering crowd, "Let us go on to the next towns, that I may preach there also; for that is why I came out" (Mark 1:38). He knew His job was much more than healing; it was to be the Savior of the world. This saving role required Him to preach the Gospel about Himself as the Son of God. It meant presenting Himself as the Good News not only for the physically sick, but also for those alienated from God, from fellow human beings, and from creation as a whole. It also meant proceeding with determination toward the final goal of death and resurrection to make divine atonement for sin.

His retreat in the early dawn helped Him maintain this perspective. The quiet moment of solitude, personal communion with the Father, and meditation on the Word provided Him with strength to keep the goal in view. Even the tug of the well-meaning but erring disciples could not deflect Him into a futile path of circling into nowhere.

Good News for Us

This is certainly good news for us. Had Jesus been so distracted by the immediate, He may have been the greatest healer who ever lived, but would He have been our Savior? However, since He did keep His perspective and stay on course, we can be sure that we do have a Savior. He is the One who healed and preached and atoned. His healing extends to our own time, reaches into your life and mine, and restores the health of an otherwise sick relationship between the Father and us. His preaching rings yet in our ears, telling the Good News that He, the Son of God, came to earth in human form on a rescue mission for humanity. His act of atonement means that all has been made right between God and us. Our sins are paid for. Our guilt is removed. We are fit to be adopted into His family.

Did you notice the words Jesus used when He gently corrected His disciples about His work? He said, "Let us go." Despite their erring attempt to drag Him off course, He did not reject them. He urged them to continue with Him in His mission. They were to go with Him throughout His time on earth, and one day He would heal and preach through them.

That also is good news for us. We are also included in His work. We are invited — yes, even urged — not only to receive the benefit of His work, but also to go along with Him as He still preaches the Gospel about Himself as Son of God, Redeemer of the world. As the Epiphany season has made clear, you and I are incorporated into the mission of our Lord and His proclamation. As He later used the minds and tongues of the disciples to be His instruments of healing and proclamation, so today He uses our hands to bring a healing touch to those who suffer from every kind of illness. He uses our tongues to proclaim Him as the Savior of the world. And when we are in danger of getting so caught up in the immediate concerns of life that we lose sight of our ultimate goal, life eternal with Him, He calls us to join Him in a quiet place where through prayer and meditation we can be corrected and put back on course.

Staying on course, keeping the right perspective, never losing sight of the final goal while also handling pressing immediate situations could have made Jesus a great corporate president — or a farmer, a sailor, or even a congregational president. But He wasn't one of these. He was — He is — our Savior. And as we now go with Him, we can be assured that with His Spirit guiding us through His Word we will stay on the course, too.

Listen to the Master's Voice

THE TRANSFIGURATION OF OUR LORD
LAST SUNDAY AFTER THE EPIPHANY
MARK 9:2-9

Eugene L. Krentz

One of the fine arts of life is the art of listening. You may have an acute sense of hearing but the question is, Are you really able to listen? Careful listening is more than merely hearing sounds. Listening opens the door to meaningful communication. It enhances our ability to understand ideas and the feelings of others.

A large American brokerage firm prides itself in the fact that when E. F. Hutton speaks, people listen. Wouldn't it be wonderful if we could make the same statement about God? In the Gospel for today the living voice of God speaks to contemporary man. But a nagging question persists. When God speaks, who listens? Let's put it more pointedly. When God speaks, do *you* listen?

St. Mark's account of the transfiguration does much more than recall an important event in the Savior's life. Here is a contemporary challenge that confronts all who profess to walk by faith in Christ. It urges us to do more than just hear our Lord's words; it calls us to become involved in a creative activity, to

Listen to the Master's Voice
Life in a World of Competing Voices

In every period of history God's people are confronted by a host of voices that compete for their attention. Frequently the messages are confusing, and trying to make some sense out of everything we hear is just not easy.

Life for the disciples was like that, too. They faced a steady barrage of conflicting views about God and the life of faith. Our Lord spent much of His time trying to help them sort it all out by teaching them about the kingdom of God. He made the word of the prophets come alive as He opened the Scriptures for them. Repeatedly He urged them not simply to hear, but to *listen* to the Good News — to take it to heart, to let it change their lives.

Just a few days before the Savior led the disciples up the mountain to the transfiguration site, He told them of coming events: "The Son of Man must suffer many things, and be rejected by the elders and the chief priests and the scribes, and be killed, and after three days rise again." St. Mark emphasizes that "He said this plainly" (Mark 8:31-32).

The Savior's voice is worth listening to. On the transfiguration mountain the meaning of many things the Lord had been saying should have struck home for the disciples. Before their very eyes Peter, James, and John saw the Lord "transfigured before them, and His garments became glistening, intensely white, as no fuller on earth could bleach them. And there appeared to them Elijah with Moses; and they were talking to Jesus" (9:2-4).

Everything about the transfiguration event calls attention to the importance of listening to the Master's voice. Besides the dazzling garments, there were voices that penetrated the silence. They were the voices of great men of old — Moses and Elijah. They too had once lived in a world of conflicting voices. They had heard voices of unbelief, voices that mocked God. But they had also heard the voice of God.

Moses had been struck with awe as he stood before a bush that did not cease to burn, and he had listened to the voice of God calling him away from the herding of sheep to the challenging task of leading a nation. On Mt. Sinai he had heard the voice of God again as He announced His covenant with the people and gave the commandments.

Elijah, afraid and despairing, had listened to the voice of God on the same mountain. That voice came to him, not in violent wind or earthquake, but in the stillness. It was the steady voice of God that penetrates the world's noise and brings an important Word to the ears of men.

Imagine the disciples at the transfiguration listening to the conversa-

THE TRANSFIGURATION OF OUR LORD

tion of Moses, Elijah, and Jesus. This was worth listening to; it should have been deeply impressed in their memories. But here St. Mark reports something interesting, something so common to us all: "They were exceedingly afraid" (v. 6). Fear got in the way of listening. Groping for words, bewildered by the experience, all that Peter can do is to blurt out, "Master, it is well that we are here; let us make three booths, one for you and one for Moses and one for Elijah" (v. 5).

Peter got sidetracked from the task of listening. He wanted to preserve the mountaintop experience, to make the precious moment permanent by building structures. But God had other ideas. From out of the cloud that overshadowed Peter and the others there came another voice. Clearly, unmistakably, this was a voice to be reckoned with. It demanded a hearing: "This is My beloved Son; listen to Him" (v. 7). It was the voice of God calling them, as He calls men of every age, to listen to the voice of His only begotten Son.

The voice of Jesus is the voice of the Good Shepherd. He speaks with authority because His words are true. In a world of noise and confusion He brings Good News to those who are bombarded by claims that the way to God is the way of works, of struggling with the Law, and of striving for personal goodness. His way is through the cross, through suffering and death, through resurrection.

Competing and conflicting voices often garble and mask the voice that we really need to hear. On my way to the parish each morning I travel past the towers of a local radio station. When the car radio is on, I always know when I am approaching the towers. The strong signal simply garbles and interferes with whatever station may be playing. It's disconcerting, to say the least, because the scrambled, irritating noise continues until the towers are left behind.

Listening to the voice of God in today's world is a lot like that. Competing voices are in the air. They not only beg for a hearing, but they also tend to garble, muffle, or blot out the voice of God that is heard in the proclamation of the Gospel and sounds forth from the pages of the Scriptures.

Think for a moment of how these mixed voices have distorted the person and work of Christ. People have attempted to explain Jesus theologically, philosophically, psychologically, and in a host of other ways. They have asserted that He was a mere man, a good teacher, a hoax, a con artist. But in the voice from the cloud at the transfiguration there was no complicated explanation, just the clear, unmistakable message: "This is My beloved Son; listen to Him" (v. 7).

The Master's Voice Is Worth Listening To

When our Lord speaks, His voice is worth listening to, not simply because He is speaking, but also because He has something extremely worthwhile to say. He talks about life and work in the world, about rescue from our sins and friendship with God, about hope and a future that reaches beyond the grave. What a word for disciples who would have to face the reality of life down in the valleys and along the dusty, crowded streets of the cities! The site of the transfiguration could be no permanent home in spite of their personal desires. God had work — rewarding and challenging work — for Peter, James, and John to do. The first step was for them to pay attention, to listen to the Master's voice.

What would happen in your life and in our world if we would seriously practice the fine art of listening to the many important things our Savior has to say? If we began each day by taking to heart the message of the cross that He shares with us? Would we not be less fearful, less confused by other voices, more able to deal with the world's confusing noise? How much more peaceful our lives might be if our hearts and minds were finely tuned to the voice of Him who says, "My sheep hear My voice, and I know them, and they follow Me; and I give them eternal life, and they shall never perish, and no one shall snatch them out of My hand" (John 10:27-28).

Listening to the Master's voice would help us understand the deeper meaning of the Savior's words: "If any man would come after Me, let him deny himself and take up his cross and follow Me. For whoever would save his life will lose it, and whoever loses his life for My sake and the Gospel's will save it. For what does it profit a man, to gain the whole world and forfeit his life?" (Mark 8:34-36).

You may remember seeing the old corporate seal of the RCA company on some of their record labels. It pictures an old record player with a big horn from which the sound emanates. A dog sits in front of the horn listening intently, and below are the words, "His Master's Voice." Isn't this what our Lord emphasized that day in the home of Mary and Martha? "Mary... sat at the Lord's feet and listened to His teaching. But Martha was distracted with much serving, and she went to Him and said, 'Lord, do You not care that my sister has left me to serve alone? Tell her then to help me.' But the Lord answered her, 'Martha, Martha, you are anxious and troubled about many things; one thing is needful. Mary has chosen the good portion, which shall not be taken away from her'" (Luke 10:39-42).

People frequently engage in small talk, filling up time and space with words that don't really matter. God never just makes small talk. He always has significant things to say. What He says matters; it is worth listening to. However, the fact that God is speaking and has important things to say about life doesn't make the task of listening any easier. Our Lord was aware of the difficulty we have, and so He punctuated His teaching with the words, "He who has ears to hear, let him hear" (Luke 14:35).

The shallow thinking of our time and the difficulty that people have in listening to the Master's voice is seen in the willingness of some to believe that one voice is as good as another. Every person certainly has the right to choose what to listen to, what to believe or not believe. But it is also true that every choice has its own risks and consequences.

The idea that every religious road will ultimately lead to the discovery of the one God simply isn't true. Theological truth is not relative. One view about God is not just as good as another. We must listen to the Master's voice precisely because what He says has eternal significance. Only His voice tells of God who sent His Son to save us from sin and death. He is the Way, the Truth, and the Life, and "there is no other name under heaven given among men by which we must be saved" (Acts 4:12). A person may have the best of intentions and be completely sincere, but to believe that just any view about God will open the gates of heaven is equally as unreasonable as believing that any liquid poured into the tank of your car will make it run.

Upsetting events and hard experiences of life may press in on us. Competing, contradictory, and distracting voices may confuse us as we face life's sometimes bewildering madness. The self-seeking life-style of many would suggest that life must always be filled with "gusto." Listen to the gentle voice of the Master who invites you to take up your cross and follow Him. Crass self-indulgence is not really living. Security and hope for the days to come are not simply by-products of "something to believe in" — no matter what it may be. Listen to the voice of Him who said, "If you continue in My Word, you are My disciples, and you will know the truth, and the truth will make you free" (John 8:31-32).

As we move through these holy days, we need not despair. The voice of God is still to be heard. No noisy or boisterous voices shall overcome the sure, still, yet strong voice of the Lord. Luther and the other reformers offer good counsel: "Let the man who would hear God speak read Holy Scripture." As we daily search the Scriptures, we will hear the living voice of Him who calls us sons and daughters. This is the voice of a loving and gracious Father who does not despise a broken and contrite heart. By the power of His Spirit He opens our ears so that we can listen to the Master's voice.

God's Son Under Pressure

FIRST SUNDAY IN LENT
MARK 1:12-15

Eugene L. Krentz

More than one person I know is convinced that facing the realities of life is like being in a pressure cooker. Is that the way you feel? There is plenty of evidence that the pressure of life squeezes in on people. The voice of a college student is filled with exasperation as she exclaims, "I wish that I could escape the pressure of life for just one long weekend!" A bumper sticker on a passing car invites motorists to "Honk, if you can cope." A book written expressly for Christians poses the troubling question, *Why Do Christians Break Down?*

The pressures of life are real, and they make the days difficult for all of us. Children, you may face the pressures of growing up, of making difficult decisions. Teenagers, for you the pressures might involve the struggle of living your life for God when friends all around you encourage a life with no restraints — a life for which the guiding principle is "Do your own thing." Singles, you have the pressures of trying to make your way in a culture that caters primarily to families and couples. Parents, for you the pressures include the challenge of maintaining a home where love prevails and Christ is at the center of things. Aging saints, yours may be in the ongoing battle of enduring loneliness and maintaining your confidence that life is still important and worthwhile.

Pressures do crowd in on people who live in a broken world where sin wreaks its persistent havoc. God's Word sweeps away our illusions about life when it states in the Book of Job, "Man is born to trouble as the sparks fly upward" (Job 5:7). Life, even for Christians, is not lived on some easy street far from pressure. In the face of this reality St. Mark says something that we must hear. He offers help, hope, and direction as we make our way through life because he ushers us into the presence of Christ, who said, "Come... and learn from Me" (Matt. 11:28-29). In His presence the struggle of life takes on different dimensions because we meet

God's Son Under Pressure

Jesus Faces the Harsh Realities of Life

Does it seem strange to suggest that Christ lived under pressure? Listen to the words of the Gospel: "The Spirit immediately drove Him out into the wilderness. And He was in the wilderness forty days, tempted by Satan; and He was with the wild beasts" (Mark 1:12-13). St. Mark had just reported the baptism of our Lord. At that time the Father decisively affirmed the sonship of Jesus: "Thou art My beloved Son," He said; "with Thee I am well pleased" (v. 11).

Our Lord was holy, absolutely perfect, the possessor of all power and authority, "very God of very God." But He was, as the Scriptures make plain, also a real man, "born in the likeness of men" (Phil. 2:7), flesh of our flesh and bone of our bone. He was bound up in the fabric of life as a *man*, enduring what you and I endure, tempted as we are tempted, under the real pressures of life in a real world.

In describing the temptation of our Lord, St. Mark is not rehearsing some staged drama, nor is he talking about a fictitious, horned and hooved, paper Satan. This is real drama of the God-man, Jesus Christ, under pressure. Here is the excruciating battle of a Savior who, in body and soul, is struggling for His life. All the harsh realities of life closed in on Him during those 40 long days and nights in the wilderness. This was the hostile environment where man cannot live, the place of the curse where loneliness is a burden, where thirst and hunger are constant companions, and where animals once called into being by His voice seek to make Him their prey.

St. Matthew and St. Luke provide the vivid details of Satan's cunning attempts to ensnare our Savior: the taunt to turn stones into bread, the challenge to leap from the temple wall to test God's ability to care for His own, the offer of the world's power and glory in return for fleeting moments of worship.

The wilderness experience was not the only test He faced. Our Lord's whole life and ministry were burdened by the pressures of loneliness, heartache, disappointment, and temptation. "Foxes have holes, and birds of the air have nests," He said, "but the Son of Man has nowhere to lay His head" (Matt. 8:20). Forty days in the wilderness were only the prelude to a struggle with Satan that dogged Him every step of the way and finally ended on a rough cross with the cry, "It is finished" (John 19:30).

First-century Christians who read St. Mark's gospel knew something about life under pressure. For them it sometimes involved martyrdom. They remembered well the brutal beheading of John the Baptist, not because he was evil but because he called people to faith in Christ, the Lamb of God, who had come to rescue and save the lost. The pressure was really on for those early Christians. Heavy taxation was the rule. They faced the boiling hatred of others because they stood up for what they believed and refused to participate in pagan feasts where idolatry and immorality were practiced.

Fire swept Rome in A.D. 64. The historian Tacitus records that many people believed that Nero, the Roman ruler, was himself responsible for the blaze that caused widespread destruction and loss of life. Christians, however, were the ones who felt the pressure. To divert attention from himself, Nero blamed them for the fire. Many were arrested, unjustly judged, and condemned to death. Some were clothed in the skins of wild animals and then torn to pieces by enraged dogs. Others were covered with pitch, ignited, and used as torches to provide light for Nero's darkened courtyards and gardens.

"What does all this have to do with *me*?" you ask. Just this: Christians do not escape the tough battle with Satan and the harsh realities of life. Jesus never offered life without pain or suffering. He never encouraged a rose-colored-glasses approach to living. His theology is a theology of the cross. He held up His life as the reflection of our own and stated honestly, "Truly, truly, I say to you, a servant is not greater than his master" (John 13:16).

The world is still a tough place. Pressures and troubles are not just abstract ideas or things that always happen to someone else. Satan is alive and well in these contemporary times. We all have done business with him, and we can apply to our own lives the Lord's caution to Peter: "Simon, Simon, behold, Satan demanded to have you, that he might sift you like wheat" (Luke 22:31).

Satan's cunning invitations have tricked us. The dust and the ashes of our readiness to heed his voice are all about us. Husbands and wives cast their marriage commitments aside because they believe the grass is greener somewhere else. Young and old wallow in self-pity because they are convinced that only bad things happen to them. Youth and adults fool themselves into believing that drugs and alcohol will solve serious problems.

What about your life? Are the pressures pushing you beyond the limits of your endurance? Are temptations getting the upper hand? Does your way of handling the pressures of life rise up to accuse you? Are you convinced that you cannot go another day or another step? Is the cry of your heart one that pleads, "O God, where are You when I need You most?" Do you identify with the Psalmist who exclaimed, "Hear my cry, O God, listen to my prayer; from the end of the earth I call to Thee, when my heart is faint" (Ps. 61:1-2)?

We all need help and strength for life's daily struggles so that we can face the pressure and keep going. What we desperately need, Jesus, the risen Lord, can and does provide. Look to Him. He sets the pattern that makes it possible to overcome and prevail, whatever the pressure.

Jesus Prevails in the Midst of Life's Struggle

Our Savior withstood the pressure. He did not crumble or wilt when the going got tough. He refused to compromise with temptation and fought the devil with firm resolve and all His strength. The battle in the wilderness was not the entire campaign, but it was a sweeping victory in behalf of you and me. At the conclusion of this fierce struggle St. Mark reports, "The angels ministered to Him" (Mark 1:13).

Even though the angels cared for and served our Lord, it is important to note that Jesus never separated Himself from the real hardships, temptations, and struggles that ordinary folks also endured. He prevailed as He used the power that is also available to each of us — the power of the Word of God. How strong and majestic are the words He used to fell the evil one: "It is written, 'Man shall not live by bread alone, but by every word that proceeds from the mouth of God'" (Matt. 4:4). "You shall not tempt the Lord your God" (v. 7). "You shall worship the Lord your God and Him only shall you serve" (v. 10). Not only did our Lord use the Word, but He also undoubtedly remembered the context of the words spoken to the people of Israel in a former age: "He [God] humbled you and let you hunger... that He might make you know that man does not live by bread alone, but that man lives by everything that proceeds out of the mouth of the Lord" (Deut. 8:3).

Our Lord Jesus never compromised with evil. He stood strong before it and prevailed even when the struggle was fidrce, painful, and long. He moved forward because there was work to be done, work that He alone could do — forgiving those who had been tricked by Satan, picking up those who had crumbled under the heavy load of their sins, encouraging those who doubted His word and promises, lifting those who were weary and desperate for help.

With a Savior like that, it is no surprise that the first-century Christians did not cave in to the threats and pressures of martyrdom. They met death with boldness, the words of forgiveness and hymns of praise on their lips. How could they do it? Simply because their faith was built on the "Gospel of God" (Mark 1:14). The world in which they lived was not Nero's world but

God's. Time was fulfilled in the coming of Christ, and the rule of God brought power, courage, and strength to those who believed the Gospel.

Is your life under pressure? Are you hurting in the midst of the struggle? Do you feel as though Satan is winning the battle? Are you worried about whether you can cope or thinking about giving up on yourself — and God, too? Take heart and find strength in the Savior, who faced life's struggles. He prevailed and makes it possible for you to prevail also. He is the living Lord. He cares for His own as a father cares for His children. He will not abandon those whom He has forgiven and made His own through His death and resurrection.

Whatever your circumstances may be, His assurance rings out in the words of Paul that "in everything God works for good with those who love Him" (Rom. 8:28). Take heart from the fact that Christ is the "Seed of the woman," who crushed Satan's power. Boldly exclaim with St. Paul, "We are more than conquerors through Him who loved us." Nothing in all creation "will be able to separate us from the love of God in Christ Jesus our Lord" (Rom. 8:37, 39).

A few years ago a young lad was running across the open fields not far from his home. Life was carefree and smooth, but everything changed in seconds when he tumbled down an old abandoned mine shaft. Down at the bottom, where the shaft narrowed, he was wedged in. There was little he could do to free himself from that cold, dark, damp, and foreboding space. In desperation he shouted for help, and someone heard. People came to the top of the shaft. Looking down they spoke reassuringly: "Everything will be all right. We will get you out. God will take care of you."

None of those well-intentioned words could free the lad. It was only when they tied a strong rope around the ankles of a man and lowered him headfirst down the shaft that the lad knew he would be helped. Strong hands grasped his shoulders and held on tightly as the two were pulled to the top of the shaft.

This is what Jesus Christ has done for you! He does not simply speak from a distance to people facing the real pressures of life. He comes down into the dark shaft of this sinful world to be with us. In the tight spaces where we are trapped, He reaches out to grasp us and hold us tightly in His everlasting arms. In the crucible of life's most severe pressures He makes it possible for us to keep going. Cheer up! You are not alone in the struggle. Christ, through His death and resurrection, won the battle. He loves you. The psalmist found help and hope in the Lord, and today you can, too. "Wait for the Lord; be strong, and let your heart take courage" (Ps. 27:14).

The Not-So-Secret Secret

SECOND SUNDAY IN LENT
MARK 8:31-38

Oswald F. Wagner

Today's Gospel speaks of a secret that is not so secret. That seems to be the point of St. Mark's distinction between those who heard Jesus' teaching about His suffering, death, and resurrection and "the multitude with His disciples" to whom He spoke about taking up one's cross and saving one's life.

Words for Disciples

Jesus first speaks to the 12 disciples alone. What He tells them is a private matter, something very important for them especially to understand.

Startling Words

We listen in on the private conversation because we dare to include ourselves in the disciples' number. We have come to believe what the Twelve for the first time confessed about Jesus — that He is the Christ, the Son of the living God. It was only after this confession that Jesus "began to teach them" the surprising secret "that the Son of Man must suffer many things, and be rejected. . . and be killed. . . and after three days rise again" (Mark 8:31).

Mark emphasizes that Jesus "said this plainly" (v. 32). Do you sense that He realized how difficult it would be for the disciples to accept these facts? Remember that the Twelve had been conditioned by popular Jewish religious expectation to look for a powerful political Messiah who would restore Israel's independence and prosperity through a national uprising against foreign oppressors. The people might have to die in support of such efforts to overthrow an empire, but the Messiah could not die if he hoped to do any good for the people.

Peter's rebuke of Jesus probably had an argumentative sound to it. We can almost hear him saying, "Common sense will tell you, Jesus, that only those who take fullest advantage of their enemies and conquer them ever get any recognition in the world. The Messiah must be like that, too. Your proven ability to do great miracles will accomplish what we need and want from you. So don't let thoughts of defeat and dying in the face of mounting opposition cause you to give up now — especially not now, when we've just discovered you as the center of our hopes for our nation. You can count on us to further your cause. There will be many more like us." No wonder Jesus called Peter the very devil himself!

Words of Rebuke

In all His person-to-person teaching of the disciples from this point onward, Jesus insisted that God brings His desired intentions to pass in ways that are exactly the opposite of the world's idea of success. The Christ must go through the total self-denial and self-sacrifice predicted by Jesus in order to atone for the self-centeredness of human existence. Peter, in wanting nothing like that for Jesus, was, without realizing it, cutting himself off from the ultimate good Jesus wanted to do for him and all mankind.

Although we are disciples of Jesus, our circumstances are considerably different from those of the Twelve when Jesus first spoke about His suffering and dying. We know that what Jesus predicted came true in horrible reality. We have the benefit of the Gospel proclamation of what the betrayal, the crucifixion, and the resurrection of Jesus actually accomplished for our salvation.

So we no longer protest against Jesus' talk of suffering and dying. We hold it as the heart of our Christian faith, and we confess the saving significance of all He endured in His love for us. But we can, like Peter, still be cutting ourselves off from the good that God intended for us if we reject the principle of self-giving by which the kingdom of God takes form in this world.

As long as we are hesitant to forgive and unwilling to help an enemy by acts of love, Satan's will is being done, not God's. While Christian disciples today speak much about trusting God to take care of them when they die, many aren't so ready to trust Him to take care of them throughout a life of self-denial and self-giving. Insofar as we Christians act on impulse or with selfish common sense according to traditional worldly value systems, Jesus will have to respond to us as He responded to Peter. That response is in fact a part of His secret caring for us and sharing with us.

We must appreciate the fact that rebuke from Jesus, as from God Himself, is part of His secret ministry to His disciples. He cares deeply about His inner circle. We need to sense very clearly that whatever causes us to resist God's way of self-giving love is Satanic and deadly indeed — in fact, the real cause of Christ's dying. That awareness of being "dead in sin" involves us in the death of Jesus *as* our Savior.

Words of Promise

But Jesus had more than rebuke for Peter and the Twelve. Part of His prediction was that, although He would "suffer many things. . . and be killed," He would "after three days rise again." The disciples didn't really hear His promise of a resurrection, nor could they consider its significance, as long as they were so set against the possibility of any good coming to them through His death. But Jesus persisted in His secret way, always including the promise of resurrection with every prediction of His rejection and death.

As part of His ministry in secret among us, Jesus also wants to impress on us the importance of the resurrection. Because we live after Easter, we have heard the full Biblical witness to His resurrection as His promise to us of a life in blessedness beyond the grave. The Holy Spirit has used that Good News to fill us not only with hope for the future beyond the grave but also with the impulse to love and serve our Savior here in this world. But this aspect of the resurrection message often tends to have the weakest impact on us, just as it was with the disciples of old. Great is our loss when we fail to hear fully what Christ's and the Christian's resurrection are all about.

The personal, secret thing that goes on between Jesus and every true believer centers first on His dying *and rising* for us and then on our dying *and rising* with Him. Through the Gospel that tells of the Savior's dying to take away all sin, we believe that our sins are fully forgiven. We are also stirred in the power of the Holy Spirit to trust God more and more as the Father who cares for us so perfectly that we are able and willing to act in a more and more forgiving and self-giving way—just the way our Savior Jesus has acted for us.

But life for us as Christians is not one of effortless self-improvement. It is rather a constant process of recognizing that we are by nature dead in sin and having our hope directed again and again to our Savior and the forgiveness of our sin through His death for us. It means being joined in Baptism with His death and resurrection so that with Him we die to sin and are raised to newness of life. The life of God within us directs us in this daily process of dying to sin and living the new life in firm confidence that we are His both now and eternally.

The world, of course, can't comprehend what really goes on between us and our Savior, Jesus the Christ. It can't understand the significance of His dying and rising and their effects in us. The joy we have in our baptism, our eagerness for the Eucharistic fellowship, our churchgoing and Bible study seem to be mere pious nonsense. It really does no good to argue with the world about any of these secret things. Trying to prove their reality only arouses unbelief's skeptical resistance.

Words for the World

But there is something about the Christ and Christians that the world can understand. Jesus therefore speaks also to "the multitude with His disciples." He would give the world a way to judge whether His life and teaching and promises are of any value. He offers the world a proper way in which to judge whether Christians' claims of being followers of God in Christ are valid.

Jesus also wants any would-be follower of His to consider well what is involved in such following. So He directs His words especially to the disciples who are among the multitudes, to help them to do those things that bring honor to Him and His heavenly Father.

Jesus describes three radically unique things that disciples, through prayerful, continuing effort under the means of grace, can do. Denying oneself is the first. That has to do with trying day after day to not let selfishness rule us in our relationships with others.

Losing life for the sake of Christ and the Gospel — the second thing — involves struggling to use our personal, social, and economic position, not merely for our own satisfaction and enjoyment, but for the good of others.

The third thing is not being ashamed of Jesus. This includes a willingness to live as Jesus did, in defiance of cultural standards that tend to exclude people. It means including in our fellowship the social outcasts despised by the world, regarding them as beloved of God, people for whom the Savior also died.

These three things are the underlying attitudes and actions by which Christians actually let the world in on the mystery and the secret of godliness. Here is the visible demonstration of what it means to be saved through the grace of God in Jesus Christ.

As our joy in being God's forgiven people is reflected in such a Christ-honoring life-style, we will not only have more opportunity than ever to talk about the secret happenings going on between Christ and the believer, but we will also have more reason than ever to know that our Gospel words do lead others to really find the blessing that comes from being in on the secret of dying and rising with Christ.

How much greater our joy and blessing will be as we continue to be more and more a part of letting God's secret out. For He really wants what He does in forgiving grace to be a secret that is not so secret. He really wants all the world to know it and to be blessed through His dying and rising, His gracious forgiving and caring for all who believe in Him.

Three Temples Through the Eyes of God

THIRD SUNDAY IN LENT
JOHN 2:13-22

Oswald F. Wagner

Tour guides try to show their travel parties places of historic importance from the best possible vantage point. As they approach an object for a closer view, they usually will describe the dimensions, the age, and the significance of what is being viewed.

Today's Gospel gives us an opportunity to view three temples of the Lord from a viewpoint that the Holy Spirit has chosen and to grow in our awareness of the significance of what we are seeing. The Holy Spirit in fact serves as the very eyes for our viewing. While no tourist guide would presume to say to his travel party, "I want you to look at this particular site through God's own eyes," that is what we have the opportunity to do through this text.

The Jerusalem Temple

Our attention is first directed to a building that Jesus saw and entered one spring day. It is the impressive temple of Herod that once stood on Mt. Zion in Jerusalem.

We can't actually see the building that Jesus saw. It no longer exists, and no precise images of it have been developed through archaeological digging. Seeing this temple with the eyes of God is not merely a matter of trying to imagine what Jesus saw or to feel what he might have felt when He saw it. We would not really be viewing the temple through the eyes of God, even if we could see it with the heightened thankfulness Jesus probably felt toward His Father for all His marvelous works that fill the world with beauty.

God's seeing penetrates to the essence of things. In the busyness and grandeur of this temple Jesus saw evil rather than a godly purpose being served. If a building was truly to serve as the temple of the Lord, it would have to be a place where God was made known and worshiped as the merciful bestower of undeserved blessing on His chosen people. Everything said or done by that people in their temple would have to be in response to the love of God proclaimed to them through word and ceremony within the place. Jerusalem's temple was supposed to give glorious recognition to the one true God and the ways of His grace. The sacrifices and the ceremonies performed there were to be reminders of how good God was to Israel— always in measures beyond their deserving— and responses of praise and thanksgiving to Him.

The temple's purpose, however, had been perverted. It had become a place where the people dutifully performed carefully regulated rituals in hope of meriting God's favor and not as a response of dedication and obedience to the unmerited favor of God. Jesus saw all the business being carried on in the temple complex as a product of perverted twists in the theology of the scribes and Pharisees. What angered Him more than the smell and noise in the courtyard was that His Father's house had been made into a house of trade in the inner sanctuary and in the hearts of the worshipers. It was a priestly trade talk, implying that the people's maintaining of the building, the priesthood, and the ritual use of the facility guaranteed God's favor on the nation, that was most offensive to Christ and His heavenly Father. If our viewing of any temple building is to be through the eyes of God, we too must assess its godly worth as Jesus did, considering the purpose of the worship done there.

This is a good reminder for us that our maintaining a place of worship and our attendance at its services can also become an unholy, Christ-angering thing if we suppose that we are engaged in trading some of our time and the support we give to the church for some further outpourings of God's favor. We meet here today, and this is our temple of the Lord, because through our baptism and the unfailing forgiveness that is ours in Jesus Christ we are God's believing and already favored people. We come together because we want to be assured through Word and Sacrament that God does love us without our deserving. We come to increase our love toward God according to His deserving.

Jesus, the True Temple of God

Such worshipful, believing reflection on God's always prior, undeserved, and continued grace brings the second temple of the Lord into our view. This temple rises before us in amazing and even more glorious beauty than the temple that once stood on the heights of Jerusalem and is certainly more glorious than this building in which we gather. Today's Gospel, in fact, has its primary purpose that we recognize this temple as supreme, towering over heaven itself. We want to get a properly focused and never-fading picture of this temple as something to carry with us always, not as a photo in our billfold or purse, but as the Treasure of treasures imprinted in our hearts.

This second Temple of the Lord is a living person, not merely a building. The true Temple of God is the man Jesus. We don't usually speak of Him as the Temple of the Lord, but that He truly is.

Note how Jesus identifies Himself as the true Temple of the Lord God's presence on earth among men. He was so upset by the religious trading carried on in the temple building in Jerusalem that He drove the merchants and money changers out of it. We picture Him with whip still in hand. He breathes deeply from His angered exertions. He says to those challenging His actions, "Destroy this Temple, and in three days I will raise it up." "This Temple" was a reference to His bodily self. John wants us to see Jesus as the very One in whom God has chosen to dwell among men. The fullness of God is templed, as it were, in Jesus, God's son.

We can see Jesus in this way only through the eyes of God. God has given us His eyes in the person of the Holy Spirit. Here and now, and in all Christian worship, God is enabling us through the Spirit to see the Christ in faith.

When we see Jesus in this way, we remember that He came to earth to replace the building that previously was to have drawn the people of Israel to the proper worship of the one true God. The building in Jerusalem had already been under construction for 46 years in Jesus' day. It was not to be completed before A.D. 70 when Jerusalem and the temple on Zion would be totally destroyed. While the body of Jesus was also to be broken in death, it would be eternally restored, as Jesus was here foretelling, to the fullness of heavenly beauty and being through the resurrection of Easter morning. And now He who is the Christ stands as the true Temple of God, yearning to bring the world to Himself under His Father's grace and blessing. Thus He and His Spirit have drawn us in trust and love to Himself as the One in whom the "fullness of God" has its dwelling.

Just as people of old were expected to approach the temple building in Jerusalem without thought of earning favor from God thereby, we now approach Jesus in the same way. Our naming His name in prayer, praise, and witness is done without any self-seeking intention. We acknowledge Him as Savior and Lord, not in some sort of bargaining arrangement with God, but only as beggars who know we have nothing to offer Him but simply desire His assurance of free and full forgiveness. His acceptance of us in this way becomes the impulse for our ongoing loving service done to honor Him.

Believers as the Temple of God

Whenever we come to Christ in worship, drawn by God's love and desiring to live in His ways, another of the true temples of the Lord comes into view. Admittedly and obviously, it's a lesser temple than the one we've just been describing—Jesus Himself—yet it is very closely related to that Temple. Although not called such in the Gospel, this third temple appears in the words that describe Jesus' disciples as those who "remembered" and "believed the Scripture and the word which Jesus had spoken" (John 2:22). All believing hearers of God's Word are the third temple of the Lord.

These disciples might look like ordinary folk, but when we see them through the eyes of God, we recognize them as temples of the Lord's presence on earth. Through them God's loving ways of grace continue to be visibly active and effective for this world's good. Take an appreciative look around at all of them. When we see our fellow believers, we are to regard them as temples of the Holy Spirit. And we should also see ourselves as one with them—temples in which God truly dwells. As such living temples of the Lord, we are beneficiaries of God's saving grace through Word and Sacrament, and we are also bestowers of God's saving grace by our involvement in and support of the ministry of the means of grace.

Let us remember therefore that our approach to this third temple of the Lord must be fully in keeping with what we said about approaching the other two temples—our place of worship and the Temple whom we worship as God and Savior. The Spirit will not let us approach this third temple with the idea of getting something for our advantage from it. In other words, we do not approach other Christians—giving them our welcome, our attentive ear, a shoulder to cry on, or some other help and care—with the thought that once they are obligated to us, they will owe us even greater favors. When we rightly regard fellow believers as the very temple of the Lord, we show our love and do our service toward them purely and patiently in view of the will of God for their well-being, concerned only for their gain and joy.

There is a big problem, then, if we talk of trying to win new church members, if not in the hope of personal gain for our efforts, then at least in the hope merely of organizational or program gains, while we claim to honor Christ. Any programmed manipulating of people, even if done to serve the growth of the church, can comes dangerously close to profaning the holy temples that believers in Christ really are.

So there are three temples of the Lord that today's Gospel has provided for our viewing. In a sense the Holy Spirit has offered Himself as the eyeglasses to make our proper viewing possible. But the Spirit doesn't merely want to be eyeglasses or contact lenses, which can be laid aside or lost. Here and now, in these words and in the Eucharist, He would once again be an eye transplant for us. Through His enlightening we can see all three temples — our temples of godly worship, the Temple who is our Savior Jesus Christ, and those who have Jesus as Lord in their hearts — as having God alive and present in them for the blessing and salvation of the world. Most blessed are we in honoring and serving these three temples. for to serve one is to serve the others. When we serve Christ, we are intimately involved with the other two as well.

Indestructible — and More

FOURTH SUNDAY IN LENT
JOHN 3:14-21

Victor A. Constien

The editor of *Prevention* magazine was being interviewed for a television talk show. It was being taped for later showing. The interviewer commented that the editor was still so active and healthy at 70 years of age. The editor responded that he didn't see any reason why he shouldn't be working when he was 80. Before they finished the taping, the editor had a heart attack and died on the set. They didn't use the tape.

We would all like to think that we will live forever here in this world, that we will not die, that we are indestructible. But when we hear about people like the editor of *Prevention* magazine or our friends and relatives who die, we realize that life on earth does end. It is destructible. The Gospel for this Fourth Sunday in Lent deals with a different kind of life, a life that is indestructible — yes, and even more.

Indestructible — and More

Life that is indestructible — and more? Yes, but only for those who believe. It is not for those who reject Jesus Christ, Son of God and Son of Man. This was the issue for Nicodemus, with whom Jesus had a one-on-one confrontation. This was the issue for the first readers of John's gospel. It is also the issue for us. It's a matter of faith or unbelief.

John wrote, "He who does not believe is condemned already, because he has not believed in the name of the only Son of God" (John 3:18). The wages of sin is indeed death. Death is the very enemy that Jesus, God's only Son, was sent to conquer. But those who do not believe that He has overcome death for us remain condemned by God. The verdict has already been leveled against those who do not believe. They are guilty and judged because they do not believe in the name of the only Son of God.

Have you ever read of disturbed persons who try to injure or even kill the doctor who has spent hours providing personal treatment? We hardly know how to describe such a tragedy. The doctor is able to provide help in the form of therapy or surgery. He can prescribe a remedy to cure the illness.

But we shake our heads in distress when the patient rejects the help, refuses to admit the illness, pours the medication down the drain, and turns on the doctor. Surely such a person has gone totally berserk!

Yet some situations are even more tragic because they have eternal consequences. As John observed, "The Light has come into the world, and men loved darkness rather than light, because their deeds were evil. For everyone who does evil hates the light and does not come to the light, lest his deeds should be exposed" (vv. 19-20). Jesus Himself is the Light that has come into the world. God's revelation of hope and salvation is embodied in Him. With the light of the glory of God's grace and forgiveness, Jesus is sent to enlighten the hearts and minds of all people. John and all the other New Testament writers bore witness to the light. They knew that the light had come in Jesus and was present in the world then and there. We know that the light is also present here and now. Wherever God's Word is preached and taught, the light shines.

If we do not believe, we cannot see the light. But why would we reject the light, preferring darkness? The reason is that deep within we love the darkness. We prefer the evil. We want to be selfish, to make decisions independent of other people's interests and needs, to take advantage of the weaknesses of others, to advance at the expense of others. Dethroning God, we want to deify ourselves so that we can live by our own rules.

Life Is God's Gift of Love Through Faith

Can there still be life for us, indestructible and more? Not under God's law. By His law God exposes our evil deeds as works of darkness. If we put our hope in the Law, we are condemned already because we do not put our trust in Jesus and His forgiveness. Severed from God by our unbelief, we are condemned to endless punishment in hell.

Yet, there is indestructible life for us — and more — because of God's love for us. God committed His Son to the mission of redeeming us from sin and death. Through faith in Jesus' completed work God grants us eternal, indestructible life and more — the fullness of joy that is still to be revealed when we come into His presence at the Last Day.

Remember how God awakened faith in the people of Israel as they trekked through the wilderness? Jesus recalled the event for Nicodemus: "Moses lifted up the serpent in the wilderness" (v. 14). Everyone who reads the Book of Numbers is startled by the record. First came God's judgment on Israel because of their impatience and disobedience. They did not want God to bring them out of Egypt. They loathed the food God gave them and complained that it was not enough. They spoke against God and against Moses, the leader God had appointed. "Then the Lord sent fiery serpents among the people, and they bit the people, so that many people of Israel died" (Num. 21:6).

As the people repented, they begged Moses to ask God to take the serpents away. In answer to his prayer God said to Moses, "Make a fiery serpent, and set it on a pole, and everyone who is bitten, when he sees it, shall live" (v. 8). And that's what happened. "Moses made a bronze serpent, and set it on a pole, and if a serpent bit any man, he would look at the bronze serpent and live" (v. 9).

Referring to this Old Testament type of Himself and His work, Jesus said to Nicodemus, "As Moses lifted up the serpent in the wilderness, so must the Son of Man be lifted up, that whoever believes in Him may have eternal life" (John 3:14-15). Nicodemus may not have understood Jesus immediately. But what kind of lifting up would God awaken faith in those who would look to Jesus as the Israelites looked to the bronze serpent? Jesus explained it Himself in a later conversation with His disciples. As He readied them for His death, He said, "I, when I am lifted up from the earth, will draw all men to Myself" (John 12:32) Then John observed, "He said this to show by what death He was to die" (v. 33).

When it was all over, things were much clearer to the disciples, of course. After His crucifixion and resurrection they could see the meaning of His words. Nicodemus could, too. God the Father lifted Jesus to that cross just as surely as God instructed Moses to lift that serpent on the pole. In God's plan it was necessary. Only through the death of His Son would God in His love offer eternal life to those who believe. "So *must* the Son of Man be lifted up, that whoever believes in Him may have eternal life" (John 3:14-15, emphasis added).

When Jesus used the word *must*, He went straight to the heart of the matter. In the final analysis Jesus did not die because angry and proud people nailed Him to the cross. He died because of God's love. That love must show itself so that people can experience it and know that it is for them. This is how we recognize God's compassion for us: "He. . . did not spare His own Son but gave Him up for us all" (Rom. 8:32). "In this the love of God was made manifest among us, that God sent His only Son into the world, so that we might live through Him. In this is love, not that we loved God but that He loved us and sent His Son to be the expiation for our sins" (1 John 4:9-10).

All the work by which God calms distressed hearts, forgives guilty consciences, and awakens confidence for the future is summarized in John 3:16: "God so loved the world that He gave His only Son, that whoever believes in Him should not perish but have eternal life."

Martin Luther was especially intrigued by the words *not perish*. What does it mean that whoever believes in Jesus will not perish? Calling the words "inexpressibly glorious," he suggested that they mean

> to be rid of sin, to have a good conscience, and not to be under the Law. Otherwise the Law punishes sin; but now, even if someone feels sin and the wrath of God, sin will not give him a bad conscience, because his sin is forgiven. The Law will not accuse him; sin will not bite or plague him; death will not devour him; for if he believes these words, he is safe and secure. (*Sermons on the Gospel of St. John, Chapters 1-4* trans. Martin H. Bertram; ed. Jaroslav Pelikan. *Luther's Works*, American Edition, Vol. 22 [St. Louis: Concordia Publishing House, 1957], p. 369)

Shortly after the terrible crash of Air Florida's Flight 90 in January

1982, *Time* magazine printed an essay entitled, "The Man in the Water." The man in the water was the unnamed hero who was one of the survivors clinging to the tail section of the plane in the Potomac River. Every time the rescue helicopter lowered a lifeline, he passed it to one of the other passengers. When the helicopter had rescued all the others and finally came back to get him, it was too late. He had gone under the icy waters. He knew as he passed the lifeline, especially that last time, and the helicopter pulled the passenger to safety, that he was giving up his chances for life. He sacrificed his life to a cold death in the river so that the others could live. Jesus Christ, God's Son, gave His life on the cross so that you and I do not have to perish but can have life — life that is indestructible, that never ends, that is eternal.

God offers that salvation, that indestructible life, to everyone. But that life is received only by faith. On the one hand, it's true that *whoever* believes in Jesus will not perish. Everyone is included in God's plan. No one is omitted or excluded from God's offer. But on the other hand, only those who personally believe can receive His gift of life. "*He who believes* in Him is not condemned" (v. 18, emphasis added). The faith that is needed to receive the promised life is itself a gift from God as His Spirit uses the Word of the Gospel to reach and change our hearts.

In His Son Jesus God gives eternal life to this community, to this congregation. It is for you, Mary, who believe in Him and are not condemned. It is you, John, who believe in Him and will not perish. It is you, Camille, who believe in Him and have eternal life. When Mary, filled with trust, says, "I believe in Jesus," her sins are drowned in the depth of the Father's love for her. When John says, "I believe in Jesus," and says it from the heart, Satan and temptation must give way. When Camille sincerely says, "I believe in Jesus," fears and doubts fade in the presence of the powerful Jesus, who holds her fast. The person who belives in Jesus is not condemned, but has new life — indestructible life.

Life Can Be Clearly Seen
in Those Who Do What Is True

How obvious is it that a person believes in Jesus and has the indestructible life God gives? "He who does what is true comes to the light, that it may be clearly seen that his deeds have been wrought in God" (v. 21). The indestructible life God gives us in Jesus has its effects. When we believe, we are born again (v. 3). God creates new life in us and lives in us. This is the indestructible life — God alive in us.

People who have the life of Jesus, who is the Truth, within them begin to *do the truth*. Having received the truth of their salvation by grace through Christ, they put that truth into action. Their lives are marked by a spirit of repentance. They openly confess their faith in Christ. They worship God in public and in private. They nurture and instruct one another in the promises of God and in His will for them. They pass the lifeline to others by telling them of God's offer of life. They care about people, both those who are oppressed and those who do the oppressing. In imitation of Christ they love all people, even their enemies.

Indestructible life and more is yours and mine through faith in Jesus. It is life that never ends. Our bodies will die, and this physical earth will pass away, but our life with God will never end. It is indestructible. It is an abundant life, as Jesus called it (John 10:10), because it is lived in fellowship with God day by day.

But it is even more. One day it will be life in the full presence of God in His glory and majesty where there is complete joy forever. Enjoy your life with God today and every day. It is a foretaste of the fulfillment we will know in heaven.

An Hour of Power

FIFTH SUNDAY IN LENT
JOHN 12:20-33

Victor A. Constien

One of the most popular religious programs on television in terms of the number of people who view it Sunday after Sunday is called the "Hour of Power." When some people first hear the name, "Hour of Power," they have a negative reaction because they think of power as pressure or force applied from a position of influence in order to gain one's end. However, a different kind of power is meant in that name—a power that comes from God. The program is intended to be an hour in which viewers are exposed to the unseen power of God.

In that sense this worship service is an "hour of power." We are drawn here to be exposed to the power of a gracious God and a loving Lord and Savior, Jesus Christ. Wherever His Word is read and His sacraments of Baptism and the Lord's Supper are administered, God communicates His power into the lives of those who put their trust in Him. So we Christians gather around His means of grace so that we can receive His strength for our lives.

That's the purpose of our meditation on the Gospel for today—to help make this an "hour of power" for you. May God grant us His Spirit so that we understand, believe, and put into action the power He gives as we examine these points:
1. Self-love robs us of power.
2. The power we need is in Christ's death for our sins.
3. His power is for everyone, regardless of national origin or social status.
4. When we are empowered by faith in Christ, we learn to gain life by losing it.

Self-Love Robs Us of Power

"He who loves his life loses it" (John 12:25), Jesus told His disciples as they prepared for the feast of the Passover just prior to His death. Those words were a strong warning. They expose a tender spot in each of us. We love this life of ours so much that we cling to it with a passion. We devote ourselves to preserving it. We worship the happiness, success, treasures, and pleasures that we seek from life.

That's our undoing. We put the love of self first. But to choose self over God and our Lord Jesus Christ; over wife, husband, or children; or over any of those people who count on us to be a neighbor to them is to let life slip away from us. Self-love robs us of power because, as we serve ourselves, we are drawn away from the source of power — God and His love. If we do not love God with all our heart, soul, strength, and mind, we lose life. Without God's life through faith in Jesus we have no power.

True Power Is in Christ's Death for Us

In quiet conversation with His Father our Lord Jesus Christ revealed where the power is:

> [He said,] "Now is My soul troubled. And what shall I say? 'Father, save Me from this hour'? No, for this purpose I have come to this hour. Father, glorify Thy name" The crowd standing by heard it and said that it had thundered. Others said, "An angel has spoken to Him." Jesus answered, "This voice has come for your sake, not for Mine. Now is the judgment of this world, now shall the ruler of this world be cast out; and I, when I am lifted up from the earth, will draw all men to Myself." He said this to show by what death He was to die (vv. 27-33).

Jesus sensed fully what He was up against. He knew and could feel that God had laid on Him the iniquity of us all. The sin of each person in this congregation today increased the pain of His physical and emotional suffering. He was altogether aware that He would die. The sting in His death would not be His own sin, for He was spotless. The sin of the world would squeeze Him lifeless in its grip.

Totally human, He naturally expressed His anguish: "Shall I ask My Father to deliver Me from this hour?" Then with divine resolution He answered His own question: "No. This is the very reason I came to this hour. The Father sent Me to die for the world. This is My mission. I am committed to it."

Blending His own will with that of His Father's, Jesus prayed not that He might be released from His mission but that His Father might be glorified. When His Father answered, the crowd heard the voice from heaven and thought that it had thundered or that an angel had spoken. But the Father had said that His name had been glorified and would be glorified again. That answer confirmed for the disciples that Jesus was indeed the Son of God. Whoever believed in Him would be saved.

Jesus wanted His disciples to experience the hour of His power with Him. In Him the world would be judged, and the ruler of this world, Satan, would be thrown out. At first glance it would appear that the world had judged Christ, found Him guilty, and punished Him with death. But things were not as they appeared to be. This world was not judging Jesus. God in Jesus was judging the sin and unbelief of the world.

This is where we see the power of the almighty God. In *When Bad Things Happen to Good People* Rabbi Harold Kushner seeks to solve one of life's mysteries by changing God. When his 14-year-old son died of a tragic illness, he said he could no longer believe in God as he had learned to know Him in the Bible. He therefore has decided that God is indeed all-loving, but not all-powerful. God hates suffering but He is powerless to eliminate it.

For many people this helps them to believe in God because it seems to be a more "realistic" way of thinking of God. But this is not the God of the Bible, who is all-powerful as well as all-loving. The Bible tells us that sin and evil are real. But God sent His sinless Son to die on the cross for all sin and affirmed His victory over sin and death by raising Him from the dead.

That is the source of power for us, a power that draws us to Jesus. By being lifted up on the cross in crucifixion, by being lifted from the grave in resurrection, and by being lifted again into the Father's presence by His ascension, Jesus has drawn more people to Himself than can ever be computerized. The number is known only to the Father and will be revealed only at the Last Day. Only in the willing death of Jesus, the Son of God, who loved us and gave His life a ransom for us all, have we seen and been possessed by such a magnetic power.

Christ's Power Is for All People

Among the people who came to Jerusalem for the feast of the Passover were several who were not of Hebrew origin. John recalled, "Now among those who went up to worship at the feast were some Greeks. So these came to Philip who was from Bethsaida in Galilee, and said to him, 'Sir, we wish to see Jesus.' Philip went and told Andrew; Andrew went with Philip and they told Jesus" (vv. 20-22).

In the prior verse John had recorded how frustrated the Pharisees felt because they were not able effectively to oppose Jesus. They said to one another, "You see that you can do nothing; look, the world has gone after Him" (v. 19). As if to support their contention, John immediately observed that even Greeks were at the feast with the request to see Jesus. What these Greeks asked, people of all the nations of the world have been asking ever since: "We wish to see Jesus."

We don't know what happened to the Greeks' petition. Did they only seek Jesus' autograph? That's the one thing on the mind of many people who want to be able to say that they shook hands or rode the elevator with a famous person. But they could have done that while Jesus was teaching in the temple.

Perhaps they wanted to talk with Jesus personally because they wanted to know for themselves whether the rumors were true. Was He indeed the Messiah God had promised? Was He truly the Son of God and Savior of the world? Was He the Word made flesh in whom people might see the glory of God, who made the world and would redeem it? While we do not learn their true intent from the Scriptures, we do know the intent of God and His Son Jesus: "In Christ God was reconciling the world to Himself, not counting their trespasses against them" (2 Cor. 5:19). God wants everyone in the world "to be saved and to come to the knowledge of the truth" (1 Tim. 2:4). Jesus intensely yearned also for the salvation of the Greeks who asked to see Him.

Jesus still draws all people to Himself. If the church's world mission is faltering, the fault lies with those of us who have already been drawn to Him. We have become complacent, selfish, and dull. We are not revealing Jesus to those who need to see Him in order to believe in Him. Do we genuinely long for peace, love, and hope for our world? Then we are called to the mission of our Lord Jesus Christ to redeem the world and restore to those who believe in Him the power He gives to be children of God.

Let's rehearse for ourselves the power of Jesus' death: "Jesus answered them 'The hour has come for the Son of Man to be glorified. Truly, truly, I say to you, unless a grain of wheat falls into the earth and dies, it remains alone; but if it dies, it bears much fruit'" (John 12:23-24). Do you remember those elementary school experiments? We watched the kernels of corn planted in the soil deteriorate and die as new life sprang from the seed. A stalk grew. Later it produced ears of corn that multiplied fifty- and a hundredfold the single seed from which the stalk began. Had the seed not died, it would have remained alone. Had Jesus not died, He would have remained alone. But He knew the Father's plan and concurred willingly in it. Power for new life, multiplied in the lives of all the people who believe in Him, is found in Jesus' death for our sins. The death of Christ has borne much fruit. By His death many are saved for life.

Empowered by Christ, We Gain Life by Losing It

From Jesus' death and from His instruction in His Word we discover His power for our lives. Through faith in Him we have our own hour of power as we meditate on His completed work for us and also learn how to make the most out of our lives. "He who loves his life loses it," Jesus said, "and he who hates his life in this world will keep it for eternal life. If anyone serve Me, he must follow Me; and where I am, there shall My servant be also; if anyone serve Me, the Father will honor him" (vv. 25-26). How can any person who hates life in this world keep it for eternal life?

Kurt became a heavy user of drugs while he served in the army in Vietnam. When he returned to his home town in Ohio, he met a young girl who introduced him to Jesus. He said, "I was raised in that town. It has 15 churches, but I had not met Jesus. When my girl friend introduced me to Jesus, it was like the Bible says, 'I was in the land of the dead and now I'm made alive.' I was really far out — out of touch with reality. It was like walking from darkness into light. Everything became real to me."

"Isn't it strange?" Kurt continued. "I was looking for love and peace through drugs. What I got was sex and violence. Now in Christ I receive what I sought — love and peace."

That is what it means for the old life to die, for the kernel to die so that there can be new life. For most of us that happened at our baptism, but the old nature that is so sinful keeps coming back and trying to control our lives. So by daily repentance we need to drown that sinful flesh and let the new life come forth.

That's what it means to be a disciple. To follow Jesus is to have within us the mind of Christ and become servants of God as He was, to walk in the way of truth and life that He gives, to be obedient to Him, and to listen carefully as He speaks to us in His Word so that we trust the guidance of His Spirit and do not lean on our own weak understanding.

This is our hour of power every time we get together around God's Word and Sacrament. Here our Lord judges our self-love. He who loves his life loses it because self-love robs us of God's power. The power we need is in Christ's death for us. His death for our sins brings forth fruit a hundredfold. Christ's power is for all people of every nation, kindred, and language. Empowered by Him we gain life by losing it as disciples of the living Lord for the sake of the Gospel.

Smile, God Loves You

PALM SUNDAY
SUNDAY OF THE PASSION
MARK 15:1-39

Theodore W. Schroeder

That crucifixion account we just read as the Gospel for today is not a very nice story. It is full of evil people, evil deeds, suffering, and death. It has a mood of gloom about it. It projects the ragged image of a cross — a cruel instrument of execution. But yet we read it — again and again, year after year. And we place the image of that cruel cross in a central position in this sanctuary. Why?

After a service that featured this same Gospel reading, a young man came forward. He had a grin on his whiskered face. He would offer a little advice, he said. "It's too grim," he said. "It's all too down, too depressing — all this sin and suffering talk. It's too bleak, man. That's not what people want to hear. People know about hurt and all of that. What they need is a little joy. They need someone to happy them up, to tell them everything will be all right. Listen, I'll tell you what you do. Take that cross down from up there; it's too gloomy. In its place put up a big smiling face that says "Smile, God Loves You" in big letters. That's what people want to hear."

Enough Gloom and Doom

Well, maybe the young man had a point. Certainly there is enough gloom and doom in our world today. All you have to do is listen to the news, and you'll get a picture bleak enough to depress Pollyanna. Suffering and death we have in abundance.

Perhaps the young man was right. We know enough about hurt and confusion and pain in our own lives. We sometimes reflect on the dark corners of our lives and find them unnervingly populated with specters of past failings and ghosts of carefully nursed angers, unresolved sins, and submerged conflicts.

Perhaps the young man was right. Why come to church to hear this suffering and death story again? Why read it over and over? Why bother? We know what it is about. Let's get to the good stuff. Let's hear the happy news, the everything-is-going-to-be-all-right news — the "Smile, God loves you" news. After all, don't we all need more joy, more happiness? Don't we all need to have our lives brightened, our troubles covered, our mistakes set aside. Isn't that what all this is about anyway? Smile — God loves you anyway. Just do your best, keep your chin up, keep on trying, and He'll be on your side.

Smile-God-Loves-You Religion

Some forms of popular American religion would have us believe that God is a nice old man in the sky who watches us with a careless eye, pats us occasionally on the head, and says, "Listen, My child, just try your best, and everything will be fine. Just keep trying, and I'll be around somewhere if you ever need Me."

If that is God, then "Smile, God loves you" is the good word, and the task of the proclaimer of the Gospel is made simple. "Listen," we can say, "don't worry. God isn't mad. He's on your side. Just keep trying, and everything will work out. Get hold of yourself. Do your best. God will overlook the mistakes."

That is what a kind old man in the sky would do, wouldn't he? Overlook our mistakes? Isn't that what forgiveness is? Forgiveness is easy for God, as easy and simple as the formula we exchange in the confession.

"We are sinners," we say.

"That's all right," the preacher says. Doesn't he? Doesn't he say that it doesn't really matter to God. God overlooks our little errors and failings. He pats us and pushes us and smiles on us and assures us that everything is really pretty good after all — doesn't He?

There is a popular misunderstanding of forgiveness that lies at the bottom of the smile-God-loves-you religion. Sometimes when we bump someone or accidentally jostle them, we say, "Forgive me." And most often, the person jostled responds, "That's all right. It doesn't matter."

Excusing or Forgiveness?

In such a case we misuse the word *forgive*. What we mean is *excuse* me. Forgiveness and excusing are not the same.

A man lost his wife and attempted to raise his young son alone. The man was busy and really didn't have much time to spend with his son, but he was well off enough to give the boy everything he needed as he grew up. As the young man moved through high school, he began to get into trouble, first with the school authorities and then with the law. Every time the son would get into a jam, his father would come, pay for the damage or pay the fine, and set the matter straight. Each time the son would say, "I'm sorry, Dad," and his father would respond, "That's all right. It doesn't matter. I forgive you."

Finally the son got in real trouble and ended up in jail. Again the father paid the fine and came to the jail cell to retrieve his son. "I'm sorry, Dad," the young man said. "That's all right," his father responded. "It doesn't matter." At that moment the son flew into a rage. He screamed at his father and struck him in the face. "You don't love me," the son cried, "and I hate you!"

In that instant when the pain of the boy's hand brought tears to the father's eyes, when he raised his own hand to strike back, when the pain of the words cut him to his heart — in that instant the father began to know the meaning of the word *forgive*. For years he had been excusing his son; now he had to forgive him.

A God who excuses does not care. A God who watches us do our best and says, "It doesn't matter," does not love. For it does matter. With St. Paul we stand astonished at our inner weakness and say, "I know that good does not live in me — that is, in my human nature. For even though the desire to do good is in me, I am not able to do it... What an unhappy man I am! Who will rescue me from this body that is taking me to death?" (Rom. 7:18, 24 TEV).

What we are and have done does matter. That wretched darkness in ourselves, the dark specters of the past that haunt us and drag us down to death will not be changed by the passing fancy of a God who pats us on the head and tells us that it doesn't matter.

The Real Sign of a Loving God

Our God loves. He loves with a love so immense that He is able to forgive instead of merely excuse. And it is only His re-creating forgiveness that will make a difference in the dark and deadly corners of our lives.

That is the reason for our trek to the cross. It is not just to recount the grim and gloomy story again or to make us feel bad and rob our lives of joy. The cross over the altar does not just preserve the memory of the dismal death of a brave man. It is at the cross that we discover once more the enormity of God's forgiveness. "When we were still helpless, Christ died for the wicked at the time that God chose... God has shown us how much He loves us — it was while we were still sinners that Christ died for us! By His death we are now put right with God" (Rom. 5:6, 8-9 TEV). How much greater can love be?

"It does matter," God says. "It does matter that the sins of the past haunt you, that you fail and fall and sometimes cannot find the resources in yourself to go on. It does matter that you hurt others and bear the guilt of past deeds, that you are troubled and confused, that you cannot find your way. It does matter than sin separates you from Me and from others and threatens to take your life. It matters so much that I am willing to offer My Son — My beloved on the cross for you, that you might have life."

The Real Love of God

That is forgiveness — the forgiveness we so desperately need. That is what it means to say "God loves me." That statement is not a pious platitude to be plastered on a silly smiling face. His love in Christ's death on the cross reaches to the very depth of my being. His love ransacks the corners of my life, my spirit, my self. There He brings light and life. There He forgives, because excusing would never be enough. There He saves, because I will never be able to save myself.

The young man was right. What we really want to hear is the Good News. We want to be made happy and be told that everything is all right. And that is exactly our message today.

But our Good News is not a silly wish offered to desperate hearts in an attempt merely to cover the pain inside. Our Good News is the message of the cross that takes the pain away.

At the cross we are fully aware of what we have done. There the dark corners of our lives are exposed by the knowledge that He is on the cross *for us*. With St. Paul we say — no, we shout! — "Thanks be to God through Jesus Christ our Lord" (Rom. 7:25). "Thanks be to God for His inexpressible gift!" (2 Cor. 9:15). "Thanks be to God, who gives us the victory through our Lord Jesus Christ" (1 Cor. 15:57). We are forgiven.

Smile, God loves you — indeed!

Ordinary Miracles

MAUNDY THURSDAY
MARK 14:22-26

Theodore W. Schroeder

The Scriptures are full of remarkable stories about some truly extraordinary people. Second Kings tells us of one such important person. One might even call Naaman, general of the great Syrian armies, extraordinary. The Bible itself calls him mighty. He led the forces of Syria at a time when its power was at a high point.

This extraordinary man had an extraordinary disease. He was a leper. Leprosy at Naaman's time was no minor illness. At best, it was a one-way ticket to exile; at worst, it meant a lonely, lingering death.

Extraordinary Naaman and his extraordinary disease came (at the suggestion of an ordinary slave girl in his household) to the ordinary house of the ordinary (at least from important Naaman's point of view) prophet Elisha in the very unimpressive, conquered country of Israel. Furthermore, the great general came with many important gifts designed to impress the unimportant, ordinary prophet.

But the prophet would not even speak to him. Through his servant, Elisha told the great Naaman to go and wash in the Jordan River. The mighty general from the powerful country of Syria, which contained the sources of the important Tigris and Euphrates rivers and where the Abana and the Pharpar rivers flowed through the capital, Damascus, was to go and wash in that muddy creek — the Jordan.

Wash in that? Where were the incantations from the subservient prophet? Where were the ceremonious reception and the miraculous healing he had expected? Where were the pomp and pageantry to which he was so accustomed and so entitled? He went off in a huff and very nearly missed his chance at healing, for God indeed worked a healing miracle through the waters of the ordinary Jordan River (2 Kings 5).

An Ordinary Upper Room

Perhaps the disciples were bored with the seeming ordinariness of what was happening that night in the upper room. Surely the ease with which they fell asleep later in the garden would seem to indicate that they saw nothing out of the ordinary in the Thursday night events.

Together as usual, they ate the Passover in a borrowed upper room. Jesus washed their feet, but He was always doing strange things like that. He broke bread and shared the cup with them, but He had done that many times before. What had He said about body and blood? It was curious but not extraordinary. He said many things they didn't exactly follow. And what was this business with Judas? Poor Judas was always getting things muddled up. Betray Jesus? To whom? For what?

Had they not gone to the cross and visited the empty tomb, the miracle of that night at the table might have been completely lost on them. It just didn't seem important enough. After all, if the Son of God — the Messiah — was on His way to establish His kingdom (or even on His way to His death, as He kept saying), would there not be great upheavals among the people? stars falling from the skies? earthquakes and fire? legions of angels coming to protect Him? All of this Passover talk seemed so ordinary — so unimportant.

An Ordinary Event in Church

Tonight we come to His table again, and it all seems so ordinary. We have done this before, heard these words before, knelt at the rail before. We have been here. It's nothing startling. and, to be truthful, nothing extraordinary happens inside of us when we receive the bread and wine.

Is that all there is? just a warm remembering? Is it merely an ordinary reenactment of a distant event meant to prod us spiritually and make us feel that in some ordinary way God is telling us that everything will be all right some day? Can this ordinary event really bring us the presence of the Son of God? share with us His body and blood? assure us of the forgiveness of our sins?

Perhaps for most of what we recognize as our sins it would be enough. Those ordinary sins that plague us might be swept away by such an event. After all, most of the things we do wrong aren't really so bad — at least no worse than those done by others. For those day-to-day little sins and ordinary failings, perhaps this Passover remembrance is right.

Extraordinary Needs

But what about the rest? What about those extraordinary, outrageous, important mistakes that are also a part of our lives? You know the ones I mean — the ones we don't even like to think about. Think of the times when we really blow it, when we do what we intended most earnestly not to do, when we fail in the area where we promised most sincerely not to fail, when we return hurt for love and do damage instead of build up. What about the times when we are really extraordinarily wrong. What about then?

Even when we face those extraordinary failings — when they haunt us, harass us, and weight us down — we are still given ordinary bread and wine in an ordinary worship service in which the pastor speaks ordinary words. Shouldn't the rafters quake with the enormity of God's act if He forgives even the most terrible sins that we have done? Shouldn't the lights black out or the windows rattle at the truth that Christ inhabits my heart with His healing presence — that He comes to me with His body and blood? Shouldn't something happen?

Extraordinary Healing

The extraordinary truth remains: Here the Jordan healing is repeated, the plain Thursday night miracle is redone. Here in the Word, however haltingly spoken, in this place, plain as it might be, in the bread, however poorly baked, in the wine, however impurely bottled, the very body and blood of our Savior Jesus Christ are received for the strengthening of our faith, for the assurance of our forgiveness, for the healing of our hearts and spirits, for the reaffirmation of the promise of life.

Impossible! The extraordinary God comes into our ordinary lives in this ordinary event for our extraordinary spiritual healing. It makes no sense — no more sense than it made to mighty Naaman on his way to the muddy Jordan — no more sense than it made to the muddled disciples on a plain Passover Thursday evening.

God's miraculous giving only makes sense in the death and resurrection of Jesus Christ. There everything is done, and the miracle — God's extraordinary miracle of salvation — is complete. The living, risen Christ comes to us in the Sacrament. He is extraordinarily here in this place, but even more extraordinarily in the bread and wine we share. The body and blood of our risen, victorious Savior are given to us for our forgiveness and strength, for our help and healing, for our victorious daily living, and with the assurance of eternal life with Him.

This is possible because Jesus Christ, the eternal Son of God, became like us. The great God took on ordinary flesh. He came in a manger and with soiled sandals, in homespun clothes and with the gnarled hands of a carpenter. He came without the trappings of royalty or the glow of the divine — so ordinary He was offensive to his kinsmen, rejected by His townspeople, and scoffed at by the religious leaders.

But He was the Son of God — God with us. He was the extraordinary sacrifice for our sins. Through His unique act we are forgiven and free. And now in this place, in an extraordinary way He shares Himself with us.

What would it mean if God only acted in what we considered to be the extraordinary of life? Where would we go to find Him? How would we be involved with Him? If He were only present in elaborate worship events and jeweled temples, where would we look for Him? By God's miraculous grace this ordinary event becomes the vehicle of the extraordinary presence of Christ our Savior.

The miracle still happens. In spite of the fact that our homes and hearts will never be ready for Him — never be extraordinary enough to become the dwelling place of the God of the universe — He comes. Though we will never have all the magazines picked up, never have all the affairs of the day in order, never have everything done that needs to be done, never have all the sins properly acknowledged and repented, our extraordinary God comes to inhabit even ordinary hearts and lives like yours and mine. He comes to us in the commonplace to work the miraculous, in the ordinary to do the extraordinary, in the unimportant to do the important.

He comes to each heart tonight in His miraculous Sacrament. To each heart, ready or not, polished and perfected or not, He gives His body and blood. And, extraordinarily, we are recreated, forgiven, healed, and free. As a result of this miracle we again are empowered to be His ordinary miracles set loose in the world as we share His eternal love, offer His effective forgiveness, and proclaim His saving Good News.

"You are the chosen race, the King's priests, the holy nation, God's own people, chosen to proclaim the wonderful acts of God, who called you out of darkness into His own marvelous light" (1 Peter 2:9 TEV).

How extraordinary!

The King Is Dead!
Long Live the King!

GOOD FRIDAY
JOHN 19:17-30

Theodore J. Kleinhans

What do you say when the Son of God dies? Today is Good Friday. It is not yet Easter. It is Friday, and they have taken Jesus out to the Place of the Skull, and they have crucified Him, and He has died—end of text.

One may wonder what exactly it is that makes this Friday "good" and what makes this Gospel message good news. Jesus left hanging on the cross is certainly not good news in the sense of the happily-ever-after ending that we have come to expect or to hope for. Yet, strange as it may seem, God's Good News on this Good Friday is precisely this: Jesus Christ, God's own Son, died—for us.

Jesus of Nazareth, the King of the Jews

Two children were playing together and half-watching a movie about the life of Jesus on television in the background. One of the children had never heard the story of Jesus, and when it came to the crucifixion scene, he became more and more engrossed in the film. His playmate, anxious to resume their game, said matter-of-factly, "Oh, never mind about that. He gets out of it in the end."

We find that tendency to rush quickly ahead to the end of the story even among more sophisticated Christians (like ourselves). We seem to want to close our eyes and hold our breath until all the suffering of Lent and Holy Week and Good Friday is over and it is safe to come out again to Easter lilies and chocolate bunnies and the resurrection. But the gospel writer paints a picture that we cannot avoid like the priest or Levite who crossed quickly to the other side of the road, pretending not to see the beaten man from Jericho. The picture has our Lord on the cross, and above Him is the title "Jesus of Nazareth, the King of the Jews."

The chief priests of the Jews complained to Pilate about this inscription. Jesus was *not* their king—not *their* king—they insisted. To call this crucified one "the King of the Jews" was a major affront. Pilate's response was simple: "What I have written, I have written."

Given the chance, we too might voice some complaints. Of all the episodes in Jesus' life, this one seems to be the strangest time to acclaim Him as King. Would not that title be more appropriate for the Jesus who fed and preached to multitudes, or the Jesus who was transfigured with Moses and Elijah beside Him, or, best of all, the Jesus who entered Jerusalem in triumph?

"Jesus of Nazareth, the King of the Jews"—Jesus is enthroned, to be sure, but His throne is a cross, and the positions of honor at His right and left hand are occupied by common criminals. Jesus is crowned, but His crown is a crown of thorns. Can this beaten man, this humbled and crucified One, be our King?

Let us turn our attention for the moment to the soldiers at the foot of the cross. As far as they were concerned, Jesus was nobody's king—not the Jews' and certainly not theirs. He was just another person being executed, another criminal whose personal belongings were not at their disposal. The soldiers divided Jesus' garments among themselves, and they separated His life and death from any possible meaning for their lives.

Our problem with Jesus' kingship exists at two levels. First, we do not fully understand the cross. We do not understand how suffering and dying can be the marks of a king. But worse than that, to the extent that we do understand the cross, we reject it. We want nothing to do with it. We do not like to see suffering and pain in ourselves or in others. We refuse to accept it. We spend our lives trying to avoid and eliminate it. Can we really accept what it means that Jesus Christ had to die for us, that true life can flow only out of death—out of His death? Can we trust Him? Can we have faith? Or do we look another way, for a forgotten loophole or a shortcut around the cross of Good Friday?

It Is Finished!

But there is no other way than the way of the cross. Despite his hastiness, that little boy attempting to regain his playmate's attention did know one very important thing—the story was not going to change. Reading the end of the mystery first does not change the outcome when we finally sit down and read the whole book. What has been written stays written, to paraphrase Pilate, or, in Jesus' own words, "It is finished."

When John writes that Jesus said, "It is finished," and bowed His head and gave up His spirit, he is not simply flashing "The End" on the screen at the conclusion of the main feature—"It is finished"; you can all go home now. Finished does not mean simply *terminated*; it means *fulfilled, completed.*

Imagine the gospel writer still with pen in hand. After he has written in large letters "Jesus of Nazareth, the King of the Jews" as the caption to his picture of the crucified God-man, he is now underlining those words and adding exclamation points all around. "It is finished!" This is it! This is the completion for which we have been waiting, for which all creation has been waiting. This is our salvation. Here and now, today on this very cross, God is in Christ reconciling the world to Himself. It is finished. It is accomplished. It is that sure.

That is the Good News. It is certain today, and we can begin proclaiming it right now. We do not have to wait until Easter Sunday to celebrate God's victory for us. Indeed, we must not wait at all. Shout it out! Jesus of

Nazareth, the King of the Jews—our King—has accomplished God's mighty work of salvation on the cross!

And from That Hour. . .

If the King Himself dies, what does that say about us, His subjects? It seems that we too must die. Of course, the King shows us that to die is not the end of the story. Death has lost its sting, and the grave is no longer a threat, but dying is still easier said than done for most of us. We like Easter better than Good Friday. It seems so much happier. We want the glory and the lilies and the lights for Jesus and for ourselves, and we want them now. We want to be winners. We want a God who looks like a winner. We want everyone to see that we and our God are winners.

But Jesus is the only God we have been given, and He is the one into whose likeness we are to be changed—Jesus, the crucified one. In this Man, God comes to us. On this cross God is most for us, triumphing over our death and destruction. It is finished. We still have to read the story through to the last page, each one of us, but we know how it ends, for Jesus and for us. In His death there is life. In our deaths there is life also, because we die with Him, in Him, into Him.

A popular song of some years ago had the intriguing line, "To conquer death you only have to die." It really is that simple. As we let go of our definitions of successs, our dreams of glory, and our other gods — as we die to sin and live in faith — we let the Spirit of God work in us. John tells us that Jesus said, "It is finished," and bowed His head and gave up His spirit. He did not simply give up—throw in the towel—but He gave up His spirit, gave His spirit back to the Father who had sent Him, gave His spirit up in order that He might give His Spirit to us.

Mary and John at the foot of the cross understood that. "When Jesus saw His mother, and the disciple whom He loved standing near, He said to His mother, 'Woman, behold, your son!' Then He said to the disciple, 'Behold, your mother!' And from that hour the disciple took her to his own home." Mary and John could not have understood everything that was going on, but they did not need to. They did not question. They did not resist. They simply let the will of Jesus be carried our in their lives.

Jesus had said to his disciples earlier in His ministry that the greatest expression of love was to lay down one's life for one's friends. This is hard to accept and even harder to do. Most of us hope never to be put in the position of having to die for another human being. But it is just as hard, if not harder, for me to lay down my life for someone else while I am still alive — to put my own life at your disposal. Yet this is what the Christian is called to do daily.

Christ died for us so that we can live. Christ died for us so that we can die — die to ourselves and die for others, die at the end of our lives and die all through our lives, die in Him and so die into life. The cross of Good Friday shows us how Christ is King and how we are His. The cross of Good Friday empowers us with new life—His new life. For Jesus, death was not the end of His life but the fulfillment of His mission. For us who are in Christ, death — His and ours — is also not the end of life but its true beginning, both now and forever.

Seeing in Faith

THE RESURRECTION OF OUR LORD
EASTER DAY
JOHN 20:1-9 (10-18)

Theodore J. Kleinhans

The Lord is risen! He is risen indeed! Alleluia!

If the message of Good Friday is that death is God's judgment on all people — even on His own Son in our place — then the message of Easter is life — new life springing out of and flowing beyond death, forgiven life, the boundlessness of eternal life in Christ Jesus our Lord. This life is ours only through faith and is lived out in the Easter fellowship of believers.

I Have Seen the Lord

Mary Magdalene had no idea of the new life that awaited her when she went to the tomb on that first Easter Sunday morning. She was the proverbial early bird trying to catch the worm — get up a little earlier than usual, gather together the needed spices, rush off to the tomb, anoint the body, and with any luck get back to her daily tasks without throwing her schedule too far off. But the best-laid plans, even of loving followers of Jesus, do not always fall so neatly into place. Mary reached the tomb very early, "while it was still dark" (John 20:1), and already someone had beaten her to the punch. The stone was removed. There was no Jesus. So much for careful planning!

Mary, like the rest of us, wanted to be in control. If something is worth doing, it is worth doing well, we tell ourselves, and if you want something done well, do it yourself! We pride ourselves on efficiency, and we constantly try to make sure that we are getting or staying ahead of the Joneses. If only life could go as we planned it, what a wonderful world we would have.

Mary's tears as she stood beside the tomb were tears of sorrow, to be sure, but I suspect that they were also tears of frustration and helplessness. "Woman, why are you weeping?" "Because they have taken away my Lord, and I do not know where they have laid Him" (v. 13). "Woman, why are you weeping? Whom do you seek?" "Sir, if you have carried Him away, tell me where you have laid Him, and I will take Him away" (v. 15). Mary knew she could do nothing about Jesus' death, which she had witnessed so painfully just a few days before. Now even the little she thought she could do for her Lord's body was taken out of her hands and out of her power by the incomprehensible fact of the empty tomb.

But Jesus came and died and was raised that we might have life and have it abundantly. He who came for all of humanity certainly came also for Mary Magdalene, for this one woman weeping outside the tomb, crippled by her own frustrations and helplessness. Jesus revealed Himself to Mary there in the garden. He is the risen Lord of life, the Victor over death. And lest for even a moment Mary try to regain control, to fit this alive-again Jesus back into her own systems and plans, into her (and His) old life, He said to her, "Do not hold Me" (v. 17).

Do not hold Me. Do not limit My place in your life only to what you want or what you can see. Do not limit your expectations, but open yourself up to the fullness of who I am and of who you are because of Me. Give up your control, and trust in Me. "'Do not hold Me, for I have not yet ascended to the Father; but go to My brethren and say to them, I am ascending to My Father and your Father, to My God and your God.' Mary Magdalene went and said to the disciples, 'I have seen the Lord'; and she told them that He had said these things to her" (vv. 17-18).

We might be tempted to say that Mary had it easy. However much she may have wanted and planned and fought to be in control, hers was a different reality from ours because she saw and spoke with Jesus in person. It was easy for Mary to let go, we might say, because Jesus was right there, alive and very much in control. It seems much harder for us, half a world away, almost two millennia later, not to hold on to our own plans, not to try to limit Jesus to our size, really to trust and to live out the new life He offers us in exchange for our old, sin-ridden, death-haunted lives.

. . . And Believed

But not all the witnesses in today's Easter Gospel shared Mary's experience of their risen Lord on that first morning, and John's account of these others sheds much light on our own situation. When Simon Peter and the beloved disciple arrived at the tomb, it was empty, and Jesus was not there. They had heard Mary's words, "They have taken the Lord out of the tomb, and we do not know where they have laid Him" (v. 2). They now saw the linen cloths in which Jesus' body had been wrapped for burial lying in the tomb, rumpled and cast aside as if a sleeper had just arisen from his bed. John tells us that the two disciples did not yet understand the Scripture that Jesus must rise from the dead. Yet seeing nothing more than linen cloths in an otherwise empty tomb, they believed. So it should be with us.

It has often been said that seeing is believing. For the Christian, however, it might be more accurate to say that believing is seeing. To see Jesus with one's own eyes and hear Him with one's own ears is a good thing, but it is not in itself a saving thing, and it is not yet for us. But to believe in Jesus, to let all one's faith and trust rest in Him alone, is salvation and life. That is much better than any mere seeing that we might choose for ourselves. Our Lord Himself later said to Thomas, "Have you believed because you have seen me? Blessed are those who have not seen and yet believe" (v. 29). For now we see only in a mirror dimly. Full sight still lies ahead.

As Jesus would not let Mary Magdalene limit his lordship over her life to her own expectations, so He could not allow Thomas or the other disciples to control their believing in Him, and so it is with us. If we seek to limit or control how Jesus comes to us, we deny ourselves the possibility of living in and living out the fullness of the new life that He offers us. Our faith is that trust by which we live in the resurrection of our Lord, whom we have not yet fully seen but in whom we believe and hope.

Go to My Brethren

There is another facet to the marvelous Easter message of this Gospel, and that is the gift of Christian fellowship and community. While each of the disciples had an individual relationship with the Lord through faith, they also, in Christ, had each other. Hear again Jesus' parting words to Mary Magdalene: "Go to My brethren and say to them, I am ascending to My Father and your Father, to My God and your God" (v. 17). Jesus makes us His own brothers and sisters, and by that incorporation into Him we are also made brothers and sisters to each other. At Jesus' command Mary went rushing back to the disciples and told them of her encounter with Him. She witnessed to them of the resurrection. In sharing her faith, she shared her sight: "I have seen the Lord" (v. 18).

And so it should be for us on this Easter day and every day. We too are called to tell each other, "I have seen the Lord! He is risen! I believe!" As we face sin and death in our lives, as we face our own helplessness and our inability to be in control, we fall back on our Lord Jesus Christ, who took our sin and death on Himself and was raised from the tomb that He might give us life. We live joyfully in the community of our fellow believers in whose lives and witness we continue to see the Lord.

The Great Transformation

SECOND SUNDAY OF EASTER
JOHN 20:19-31

C. George Fry

A decade ago, when I was teaching on the college level, I observed an interesting change in the lives of two people. It was the custom at Capital University for one of the fraternities to sponsor a "blind date" night. John did not expect much of this. It was not the first time he had been on a blind date. He did not expect it to be his last either.

Preparing for that Friday night progressed as a fairly routine matter. There was a certain measure of fear and a great deal of doubt over what was about to happen. John assumed that the sorority girl he was about to meet would be simply another girl who passed through his life without much significance.

From the moment that John met Elizabeth in the lounge of the girls' residents hall, however, he knew that this time things were going to be different. How different he did not fully fathom right away. Little did he realize that he had just met his future wife. Three years later I officiated at their wedding in the college chapel. What had been a routine blind date became a rendezvous with destiny. Lives were changed.

Today's Gospel presents part of the greatest love story in history, that of Christ for His church. In this episode we behold a great transformation. The followers of Jesus are plagued with two problems, fear and doubt. One is emotional, the other intellectual. One is societal, the other personal. Both debilitate and depress, preventing the church from fulfilling its mission. Christ comes to His disciples, and His presence works a great transformation as they are changed from fearful to faithful disciples and from doubting to believing disciples.

The Great Transformation

From Fearful to Faithful Disciples

One great transformation that occurred on that first Easter was a change in the disciples from fearful to faithful men. In the beginning they were fearful men gathered behind closed doors. They were possessed by both external and internal fears.

The external fear was a fear of danger from the enemies of Jesus. The apostles felt that what happened to Christ might also happen to them. As He had been condemned by the religious leaders and crucified by the state, they also, because of their association with Him, might be exiled or executed. Like Peter they were not sure what they might do if they were confronted by the authorities because of their commitment to Christ. Peter had denied the Master, and the rest had fled. Only John, the beloved, had remained to stand at the foot of the cross.

There was also an internal fear. It was not connected with any specific action or attitude. In part it was generated from a sense of shame. There is a kind of guilt that causes fear. A dread of impending judgment is present as the memory of past failure haunts the mind. Failing to face up to unforgiven sin causes it to be repressed or denied. Anxiety results. Among the disciples there was the recollection that they had been ashamed of Jesus, and in the hour of trial they had fled. Reports of His resurrection filled them with the fear that Christ might come to them with punishment, not grace.

The Gospel, however, shows that band of fearful men being transformed into faithful disciples. Faith is simply trust in Christ, and that trust gave them courage. Courage is literally from the Latin word for *heart*. We are reminded of this in the Communion liturgy when the minister invites us to "Lift up your hearts" and we reply, "We lift them to the Lord." When Jesus appeared among the disciples, He gave them "heart" in two ways.

First, He forgave their sin. That meant hope for the future. John Wesley had been raised a pious son of the Church of England. He had a parson for a father, studied theology at Oxford, and was ordained a priest. As a member of the Methodist Club, young Wesley tried to lead a life of strict morality. He became a missionary in Georgia and attempted to share Christ with others. In these efforts he failed. Guilt, not grace, was the central reality in his religion.

Then he heard Martin Luther's preface to the Book of Romans and felt his fears dissolve when he realized that, while he was a sinner, he was a *forgiven* sinner. He "exchanged the faith of a servant for the faith of a son." With a new heart for his preaching, Wesley went out to witness with great effect in the England of the Industrial Revolution. Once his fear was transformed into faith, Wesley was able to transform a generation by sharing Christ. He — and England — had a hope for the future.

That was the experience of the men in the locked room on the first Easter, of Martin Luther in the tower study at Wittenberg, and of John Wesley at the Aldersgate Street meeting. It can be ours today as well.

The second way in which Christ gave the disciples heart was simply in being present with them. That meant they could cope with any situation.

Once David Livingstone was asked the secret of his ability to work for Christ as a missionary in Africa. He confessed that it was his faith: "Trust in the Lord with all thine heart, and lean not to thine own understanding. In all thy ways acknowledge Him and He shall direct thy steps. Commit thy way unto the Lord; trust also in Him and He shall bring it to pass" (William L. Colemen, "An Interview with David Livingstone," *Christianity Today*, XVII [April 27, 1973], 7). Livingstone knew the power of Christ's presence.

After the Vietnam War former American prisoners of war landed at Clark Air Force Base in the Philippines. Richard Abel was one of them. Reflecting on his experience in the "Hanoi Hilton," as they had called their prison, he said, "I couldn't have made it if it wasn't for Jesus Christ, and being able to look up and see Him in some of the trying times" (Quoted in Edward E. Plowman, "P.O.W.s: With God's Help," *Christianity Today*, XVII [March 2, 1973], 50).

That power to cope has been present in the church through the centuries. It began on that first Easter when Jesus appeared to His fearful followers as they hid behind closed doors. Assuring them of His grace, He promised to abide with them. No tribulation would be more than they could bear, for His power would transform them into "more than conquerors."

From Doubting to Believing Disciples

The second great transformation that occurred among the disciples brought them from doubting to believing. More than a week had passed since the first Easter gathering. Once more the followers of Jesus were assembled. They were sharing what His appearance had meant to them. Thomas, one of the Twelve, had not been present when Jesus had appeared the first time. Listening to the report of that event by other others, he had doubted. This time when Christ came, He brought about a great transformation in Thomas. Previously filled with skepticism, he made a great confession: "My Lord and my God!"

Thomas saw the wounds of the risen Christ and was freed from doubt. Three things happened as a result. First, Thomas achieved the right kind of humility. His problem, like ours, was that he was humble about the wrong things. G. K. Chesterton once wrote:

> What we suffer from today is humility in the wrong place. Modesty has moved from the organ of ambition and settled upon the organ of conviction where is was never meant to be. A man was meant to be doubtful about himself, but undoubting about the truth; this has been exactly reversed. Nowadays the part of a man that a man does assert is exactly the part he ought not to assert — himself. The part he doubts is exactly the part he ought not to doubt — the Divine Reason (G.K. Chesterton, *Orthodoxy* [New York: Dodd, Mead, and Company, 1936], p. 106).

Thomas had trusted in his own mental powers — common sense, reason, experience, and the report of his physical senses. A risen and living Lord, therefore, was to him an impossibility. "Unless I see. . . I will not believe." Christ confronted Thomas with what he had "known" to be impossible — life after death. The result was that Thomas became humble in the right way — about the limitations of his own knowledge. That opened him up to the power of God, for with the Lord nothing is impossible.

In a similar fashion we ought not limit God but be open to what His Son is willing and able to do in our lives. Because He lives, He lives *for us* and, in Luther's words, "is willing to give us all good things, if we are humble enough to receive."

Second, Thomas arrived at the right kind of certainty. His notion, like ours, was that faith is a kind of "divine mathematics," a sort of "spiritual algebra." Religion was to be reasoned out and set forth in foolproof propositions. Surely a well-reasoned theology is to be highly prized, but the heart of our faith is a person, not a principle. Saving faith in Jesus Christ is a matter of a right relationship with our Savior, not a logical demonstration of a metaphysical truth. As Thomas encountered his living Lord, he was moved beyond the certainty of facts to the certainty of love.

Aleksandr Solzhenitsyn, a practicing Christian, is one of the greatest writers produced by the Soviet Union in the 20th century. Because of his loyalty to Christ, Solzehitsyn has suffered imprisonment, surveillance, and finally exile. In addition to his political and religious problems, Solzenitsyn has had to struggle with illness. His novel *Cancer Ward* is based on personal experience. From his painful pilgrimage Solzhenitsyn has gained the right kind of certainty. In one of his novels Staff Colonel Verotyntsev is described as one who "brought with him, too, that passionate sense of conviction which inspires belief less by its veracity than by its origin in personal suffering." That sort of certainty is what Christ inspired in Thomas. Gazing on the wounds of his Savior, Thomas learned that truth is seen in love.

In a similar way the Easter Christ comes to us — the One wounded on our behalf. The power of His resurrection is more than logical probability or historical likelihood. It is, instead, an overwhelming love that changes us, causing us to doubt our doubts and move from confusion to confession.

Third, Thomas arrived at the right kind of ministry. His faculties — power of mind and heart, strength of emotion and soul — were not simply to serve his own welfare, but that of others. Christ saves us in order to serve others.

Jose was hoeing carrots when he heard the screams of a three-year-old boy who had fallen into a deep well. Rushing to the edge of the field, Jose saw the shaft. Looking down into that black hole, he listened to the cries of a perishing child. The pipe was only 20 inches wide, yet he knew what he had to do. The lad would quickly drown in the water.

Jose called for a rope and tied it around his feet. Even though he had a great fear of narrow places because his parents had punished him as a child by locking him in a dark cistern, he plunged headfirst into the well shaft. Other workmen lowered him by the rope attached to his feet. Blood rushed to his head. He became dizzy. The heat was almost suffocating. He struggled to remain conscious. When he reached the boy splashing in the water, he grasped for him. It took several attempts before he got a good hold. Slowly the men at the top of the well pulled them up. Jose said it felt as if his arms and legs were being torn from his body and the rough-welded seams of the pipe tore his flesh. Finally Jose and the boy emerged into the light of the sun. They stood sobbing for joy at being alive.

If Jose had considered the facts or had stopped to reason, he would not have risked his life for what appeared to be an impossible mission. Love, however, compelled him. Forgetting his doubts and fears, Jose plunged ahead in faith, seeking to help a child in distress.

This Easter Christ comes to us as He did to Thomas. Often paralyzed by doubt and torn by inner conflict, we fail to see the needs about us that we can meet. Glimpsing the Savior frees us from being self-centered and liberates us to minister to others.

A century ago the British preacher C. H. Spurgeon was reflecting on this text. Marveling at the power of Jesus to move us from indecision to confession and from confession to action, Spurgeon noted: "Many a believer lives in the cottage of doubt when he might live in the mansion of faith." This Easter Christ comes to us, speaking through His Word and touching us through His Sacrament, inviting us to move beyond where we are — to be more like Him. With that invitation comes power, a power that causes a great transformation — from fear to faith, from doubt to belief.

Christ Comes to His People

THIRD SUNDAY OF EASTER
LUKE 24:36-49

C. George Fry

A century ago Mark Twain was traveling in Europe. Reports reached America that the famous author had died. Learning of this news, Twain cabled home, "The reports of my death are greatly exaggerated."

The reports of the death of Jesus were *not* greatly exaggerated. They rested on hard evidence. Christ was crucified in a public place. The crowd included both adversaries, such as the priests and scribes, and members of His family, including Mary, His mother. There was no doubt as to the identity of the man on the cross. Nor was there any uncertainty as to His death. His life expired. He committed His soul to His Father. As proof of His death a centurion pierced his side with a spear. Before dusk the slain Master was entombed. A stone was rolled before the door. Soldiers were stationed to keep watch. As the sun set on that first Good Friday the evidence was compelling: Christ was "crucified, dead, and buried."

No wonder it was hard for the disciples to believe that Jesus "rose again from the dead." Certainly the report of His resurrection also rested on hard evidence — an empty tomb, folded burial linen, sightings in several places, the testimony of people and of angels. The news was that Christ had been seen and heard in several places, ranging from the garden of the tomb to the Emmaus road. His followers were reflecting on this news when the Savior Himself "stood among them" and gave them the familiar greeting, "Peace to you." Their response was not initially one of joy but of terror, not of love but of fear, for they "supposed that they saw a spirit." In this context of shock Jesus calms their hearts and assures them that He is alive and well and that His will is to be among His people. Christ now, as at His birth, is Immanuel, "God with us."

Today as then, Christ comes to His people, both in fulfillment of promise and for the remission of sin.

The Fulfillment of Promise

Christ comes to His people in fulfillment of His promise. On that first Easter the disciples should not have been surprised, for Jesus had assured them that He would triumph over death and return to them. He gave them that promise in both word and deed.

The Word of God promised the disciples that it was necessary for Jesus to go to Jerusalem, to be judged and condemned, to be crucified and buried. It also testified, however, that the cross was not a period, marking the end of Christ's career, but a comma, indicating that there was more to come.

As Christ ministered to the disciples He showed them that all Scripture has its center in Him. Jesus is the goal of the Law, the Prophets, and the Psalms. Christ revealed Himself as the fulfillment of the legislation of Moses, the expectation of the prophets, the adoration of the psalter, and the proclamation of the Gospel. The Lord said:

> These are My words which I spoke to you, while I was still with you, that everything written about me in the law of Moses and the prophets and the psalms must be fulfilled (Luke 24.44).

In this Easter season the same Jesus Christ comes to us through the Scriptures in fulfillment of His promise. He is the one who is able to meet the longings of our hearts, for, as Augustine mused, they are restless until they rest in Him.

Dr. E. V. Rieu was a distinguished British scholar, well known for his translations of the works of Homer into English. The publisher of the Penguin Classics asked him to try his hand at the gospels. At the age of 60, having been a life-long agnostic, Rieu agreed to attempt it. At that time his son said, "It will be interesting to see what Father makes of the four gospels. It will be even more interesting to see what the four gospels make of Father." Within a year Dr. Rieu was converted to Christianity. He observed, "I got the deepest feeling that the whole material was extraordinarily alive. My work changed me. I came to the conclusion that these words bear the seal of the Son of Man and God" (Quoted by E. M. Blaiklock, "More and More Scripture Lives!" *Christianity Today*, XVII (September 28, 1973), 18-19.)

This same living Christ also comes to us through Baptism. Our baptism is a type of Christ's death and resurrection. By the water and the Word Jesus touches us. This became real for me some years ago when I was serving a congregation in Columbus, Ohio.

Every Sunday morning Mrs. Boots was in church, but her husband, Jesse, never came. When I called on them in their home, I learned the story. She was an excommunicated Roman Catholic, removed from St. Leo's parish roster because she had married Jesse, a lapsed Baptist. That was before Vatican II. I invited Jesse to church — and he replied by inviting me to go fishing with him on Sunday morning at Buckeye Lake. So it went.

Within a year Jesse went into the hospital. His illness was serious. He was discharged and went home — incurable. Jesse started dying physically — but he began living spiritually. There was no thought of waiting until fall and the adult class. Jesse received private instruction. Now he was in church — every Sunday. One day after the service Jesse said to me, "Pastor, I don't think I'll live to finish the catechism. Can I be baptized next Sunday?"

I'll never forget that hot spring morning in that small frame church. After a hymn Jesse came forward to the font and he began to cry, loudly, with great streams of tears coming from both eyes — tears of repentance and tears of joy. Then when I baptized him, all he could say was "Thanks." To my knowledge that response is not in the formal liturgy of any of our

Lutheran synods. To Jesse, however, the risen Jesus was so real that he felt his touch in the waters and was compelled to give thanks to the God who saves.

Christ also comes to us through the Lord's Supper. Exegetes disagree as to when and how the term "breaking of bread" in the New Testament refers to Holy Communion. During the events of the first Easter Christ manifested Himself to His followers in "the breaking of bread." Today in the Sacrament of the Altar the same Jesus comes to us with life and salvation.

For me that sense of the Savior's presence was especially real when as a young minister I was supplying a rural congregation on the edge of Appalachia. About 30 farm folk attended that small "Dutch chapel" in southeastern Ohio. With weathered hands they would receive the wafer, and their faces, worn with cares and labor, would await the chalice. Lyle Carpenter was a man in his 40s, working two jobs to keep the family farm in his name. One Monday, after he had been to Communion on Sunday, he died suddenly. The tractor on which he was plowing "the back 40" turned over on him. After the funeral his wife stopped me and said, "Pastor, I know Lyle is with the Lord — because the Lord was with him." Young and inexperienced, I asked, "When?" "Why just last Sunday," she replied. No wonder we Lutherans talk of a "real presence" of the Savior in the Supper.

The Remission of Sins

Christ also comes to His people for the remission of sins. His promised presence is for the purpose of pardon.

Forgiveness is the meaning of the ministry of Jesus. John's first epistle makes the amazing statement: "I am writing to you, little children, because your sins are forgiven" (1 John 2:12). Paul, seeking to make clear the mystery of Christ, described Jesus as God's "beloved Son, in whom we have redemption, the forgivenss of sins" (Col 1:13-14). Martin Luther defined the church as an association of men and women in which God "daily and richly forgives all sins to me and all believers."

The whole life of Christ was concerned with forgiveness. In telling Joseph of His coming birth the angel said, "You shall call His name Jesus, for He will save His people from their sins" (Matt. 1:21). On the cross Christ prayed, "Father, forgive them" (Luke 23:34). In between, when He taught His followers to pray, Jesus instructed them to say "Father... forgive us our sins" (Luke 11:4).

It is against this background that Christ's appearance to His disciples takes on additional meaning. After He "opened their minds to understand the Scriptures," Jesus explained:

> Thus it is written, that the Christ should suffer and on the third day rise from the dead, and that repentance and forgiveness of sins should be preached in His name to all nations (Luke 24:45-47).

Forgiveness makes it possible to restore ruptured relationships. Whatever else sin may be, it is estrangement from self, others, and God. It is characterized by a breakdown of positive contact. Confrontation or alienation replaces conversation and cooperation. To overcome this isolation caused by harmful acts and attitudes Christ died. By His cross we are joined to God and to each other. Sin is forgiven. The past can be forgotten. The future can be welcomed.

One American poet remarked that "each spring God seems to rewrite the book of Genesis." That author had in mind the beauty of nature during this season. There is, however, a deep theological truth also involved. On Calvary God did rewrite the book of Genesis. Death is not the last act. The Fall is not the final chapter. Life has been restored because sin has been forgiven. Now we can live as God intended.

Some years ago I was talking with an old country preacher about how he understood life before the Fall. Paging through his well-worn Bible, he speculated why God made Eve out of Adam's rib. The reason Eve was made, he felt, was self-evident. Adam was alone, cursed with loneliness. "People need people," he said and then quoted Scripture: "It is not good that the man should be alone" (Gen. 2:18).

Then he wondered aloud as to why God chose a rib. "If the Lord had created Eve out of Adam's ear, she would incessantly be listening to gossip," he quipped. "If God had made her of Adam's tongue, she would incessantly be the source of gossip. If the Creator had formed her from Adam's foot, she would constantly be gadding about — or the man would try to tromp on her. Instead God took her from Adam's rib, from his side, to show that she was literally his 'sidekick,' his boon companion." Then he concluded, "That rib was lifted from next to Adam's heart. The woman was taken from the heart of man, and man's heart is restless until loved by another."

The accuracy of that country parson's exegesis I will allow others to judge. As to his theology, this I can say: That preacher had discovered a basic law of human community. All people are one flesh with a common ancestry, a common biology, a shared history, and a shared destiny. We all were meant to live together in love — black and white, male and female, young and old, rich and poor, wise or simple. Each person, whether he lives in Indiana or Nigeria, Berlin or Burlington, is capable of imaging God and is of infinite worth. The tragedy in sin is that we see that reflection distorted beyond recognition — and those intended to serve one another like the members of the same body are estranged from each other.

Christ came bringing forgiveness to the fearful disciples on the first Easter. Filled with his pardon, they later received His power on Pentecost, and the church was born. To that church was given the Word and Sacraments, and through that church Christ continues to come, forgiving sins and uniting people in love.

Recently I read an Ann Landers column about a young school teacher who had begun a new job in a New York grammar school. At first she felt herself very much a stranger. She wondered if her colleagues would ever accept her. One day while driving to work, she heard on her car radio that the DC-10 on which her sister was a passenger had crashed in Spain. Later she learned that her sister was one of the few survivors, but at the time she did not know that. Grieving and crying, almost hysterical, she arrived at school. Learning her situation, members of the faculty and staff, who had previously been strangers, now befriended her. A sense of tragedy broke down the distance. That school became a loving and caring community. Then the author concluded her letter with the reflection that "it is too bad that it took a tragedy to make of us a community."

It took a tragedy — the death of the innocent Son of God — to free the human family from sin and to prepare the way for real community. On Easter that tragedy becomes a victory, for the Crucified One now comes as the Risen One — with life and salvation for us all. It is our privilege as part of the church to be living in the happy ending of joy forevermore.

Jesus, the Good Shepherd

FOURTH SUNDAY OF EASTER
JOHN 10:11-18

Frank D. Starr

"Are you good at your work?" To have someone say so is a compliment, one we like to hear. We strive for good workmanship in whatever we do. Quality is the goal; shoddiness is something to avoid.

Many people are good at their work, but how many are so good that no one else could do their work as well? Such people are truly exceptional, so exceptional that we usually remember them by name rather than by occupation — Martin Luther, John Paul Jones, Michelangelo, Joan of Arc, Johann Sebastian Bach, Henry Ford, Walter Reed, Henry Luce, Frank Lloyd Wright, Florence Nightingale. The list could go on and on of people who did more than "good work" — whose work was exceptional. Nevertheless, even these exceptional workers did not do all that could be done. There is always someone who can carry the work in any area a little further.

The Shepherd Who Sacrifices Himself

There is One, however, who needs no successor, no one to complete His work. He is the Good Shepherd, Jesus. As the Good Shepherd, Jesus is unique, in a class by Himself.

Others have also been shepherds and still are today. The prophets and other leaders shepherded God's people before Jesus came, and the apostles, pastors, teachers, and others have been doing so ever since. Many have been leading and guiding God's people but not in the way Jesus did. One aspect of Jesus' shepherding put Him in a class by Himself. Jesus is the Good Shepherd, who laid down His life for the sheep.

Many have given their lives for others. History and legend record many heroic sacrifices. Some are particularly noble and inspiring. Some acts of personal sacrifice are widely known; some are known only to few; and some are known to no one but God. Some personal sacrifices have benefited many, some only one — though even one person's life is worth a great deal.

Texans will always "remember the Alamo," where a relatively small band of volunteers held off a far superior Mexican army at the cost of their own lives, buying time for their fellow Texans in a struggle that ultimately succeeded. Robert Louis Stevenson recorded the story of Father Damien, a Roman Catholic priest who gave his life in ministry to a Hawaiian leper colony. Many among the passengers of the Titanic stayed on the sinking ship so women and children might have the available places in the life-boats.

Men and women have given kidneys to those whose own organs no longer functioned. Lives have been risked and lost to save victims of fires, drowning, and similar tragedies. Unsung individuals have sacrificed personal advantage and material comfor in service to the poor, the homeless, the hungry, and the oppressed people who populate this world in great numbers.

Such sacrifices deservedly draw forth our admiration. But no sacrifice approaches that of the Good Shepherd, who laid down His life for the sheep. No other sacrifice cost as much as His, for He is the divine Lord of the universe, who suffered and died. No other sacrifice accomplished as much as that of the Good Shepherd. We may extend a life for perhaps seven or eight decades at the most; He saved lives for an eternity. He died so that millions, even billions, of precious human souls may live forever in the glories of heaven. The Good Shepherd laid down His own wonderully precious life for the sheep and redeemed them for a glorious eternity.

The Shepherd Who Knows His Sheep

Jesus is the Good Shepherd who knows His sheep and is known by them. There is a country music song, still popular after some decades, that declares, "You think you know me well — but you don't know me." Sometimes in self-pity we may lament, "Nobody understands me."

There is some truth to the assertion that no other person really knows our inner selves. No matter how close we are to another, no matter how long we have lived in the same house, no matter that we share almost all of the same experiences — to some degree there will always be some part of us that no one will ever really know. Only in a limited sense can we say to someone, "I know just how you feel." Some experiences are so private and personal that no one can share them with us. We may accompany another person only so far and no farther.

But Jesus, the Good Shepherd, knows us. He knows us in and out, through and through. He knows us better than we know ourselves. The desperate prayer "Lord, tell me what's going on inside of me!" is not a foolish prayer. He knows even when we don't. And He can share every experience that we have. He can feel our every feeling. Whatever step we take, He has stepped there before us; whatever path, He has walked it; whatever dark room, He has entered it. He can hold onto our hand when others must let go.

The Letter to the Hebrews assures us:

> Since therefore the children share in flesh and blood, He Himself likewise partook of the same nature, that through death He might destroy him who has the power of death, that is, the devil, and deliver all those who through fear of death were subject to lifelong bondage. For surely it is not with angels that He is concerned but with the descendants of Abraham. Therefore He had to be made like His brethren in every respect, so that He might become a merciful and faithful High Priest in the service of God, to make expiation for the sins of people. For because He Himself has suffered and been tempted, He is able to help those who are tempted (Heb. 2:14-18).

> For we have not a high priest who is unable to sympathize with our weaknesses, but One who in every respect has been tempted as we are, yet without sin. Let us then with confidence draw near to the throne of grace, that we may receive mercy and find grace to help in time of need (Heb. 4:15-16).

Jesus, our Good Shepherd, knows us, and we know Him. We know Him because He has revealed Himself to us in the Holy Scriptures. He has drawn back the mystery of His being, revealing to us the three distinct Persons in the Godhead of the Holy Trinity. He has made Himself known to us in the incarnation of Christ in human flesh, in whom the divine is united with the human. We would never have discovered such mysteries of the eternal God had He not revealed them to us. But He has revealed Himself, and we know Him. And He has made Himself known to us in His dealings with us. We know His grace, His love, His care, and His mercy firsthand as He has led and fed us through life. He is the Good Shepherd; He knows us and we know Him.

The Shepherd Who Seeks Lost Sheep

Jesus is the Good Shepherd, who seeks out the sheep not yet in the fold. There are many wonderful things to be said about God, but perhaps the most marvelous is that the Lord has visited His people. He has come down from His exalted throne in heaven to seek and to save us. St. Paul exclaims, "Great indeed, we confess, is the mystery of our religion: He was manifested in the flesh" (1 Tim. 3:16).

Sometimes we express admiration for a highly placed person who associates with ordinary people. We approve when a president of the United States pauses to join flood victims in filling sandbags, even though we know this is only a gesture. We are glad when a great person still has "the common touch." Jesus, the Almighty God, descended from heaven and took on the form of a servant.

Jesus came among us for a clear purpose. "The Son of Man came to seek and to save the lost" (Luke 19:10). This marvelous fact distinguishes the Gospel from all other sources of hope and faith. Others may exhort us to seek after God; the Gospel tells us that God has come down to seek after us and graciously to invite us into His kingdom.

Jesus is the Good Shepherd who is not content in knowing that the 99 are safely in the fold; He goes out to seek the one lost lamb, and when He has found that little lost one, He lovingly gathers it in His arms and carries it home rejoicing. The enthusiastic and joyful new Christian may exclaim, "I found God!" but no Christian has ever really found God; rather, God has found every one of us after seeking us.

It is true, of course, that the Lord uses His servants in the seeking. About to ascend into heaven and to resume His place at the right hand of God, Jesus commissioned His church to go and proclaim the Gospel, assuring them that as they went, He would be with them. Wherever the Gospel is proclaimed, the Lord accompanies this gracious message with power as through it He searches and seeks for the lost and brings them into the fold where there is one flock and one Shepherd. As we share the Gospel with family, friends, neighbors, co-workers, schoolmates, and — through our church — with people all over the world, the Lord accompanies us, seeking the lost and gathering them into His fold. He is the Good Shepherd who seeks the lost and brings them in.

The Shepherd Who Was Sent by the Father

Jesus is the Good Shepherd; He has the Father's endorsement. "The Father loves Me, because I lay down My life, that I may take it again.... This charge I have received from My Father" (John 10:17-18).

Jesus is the Christ. "Christ" is not Jesus' last name; it is His commission. It means He has been anointed, appointed, selected by God the Father to redeem us by offering the perfect sacrifice of His own precious life on the cross. Perhaps the best loved and best known passage in the Bible is that which clearly states Jesus' commission: "God so loved the world that He gave His only Son, that whoever believes in Him should not perish but have eternal life" (John 3:16). One of our hymns dramatizes Jesus' commission by the Father:

> "Go down, My Son," the Father said,
> "To free my children from their dread
> Of death and condemnation.
> The wrath and stripes are hard to bear,
> But in your death they all can share
> The joy of your salvation!"

> "Yes Father, yes, most willingly
> I bear what you command Me;
> My will conforms to your decree,
> I risk what you have asked me" (*LW* 111:2-3).

The Lord Jesus acted under commission, and His entire ministry bore the imprint of that commission. On two pivotal occasions, the Gospel records, the Father's own voice was heard, endorsing the words and activity of His Son. When Jesus' precious life ebbed out on the cross, the Father darkened and shook the earth, causing a bystander to conclude, "Truly this was the Son of God!" (Matt. 27:54). The Father's final endorsement of the Son's salutary work came conclusively and explosively when He raised Jesus from the grave, and the resurrected Lord appeared before the church in triumph.

Jesus was the Good Shepherd; He carried the Father's endorsement. We can be confident that our salvation is assured, complete, and entire; that the Gospel stands guaranteed; and that we stand free as sons and daughters of the Kingdom. We need not wonder or worry about our standing before God; in Jesus God Himself has given to us the Good Shepherd.

"What makes you so good?" is a taunt sometimes heard when our competence is challenged. In the case of Jesus, the Good Shepherd, the challenge received a conclusive reply, Jesus *is* the Good Shepherd, not on one but many counts. We who follow Him have found Him all He claims to be.

Branches of the Vine

FIFTH SUNDAY OF EASTER
JOHN 15:1-8

Frank D. Starr

A young girl and her father stepped through the outpatient entrance of the hospital. Her physician had ordered a blood test for diagnostic purposes. Though a brave girl, she said to her father, "Daddy, will you hold my hand when they draw the blood?"

We can understand her request. Most of us feel better in such a situation if we can hold the hand of someone we love and trust. Holding that hand seems to give strength and reassurance. Somehow we seem to draw on an extra reserve of courage and endurance.

United with Christ

Remembering such experiences, we can appreciate the expressive image drawn by the Lord Jesus as He speaks about our connection with Him—the picture of the vine with its branches. Much closer than merely holding hands, our connection with the Lord is our lifeline. United with the Lord through faith in the Gospel, we have God's life flowing through us and producing Christ-like love, kindness, mercy, peace, thankfulness, joy, and other godly qualities. Christ desires this union with us and dwells within us. To this end He has cleansed us and continues to train and strengthen us so we might be more effective in His service.

We, the Lord's people, are united with Him as a branch is united with the trunk of the vine. We are nourished and sustained by His love and grace just as every part of our bodies is nourished by the nutrients carried by the blood—just as every branch of a plant is nourished by the sap that flows to the end of each twig. Any branch cut off from the stem and thrown away soon dies; its leaves wither, dry up, fall off, and are blown away. So we, too, when we are no longer joined to Christ in faith, lose living contact with the dear God, who provides meaning and joy.

Perhaps one of the most meaningful phrases in the Bible is "in Christ." This short phrase is found many times in the New Testament. It describes our situation as Christians_ we live "in Christ." That relationship is behind the picture Jesus uses in today's Gospel. We are branches of the vine. Jesus does not say we should strive to *become* branches; He says that we *are* branches. "I am the Vine; you are the branches" (John 15:5).

This is the most wonderful truth we will ever learn; it is the Good News that God has come in Christ and redeemed us through His sacrificial death and glorious resurrection. The benefits of Jesus' death and resurrection are ours, given and received through Word and sacraments. "Do you now know that all of us who have been bapt zed into Christ Jesus were baptized into His death? We were buried therefore with Him by baptism into death, so that as Christ was raised from the dead by the glory of the Father, we too might walk in newness of life" (Rom. 6:3-4). Through the means of grace, through water and the Word, He has brought us into His kingdom. He has made us members of His body, the church. We have been incorporated into Him. We are joined to Him in the closest possible relationship. It is a communion in which He lives in us and we live in Him.

Jesus describes this relationship with the picture of the vine and the branches. As integrally connected as the branch is to the vine, so we are connected vitally with the Lord. St. Paul uses a very similar picture in his letter to the Christians of Rome when he compares us Christians — specifically, us Gentile Christians — to branches that have been grafted into a tree. While St. Paul intends particularly to explain how Gentile Christians are related to Israel, the underlying truth applies to all of us. Through no effort or merit of our own, we are "in Christ." We have been joined to Him and made part of His kingdom. By saying "I am the Vine, you are the branches," Jesus emphasizes the reality of this relationship, not as an ideal, not as something to be achieved by our effort, not as something that may some day happen, but as something that *is*. He assures us: "You are already made clean by the Word which I have spoken to you" (John 15:3).

United by Faith

This relationship continues through faith. St. John penned his gospel in order that "believing you may have life in His name." The faith that lives in our hearts is what joins us to Christ. When we trust His promises, we are joined to Him and enjoy communion with Him. The way is open for life to flow from Him to us.

The Lord made this connection; He created the faith that exists within us. Dr. Martin Luther described how we have come to faith in his explanation to the Third Article of the Apostles' Creed: "I believe that I cannot by my own reason or strength believe in Jesus Christ, my Lord, or come to Him; but the Holy Ghost has called me by the Gospel, enlightened me with His gifts, sanctified and kept me in the true faith."

Nourished by the Vine

And as the Holy Spirit has created the faith by which we live in Christ, so He nourishes and sustains it. St. Paul calls the Gospel "the power of God for salvation to everyone who has faith…For in it the righteousness of God is revealed through faith for faith" (Rom. 1:16-17). Daily in faith we reclaim the promises of God given through Baptism and are renewed. Often we come to the Lord's Table, where we are strengthened by His true body and blood. Nourished in this way, we draw on that strength and power, that life that Jesus speaks about when He declares: "Abide in Me, and I in you. As the branch cannot bear fruit by itself, unless it abides in the vine, neither can you, unless you abide in Me." (John 15:4).

Of course a branch cannot, by its own will, sever itself from its supporting stem. But it can be broken or cut off, and when it is severed and deprived of the nourishment it receives from the stem, it withers and dies. Its connection with its supporting stem is necessary for its continued life.

Jesus refers to this truth from nature to point us to another truth, an all-important truth for us. When we are severed from Christ, when we no longer cling in faith to Him as Savior and Lord, then we die, too.

Faith, we know, cannot be seen with the eye. Neither can the power of God that flows through the means of grace. These realities are apparent not to sight but to faith. And just as faith itself may not be detected by observation, so the loss of faith may not be apparent to human observation. It is possible for someone to appear to remain a faithful Christian while within the faith has died, and only its shell remains. Such a person is like a dried flower that once throbbed with life but is now dead. The external appearance only gives the impression of life when, in fact, no life exists.

Jesus admonishes us to remain in Him, to abide in Him, as a living branch continues to draw its nourishment from its supporting stem. We *do* have the power to sever our connection with Christ. We can actively resist the Holy Spirit, deliberately slamming shut the door of our heart to His entrance. And we are also able to allow that door to close gradually through our neglect. Jesus warns us, "He who is not with Me is against Me, and he who does not gather with Me scatters" (Matt. 12:30). He further tells us, "No one can serve two masters; for either he will hate the one and love the other, or he will be devoted to the one and despise the other. You cannot serve God and mammon" (Matt. 6:24).

A living faith is just like our living body; it requires nourishment. That is why our regular and frequent use of the means of grace is vital. That reality is behind our concern for fellow Christians who remain absent from God's House, failing to hear His word and to draw on the power of the Gospel. That is why we are so eager to enroll children in Sunday school and their parents in Bible classes. That is why we urge families to gather about the Word of God at home. That is why we encourage daily meditative Bible reading. These are the means by which our faith is nourished, keeping it alive and strong. This is how we abide in Christ, remain in Him. This is what the Lord Jesus urges us to be doing as He pictures the vine with its branches.

Living Productively

Severed from the vine, the branch withers and dies; severed from Christ, we die. But abiding in Christ we live, and we live productively. Abiding in Jesus, we glorify and honor God. As garden and orchard produce vegetables and fruit that nourish and delight us, so Christians live productively.

Branches separated from their supporting stem produce no fruit. That's obvious in the plant world, but it does not seem so obvious when we think of our relationship to God. Living a good, God-pleasing life on our own with minimal or no help from Him seems to be a distinct possibility to the human mind unenlightened by the Holy Spirit.

But the truth is "no faith, no fruit." Apart from Christ, we cannot please God. Our every effort apart from Him remains shot through with sin, like fruit that rots on the tree before ripening. But in Christ, abiding in Him, we can say and do and think things that delight God. The branch growing from the vine produces rich fruit.

Even a backyard farmer knows that plants yield more when they are tended and carefully pruned. Tomato growers will watch the growing plants for unproductive branches and will prune them so the plant's nutrients may be channeled more effectively toward the production of fruit. Jesus speaks of God the Father as a gardener who carefully tends and cultivates us; as a result we become more productive of those qualities God nurtures in His people. Knowing this often explains experiences common among God's people.

St. Peter wrote his letters to Christians who experienced frequent persecution because of their faith. Reminding them of how God had redeemed them through Jesus, he writes, "In this you rejoice, though now for a little while you may have to suffer various trials, so that the genuineness of your faith, more precious than gold which though perishable is tested by fire, may redound to praise and glory and honor at the revelation of Jesus Christ" (1 Peter 1:6-7).

While we might not have to endure much in the way of persecution, nevertheless, life seems to throw plenty at us that God uses to polish our faith and make it shine, that prunes back those habits and practices and attitudes that are unproductive of Christian graces and virtues. When we are called to suffer some hardship or burden that comes through no fault of our own, we ought not complain that God is not paying as much attention to us as He might, that His care is not as evident, His love not as warm, His blessing not as apparent. Instead, we recognize that the Father is acting as the gardener who prunes and tends and digs to stimulate growth and produce a better yield in a pure faith, in godly living, and in Christ-like attitudes. We might say with St. Paul:

> We rejoice in our hope of sharing the glory of God. More than that, we rejoice in our sufferings, knowing that suffering produces endurance, and endurance produces character, and character produces hope, and hope does not disappoint us, because God's love has been poured into our hearts through the Holy Spirit which has been given to us (Rom. 5:2-5).

Perhaps you recall walking through a flourishing, highly productive garden. Healthy plants, heavy with fruit, are on every side. Such a peaceful, picturesque scene did not just happen. It is the result of much labor, tender care, foresight, and preparation.

Some Christians are like that garden. Their lives are inspiring showcases of Christ-like qualities. Such Christians — like the garden — do not just happen. They have a vital, continuing connection with Jesus through Word and Sacrament; they have experienced the loving but sometimes painful pruning and nurture of their gardener Lord.

May the Lord make of all of us a flourishing, productive branch through whom He works and in whom He lives.

The Command to Love from the One Who Loves Us

SIXTH SUNDAY OF EASTER
JOHN 15:9-17

Daniel G. Mueller

"My God, My God, why hast Thou forsaken Me?" Jesus cried out with a loud voice. Tormented in body, soul, and mind by the torture of His passion, exhausted from hanging on the cross under the burden of the world's sin, Jesus sounded like He was reaching the end of His rope. In mortal agony He screamed, "My God, My God, why hast Thou forsaken Me?"

How very different those words of Jesus are from the opening words of today's Gospel: "As the Father has loved Me. . ." (John 15:9). And yet both were spoken by the Savior within hours of each other. Understanding how the Father loved the Son, the cross notwithstanding, is absolutely crucial for us to understand and grow from our text, for Jesus says to us, "As the Father has loved Me, so have I loved you. . . . This I command you, to love one another" (vv. 9, 17). Here we have an intricately detailed lesson in practical love — the Father's love for the Son, the Son's love for us, and, because of all that, our love for one another.

The Father's Love for the Son

In the movie "Arthur" a filthy rich young man, who had never in his life had to care for anyone, suddenly falls in love. It is a feeling he cannot describe. In order to determine if it is the real thing, he asks a total stranger, "How can you tell if you are in love? Does it make you feel funny? Does it make you whistle all the time?" The stranger, unimpressed by the joy of new love, tells him, "You could be in love; then again, you could be getting sick."

Arthur's dilemma of not knowing what love feels like is unfortunately typical. In fact the problem is even worse than that. Not only do we not know what love feels like, but it is difficult for us even to know what love is. The word itself covers such a broad range of emotions — I love pizza, I love my children, let's make love — that it is no help at all in getting to know what love is.

Scripture tells us that "God is love" and that "we love, because He first loved us" (1 John 4:8, 19). From God we learn what love is by experiencing it in the gift of His Son. The more we can know about how God loves, the more we will know what love is and the more we will be able to love.

The Father loved the Son, Jesus tells us. That is quite an assertion when you add up everything that happened to the Son of God as part of the plan of salvation. He "emptied Himself, taking the form of a servant, being born in the likeness of men. And being found in human form He humbled Himself and became obedient unto death, even death on a cross" (Phil. 2:7-8). Does that sound like something a loving father would want for his son? If God really loved Jesus, why did He let the cross happen? Was it because God loved us more than He loved His own Son — loved us so much that He gave up His only Son for us and did not spare Him? St. Paul testified to the immensity of God's love in his letter to the Ephesians: "But God, who is rich in mercy, out of the great love with which he loved us, even when we were dead through our trespasses, made us alive together with Christ" (Eph. 2:4-5).

I don't know that we can rightly say that God loved us more than He loved Jesus; that is an impossible question. But I do know that God's love for us is boundless, so great that He did give us His Son, whom He loved dearly. It's somewhat like a father who gives up his son to go to war. Does he do it because he loves his son too little? Or because he loves others more than his own son? No, he loves his son and loves him dearly, yet he gives him up because he believes it is the necessary thing to do.

Passing through the emergency room of a hospital a few years ago, I had the opportunity to witness a father's love in action. It all happened very quickly, but it made a lasting impression on me. A little boy had been injured badly. A nurse was taking him through heavy double doors into a procedure room. The boy was afraid and was crying and struggling in the nurse's arms, reaching out to his father and pleading not to be separated. "Daddy, Daddy!" he cried. The father was crying also, but he let his son go. He gave up his son to the nurse because it was necessary; it was the good thing to do. He did it because he loved his son. God gave up his Son, not for his Son's sake, but for ours. Because He loved us, He gave up His Son — the Son whom He also loved.

The Father loved the Son. How does a father love his son? It begins by sharing in the process of the son's creation; the father shares his physiology with his son so that the son is a "chip off the old block." But the Son of God is uncreated; He is God without beginning and without end. Yet God shares with Him His nature, for Scripture tells us the Son of God "reflects the glory of God and bears the very stamp of His nature" (Heb. 1:3). A father loves his son by giving him a name, and the Father has given Jesus "the name which is above every name, that at the name of Jesus every knee should bow... and every tongue confess that Jesus Christ is Lord" (Phil. 2:9-11). A father loves his son by caring for him, and Jesus testified, "All things have been delivered to Me by My Father" (Matt. 11:27). A father loves his son by being there when he needs him, and Jesus knew He could count on His Father. When He needed Him, He said, "Do you think that I cannot appeal to My Father, and He will at once send Me more than twelve legions of angels?" (Matt. 26:53). A father loves his son by giving him a home, and Jesus loved His Father's house and talked about its many mansions.

The Father loved the Son. The Scriptures don't tell us what kind of a feeling that was. Feeling is probably not even the right word to describe its nature. Instead, the Scriptures detail for us the close commitment that allowed the Father and the Son to be one, even as Jesus testified: "I and the Father are one.... The Father is in Me and I am in the Father" (John 10:30, 38). It was a relationship built on commitment, the complete commitment of the Father to the Son and the Son to the Father. Jesus also testified to this: "For this reason the Father loves Me, because I lay down My life, that I may take it again" (John 10:17).

The close commitment that exists between the Father and the Son has become the definition of love for many people. Love is a commitment, not a feeling. Love is the commitment that keeps a marriage alive even when the early surface thrills are gone, because love looks for deeper rewards than just a thrill. Love is the commitment to carry through a pregnancy that doesn't feel very good or is not very convenient. Love is the commitment that wakes a parent in the middle of the night to care for an ailing child. Love is the commitment that motivates a child to go against his friends and to do right because that's just the way he was raised. Love is the commitment that moved God to give up his only Son and that caused Jesus to give up His life for us. Feeling doesn't have much to do with any of those situations because it really doesn't have all that much to do with love.

There was a beautiful lady named Toni in my former parish for whom love was a commitment. Her husband, whom she dearly loved, was nearly killed in an industrial accident. An oil field worker, he was nearly crushed to death under a stack of drilling rig pipes. The doctors told her it would have been better if he had died. He was in a coma for six months and in the hospital 16 months. When he came home, he was not even a shadow of the man he had once been. He could barely speak. When he did speak, he told Toni over and over again, "Go away; I want you to divorce me." Sometimes the only word she could understand was "divorce." He was saying it for her, because he loved this beautiful woman and pitied her. How easy it would have been for her to divorce him and find someone else. But she didn't. She was in love, committed for better or for worse, in sickness and in health. Last I heard, Toni had to put her husband in a nursing home, but they were still married.

The Son's Love for Us

"As the Father has loved Me, so have I loved you," Jesus said. The Savior is committed to us. It was certainly not because of some "good feeling" that the Son of God came into the world "not to be served but to serve, and to give His life as a ransom for many" (Matt. 20:28). Jesus loved us, not for His sake, but for ours — commitment, not feeling.

One of my favorite illustrations of the love of Jesus is the account of His betrayal in the Garden of Gethsemane. There we see the enormity of the Savior's love. Judas, a man who had been with Jesus throughout the glorious time of His ministry, who had known the love of Jesus, led the mob that came to arrest Him. As the traitor approached the Savior to carry out his pathetic act, Jesus, whose feelings must have been devastated by what was happening, reached out to His disciple one more time in love and said to him, "Friend, why are you here?" (Matt. 26:50). Jesus called the traitor friend. He didn't call him names. He didn't curse him. He didn't forsake him. What would you have said to Judas? Jesus loved Judas, was committed to him, and called him friend.

So great was the Savior's commitment to us that "having loved His own who were in the world, he loved them to the end" (John 13:1). He loved us in spite of the cross, despising the shame of it. He loved us with His life, and He loves us still. He came to life again and is now at the right hand of the Father where He intercedes for us.

Our Love for One Another

"As the Father has loved Me, so have I loved you. . . . This I command you, to love one another." The kind of commitment the Father displays toward the Son and the Son displays toward us is what Jesus commands us to have toward one another. After He washed His disciples' feet (I wonder how that felt), Jesus said, "I have given you an example, that you also should do as I have done to you" (John 13:15).

"Love one another." In the Scriptures God tells us how: "Bear one another's burdens" (Gal. 6:2). "As the Lord has forgiven you, so you also must forgive" (Col. 3:13). St. Paul describes love in 1 Cor. 13 as being patient and kind, not jealous or boastful, arrogant or rude. It doesn't insist on its own way but is concerned about the needs and wants of others. It isn't irritable or resentful. It doesn't rejoice in the wrong but finds joy in looking for what is right and good. It endures all things, bears all things, hopes and believes all things. That sounds like we will have to put up with a lot of "stuff." It doesn't sound like it will feel very good. But feeling is not what love is all about.

If it frightens you to think about our Lord Jesus' command to love as

He has loved us, that's okay. It is a big order. We are all ready to make excuses for why we can't do it: "But we're only human!" Don't be afraid. The love of the Father empowered Jesus to obey Him. The love of Jesus empowers us to obey. "We love, because He first loved us" (1 John 4:19). We love because God abides in us and we in Him, because He has given us His Spirit. Through Baptism God has recreated us in His image, and His image is love. Therefore love is our image as well. We have known the love of God personally in our lives, and through Jesus that love is perfected in us and through us so that we do love.

After His resurrection, Jesus walked on the beach with Peter one day and spoke to the apostle about love. Three times Jesus asked Peter, "Simon, do you love Me?" (John 21:15-17). The questions made Peter remember the three times just a few days before when he swore he didn't know Jesus. Jesus was not asking Peter, "How do you feel about Me, Peter?" He asked him, "Do you love Me?" When Peter answered yes, Jesus instructed him, "Feed My sheep." We might say that Jesus told Peter to do something about his answer—to show his love by loving those whom Jesus loved.

Imagine Jesus asking you and me that question three times: "Brother, sister, do you love Me?" We answer that we do, and Jesus says to us, "Then love one another, for I have loved you as the Father has loved Me."

I Don't Know Who I Am Anymore

THE ASCENSION OF OUR LORD
LUKE 24:44-53

Daniel G. Mueller

Who am I? is a question asked often today as people seek more and more to establish their own identities. Marriages are breaking up because wives feel their identity has been swallowed up by their husband's. People change jobs, move to new locations, and do many other things in an effort to establish an identity they feel comfortable with. Great effort is expended in an attempt to resolve the nagging feeling that "I don't know who I am anymore."

A great many people do not like themselves very much. They don't like who they are. Young people feel pressured to develop an identity of their own. Mothers lament, "I'm not a mother and wife; I'm a maid and a chauffeur." Sometimes we can laugh about our identity problems; most of the time they make us tired and frustrated.

Who are you? Let me give you a definition of who I am. I am a father, husband, son, brother, friend, pastor, hunter, writer, driver, sinner, saint, uncle, nephew, carpenter, gardener. Some of those things I like to be more than others. Some of them I don't like to be at all. But all are who I am, and each of you is just as complex.

Trying to be all those things is very difficult. No wonder people get tired of it all and feel like dropping out. That's a natural reaction. The problem is not only that we try to be too many things. We forget to be who we have been called to be.

Who Is Jesus?

The disciples of Jesus suffered from an identity crisis also. They wanted to be something else than what Jesus wanted them to be. For that matter, they wanted Jesus to be something else, too. He came to be the Savior of the world. That was and still is His identity. But the disciples wanted Him to be a king. When Jesus told them who He was and how He had come to suffer, die, and rise again, "they understood none of these things," Luke (18:34). They did not understand because they didn't want to.

The disciples did not want to hear about the suffering and death of our Lord Jesus. That whole idea was contrary to what they expected of Him, and all they wanted to hear was what fit their expectations. Once when Jesus spoke of His Passion, Peter rebuked the Lord, saying, "God forbid, Lord! This shall never happen to You" (Matt. 16:22). Peter, together with the other disciples, did not want to hear about our Lord's suffering.

Unfortunately, because they refused to listen to what Jesus had to say about His suffering and death, they missed out on what He had to say about His exaltation, also. Not even the great good news of Christ's return to heaven, the ascension and all that it means for us, got through to the disciples at first. Jesus had told them, "When I go and prepare a place for you, I will come again and take you to Myself, that where I am you may be also. And you know the way where I am going." The good news of the ascension, that Jesus has gone to prepare a place for us in heaven, a place to which He is coming to take us, was news that flew right past the Twelve. "Thomas said to Him, 'Lord, we do not know where You are going; how can we know the way?' Jesus said to him, 'I am the Way' " (John 14:3-6).

The disciples did not want to hear about our Lord's dying because it created an identity crisis for them. If their Master would suffer, it probably meant that His followers would suffer, too. If the Master went to the cross, then His followers would bear the cross as well. Jesus Himself had promised that: "If any man would come after Me, let him deny himself and take up his cross and follow Me" (Matt. 16:24). And that is not how the disciples thought about the Lord or about themselves.

Their image of Jesus — of the Christ — was that He would be a king. And because of their closeness to Him, they would be His officials, persons of authority. They would be His secretaries of state, agriculture, defense, and all the rest. Each would receive a political plum for having supported Him. It was a dream the disciples found horribly hard to give up. Even after our Lord's death and resurrection, on the day of His ascension into heaven, they still dared to ask Him, "Lord, will You at this time restore the kingdom to Israel?" (Acts 1:6). They were still hoping for their political plums.

But it was not to be. Jesus opened their minds to understand the Scriptures. In effect, Jesus said: Look at all that has happened to Me — My suffering, death and resurrection. Look at the work I have done in your midst. Everything written about Me — about the Christ — in the Scriptures has been fulfilled. Once again Jesus revealed to them who He was, His true identity, and in the process He taught them who they were.

He was not the king they expected Him to be. He was a Savior, who came because of God's love to serve, not to be served, and to give His life as a ransom for many. He was the "Suffering Servant" of Isaiah, who bore our griefs and carried our sorrows, who was wounded for our transgressions and bruised for our iniquities. He was the One with whose stripes we are healed. He was the Forsaken One of Psalm 22, the "worm, and no man," whose hands and feet were pierced, whose garments were divided. And, as they were about to discover, He was the Victorious One of Psalm 68, who ascended on high, leading captivity captive and receiving gifts for mankind. He was the Savior, the Christ, the King of kings, who came, not to set up an earthly kingdom, but to establish an everlasting Kingdom of life with God now and in heaven — a Kingdom built on the good news of repentance and forgiveness of sins in Jesus Christ.

Who Are His Disciples?

Because Jesus was no earthly king, the disciples were no "big shots" either. Jesus often tried to get this through to them, teaching by word and example that the life of His followers is a life of service, not arrogance. When two of the disciples had tried to guarantee for themselves the best positions in His kingdom, causing the rest to be indignant toward them, Jesus taught them all a lesson about their identity: "The rulers of the Gentiles lord it over them, and their great men exercise authority over them. It shall not be so among you; but whoever would be great among you must be your servant, and whoever would be first among you must be your slave" (Matt. 20:25-27).

The identity of the Christ, Jesus taught His disciples, was that of the Savior, through whom God would draw all to Himself by repentance and the forgiveness of sins. Their identity, because of their relationship with Him, was that of proclaimers — witnesses — who would tell of the Christ and call people to Him. From the very beginning, when Jesus first said, "Follow Me," He called them to be fishers of men. Jesus finally got through to them that He was the Christ of the Scriptures and not of their imagination, and that they were to be His witnesses. His identity and theirs were clearly defined.

Jesus said very simply, "You are witnesses of these things" (Luke 24:48). That's all. What He said to His disciples, He says to all of His followers — to us. When a Christian asks, "Who am I?" Jesus responds, "You are My witnesses." That's really who we are. Everything else we do is just a function of who we are. I am a witness of Jesus Christ who drives a car and is married and a father and hunts and works as a pastor and sins and does all kinds of things. But who I am is primarily this: I am a witness of Jesus Christ. That is a great identity. It is an identity with which I can always be satisfied. It says something wonderful about me: I am loved by God, redeemed, forgiven, and made His own.

St. Peter wrote to his Christian friends in Rome to share with them the wonder of their identity and let them know they too were witnesses. He said it in a way that lets us know how very special our identity is. "You are a chosen race, a royal priesthood, a holy nation, God's own people, that you may declare the wonderful deeds of Him who called you out of darkness into His marvelous light. Once you were no people [you had no identity] but now you are God's people; once you had not received mercy but now you have received mercy" (1 Peter 2:9-10). That's who we are.

In Baptism God called us just as surely as He called His disciples. He called us by name and said to us, "Follow Me." "As many of you as were baptized into Christ have put on Christ" (Gal. 3:27) we quote in our baptismal rite. We have put on Christ; that's how we became His witnesses. In putting on Christ, St. Paul explains, "It is no longer I who live, but Christ who lives in me; and the life I now live in the flesh I live by faith in the Son of God, who loved me and gave Himself for me'" (Gal. 2:20). Because Christ lives in us, we are His witnesses. People look at us and see Christ. That's what being a witness is all about.

To empower us to be witnesses, God has given us the Word and the Sacraments. In the Word we learn what we are witnesses to: God's almighty power and endless love. In the Word we see all that Christ Jesus did for us and are then able to give a testimony of it. Through the Word the Holy Spirit comes to us, the One who calls us by the Gospel, enlightens us with His gifts, sanctifies and keep us in the one true faith. What God begins in us through the Word, He strengthens and confirms in us through His sacraments.

Our Savior promised to send the Holy Spirit, and send Him He did. With Luther we confess that the Spirit daily forgives all sins to me and all believers. Daily He calls, gathers, enlightens, and sanctifies the whole Christian church on earth and keeps it with Christ Jesus in the one true faith. Every day He does this.

How much easier life would be if we just remembered who we are. Can you imagine the difference it would make in all that we do, if we always did it as witnesses of Jesus Christ? What if we dated as witnesses of Jesus Christ and chose our marriage partners that way? If we drove as witnesses of Jesus Christ, I know insurance rates would go down. If we lived as witnesses of Jesus Christ in our homes, our marriages and our performance as parents would be that much better. If we worked as His witnesses, our job situations would improve tremendously. Everything we do would be greatly improved and enhanced. When we forget who we really are and fail to be who we have been called to be, all kinds of problems develop—guilt, hurt, unhappiness, disappointment, jealousy — all the fruits of sin. It's good to know who we are.

It was good for the disciples. St. Luke tells us that after Jesus got through to them who He was and who they were, He ascended into heaven. "He led them out as far as Bethany, and lifting up His hands He blessed them. While He blessed them, He parted from them, and was carried up into heaven" (Luke 24:50-51). The disciples were left behind, not with sadness such as they had when Jesus first left them and their dreams seemed to die with Him, but with great joy because they knew who He was — their crucified Savior, risen Lord, and ascended King. And they knew who they were — His witnesses. They got started with their job right away, St. Luke tells us, for they "were continually in the temple blessing God" (v. 52).

Through the record of His holy Word God tells us who we are. We are Christ's witnesses. That's our identity. The more we practice being who we are, the more we will know great joy.

This High Assignment

SEVENTH SUNDAY OF EASTER
JOHN 17:11b-19

George H. Beiderwieden Jr.

As the body of David Livingstone was being brought back to London to be buried in Westminster Abbey, throngs lined the streets of the route. One man was obviously much moved. Someone standing next to him asked, "You knew the missionary well?"

"Yes," was the reply. "David and I were boyhood friends. Later we went to Africa together. David went for Africa's souls, and I went for Africa's gold. And today I realize I concentrated upon the wrong world!"

It's so easy. The Lord in His high-priestly prayer helps us again to set our priorities in proper order. He points us to

This High Assignment
The Challenge

The nub of this section of His prayer is verse 18: "As Thou didst send Me into the world, so I have sent them into the world." Let's not allow the details to obscure the chief directive here. The Lord Jesus sent the Twelve — and now sends all believers — into the world. They are not to wait for the world's invitation or for ideal circumstances. He provides the initiative. His command is "Go!"

His marching order is characterized by the mission His Father gave to Him: "As Thou didst send Me into the world, so I have sent them" (v. 18). That implies commitment and dedication. How often He has declared His complete, unquestioning surrender to His Father's will earlier in this gospel: "The Son can do nothing of His own accord, but only what He sees the Father doing" (John 5:19). "I seek not My own will but the will of Him who sent Me" (John 5:30). Now do you catch the weight of the *as*? Just as He was absorbed with carrying out His heaven-directed commission, so He wants us to be absorbed in carrying out the mission He hands us.

And He here indicates the power, the push, the incentive that will get us on the road out to our world. "As Thou didst send Me into the world." We know what the goal of that mission was. "God sent the Son into the world, not to condemn the world, but that the world might be saved through Him" (John 3:17). He left the mansions of glory, turned His back on the adulation of all the hosts and the endless hallelujahs of the ten thousand times ten thousand, spent 33 of what must have been the loneliest, most miserable years ever here below in our world, and then went to the cross in the face of spit, mockery, and beating—all for us. He did it for our forgiveness, our adoption, our peace, and our eternal glory. Surely whatever He now asks will be easy! "As Thou didst send Me . . . so I have sent them" (John 17:18).

There is something else here. He was sent by the Father to *save*. On this almost identical mission He now sends His people. Now, of course, believers are not sent to pay for anyone's sins. He did that once— adequately, completely, entirely. "Where there is forgiveness of these [sins], there is no longer any offering for sin" (Heb. 10:18). Believers are, however, given a critical part to play in the salvation of their contemporaries. The Spirit converts. And He has decided to do that through the Word. That's where we come in! We are to speak that Word. "You shall be My witnesses" (Acts 1:8). We believers are also to persuade our world to come where that Word is proclaimed—to the worship service, Bible classes, adult instruction sessions. We provide the students. The mighty Spirit of God is the effective Teacher. Do you begin to see our challenge?

The Challenged Ones

Why don't we do it? Or why don't we do it more? Is it possibly because we're not keenly enough aware of all that we have to share? Are we not the "satisfied customer" we ought to be? Our Lord reminds us of a few facets of what we have received.

"The world has hated them because they are not of the world, even as I am not of the world" (John 17:14). He evidently figured that was important, for He repeated it: "They are not of the world, even as I am not of the world" (v. 16). At first blush that doesn't sound much like an advantage. Being different isn't exactly what modern people strive for—especially not being otherworldly. But this different is *different*! He says we're like Him: "Even as I am not of the world" (v. 14). Think of just one distinction: We have peace. He had just told His disciples, "My peace I give to you; not as the world gives" (John 14:27). The world and all its followers are torn with strife. But all the wars and the scratching and all competing is minor beside the deeper strife — the guilt over sin. We have peace — His peace. It comes from the forgiveness He has bought for us. Are we ever different!

We have something else. "These things I speak in the world, that they may have My joy fulfilled in themselves" (John 17:13). We have joy. Joy isn't the same thing as happiness. Happiness depends on what happens. No one is happy all the time. Remember that our Lord predicted: "'In the world you have tribulation" (John 16:33). Adverse circumstances of life will, at times, produce great sorrow.

Joy is deeper. The object of the believer's joy is the Lord Jesus Himself. Paul writes: "Rejoice in the Lord always' again I will say, Rejoice" (Phil. 4:4). Having Jesus gives us deep down joy as we know His Calvary payment and the forgiveness that is ours as a result. All the promises of the heavenly Father are ours through Him, including the assurance of eternal glory. It's like the difference between riding in an airplane and riding in a jeep. The rough road affects the air passenger differently than the jeep rider. Had you forgotten? We have an airplane ticket! What do we have to share? Joy — real joy — no matter what!

I like Luther here. He does a little imagining. In explaining why the Lord said, "These things I speak in the world," Luther wrote, "In order that through the Word, caught with the ears and held in the heart, they be comforted, joyfully rely on it, and be able to say: See, this is what my Lord Christ said; this faithfully and fervently He prayed for us; this have I heard from His mouth, etc. What here is needed is that one hold to the Word with his whole heart and take comfort in that."

We have another advantage to share. With Jesus comes the ability to resist all the world's evil. "I do not pray that Thou shouldst take them out of the world, but that Thou shouldst keep them from the evil one" (John 17:15). Even many who are without Jesus are recognizing the enemies of human well-being. Modern man's materialism and greed sets labor against capital and capital against labor. But what can we do about it? Only Jesus can change getters into givers. We hear so much about ever-increasing crime, overcrowded penal institutions, cries for sterner penalities, and frequent repeaters. Only Jesus can change the heart. We have the drug problem. Only Jesus can alter the will. So we, the challenged, have plenty to share, don't we?

Meeting the Challenge

Then how can we meet the challenge? The Lord here suggests three avenues. He directs us to the first by His example: "Holy Father, keep them in Thy name, which Thou hast given Me" (v. 11). Our Lord is here urging us to pray. He once told His followers: "Pray therefore the Lord of the harvest to send out laborers into His harvest" (Luke 10:2). Haven't we too often thought of that prayer as referring only to more foreign missionaries? There's also so much need right here. "The fields are white" also in our town. We need to pray, "Lord, reform Thy world, beginning with me!" We need to respond with the words of the hymn, "Here am I, send me, send me!"

Oh, what need there is among us for more prayer! There is no more urgent plea than for the burden laid on us of those still lost. A foreign missionary sobbed, "They tramp over my breast at night; it seems I can never be happy again!" But they don't keep us awake nights — not even their fearful future if someone doesn't share the Gospel with them! We need to pray that our eyes be opened to our opportunities. So many today seek something they do not know. We know they really are seeking a Person — our gracious and merciful Lord. We need to pray for courage, for less fear of doing it poorly. We need to remember that "he who makes no mistakes makes nothing!" Oh, let us *pray*!

Our Lord also says, "I have given them Thy Word" (John 17:14). That's a cue, too. We, the challenged ones, will meet the challenge better the more we are in His Word. Part of it is the mirror of His holy law. Looking into it we see ourselves as He, the holy God, sees us, and our relief at having our sins paid for increases measurably. Looking into the mirror of the Law also helps us appreciate better the fearful plight of those who do not know the Savior. "It is a fearful thing to fall into the hands of the living God" (Heb. 10:31).

But the more we hear His Word — the more we read it and study it — the more clearly will the most important fact stand out. When St. John reported the events of Easter Sunday night, he noted, "Then the disciples were glad when they saw the Lord" (John 20:20). When we see the Lord in His Word, He will become more than just a catechism answer, more than a figure in a stained-glass church window, more than a name we mumble before and after meals. Jesus will become a Person for us — a living, acting, and reacting Lord. He becomes someone to whom we own infinitely more than we can ever repay, but also someone whom we most earnestly desire to please. "Lord, what will You have me do?" And we know what He wants most. We've caught His bottom line. He want us to share Him with all the world.

One thing more: He prays for our aid. "Sanctify them in the truth" (John 17:17). *Sanctify* means "set apart." That points to growth. The beginning is that Jesus is our payment for sin. But do we not often leave it at that? "I'm converted! I trust Jesus!" To be set apart involves more. It means that Jesus is Lord of my life. He has bought that right on Calvary. The ability to let Him be Lord in our lives comes from absorbing His Word.

What He wants from us is what He did Himself. "For their sake I consecrate Myself, that they also may be consecrated in truth" (v. 19). He set Himself apart. Only He could do it voluntarily. Truly and completely God, He took on Himself our humanity. He substituted for our race beneath the awful wrath of God. He died. And now the truth of all that He has done can enable us to be set apart for His purpose. With St. Paul we can say, "I have become all things to all men, that I might by all means save some" (1 Cor. 9:22).

> When I enter that beautiful city,
> And the saved all about me appear,
> I want to hear somebody say to me:
> It was you who directed me here!

The Good Life

THE DAY OF PENTECOST
JOHN 7:37-39a

Dean O. Wenthe

The good life — think about it for a moment. Our culture is constantly calling us to live it. More than that, the media offers many suggestions on how we can achieve it. The good life will be yours if your children acquire that particular toy that was so neatly demonstrated during the Saturday morning cartoon commercials. If you teenagers will only wear the right designer clothing, popularity will envelope you even as the fabric surrounds you. And of course every adult has a secret shopping list that fills our daydreams with everything from exotic vacations to custom cars. The irony of it all is that such a selling job frequently robs us of the *real* good life.

If with the wave of a wand all our wants could be met, possibly by next Sunday — certainly by the following week — we would then have a new list and again be on the quest for "the good life."

Good Christian pilgrims, do you really want "the good life" — not just the life that means tomorrow you have more than you do today, nor even some remote world portrayed for us by a Madison Avenue advertising firm, but never to be found? For anyone in search of "the good life," Pentecost provides all that your heart desires, and it does so right now.

The Need for the Water of Life

Jesus addresses each of us: "If anyone thirst, let him come to Me and drink. He who believes in Me, as the Scripture has said, 'Out of his heart shall flow rivers of living water'" (John 7:37-38).

The picture of the good life that Jesus holds before us does not at the same time enslave us by fanning our desires for what we don't have. Rather, Jesus presents Himself. "Come," He says. "Drink from Me." Jesus' invitation is aimed precisely at our deepest longing for happiness and the good life.

The land where Jesus walked was dry, dirty, and dusty. Sandaled feet needed repeated cleansing as they collected the grime of Palestine's pathways. In such a world, water meant life. From ancient times to the present, the hiker who becomes lost without water faces imminent death. The dry desert wind whips around a person, and the sun creates a crucible in which the body is quickly dehydrated. To have water is to live; to lack it is to die.

Jesus knew that the world through which He walked was parched by a force more severe than the power of the desert wind. He knew and faced the power of sin. It was the furious force of their rebellion against God that ruptured the relationship of Adam and Eve to the world around them. God had planted a grand garden; flowers, fruits, and foods were close at hand. But man's hand, reaching out against God, simultaneously planted thorns and thistles. Now the desert's dryness and winter's cold are threats to human life. Constant effort and caution are required, and in spite of all the sweat of our brow and our modern technology, we and the land we inhabit remain under the curse of our rebellion.

Luther aptly portrayed our plight when he stated that the human being, even without Christ, will encounter God in such basic elements as water, fire, and rope. The water, however, will drown him, the fire will burn, and the rope will hang him. But, the Reformer continues, the person who has seen God in the manger and on the cross "will use the rope to haul water from the well and the fire to boil that water to cook the family dinner."

Our lives are not "good" because our own sin — our refusal to behold Christ first — has dehydrated us of purpose and meaning. The junk food of gossip and grudges, the deceptive delicacies of infidelity and indecency, the main courses of pride and power — these poisonous provisions are offered to us by the prince of this world as the answer for our hunger. Each of us has been invited to his banquet; each has sampled the fare. Some have eaten to the full, but all of us have failed. Our tongues are tainted with the taste of sin. We know how incapable we are of our resisting those delights that are specifically served to suit our strongest appetites. If we formed a self-help group this morning and dubbed it "sin-watchers," it is doubtful whether anyone of us would lose even an ounce of sin, let alone the pounds that have accumulated through the years. None of us is fit. We are all obese with sin.

Nothing short of a radically different diet will save any of us from certain death. Someone must come to us from outside and change us within.

The Living Water of the Spirit

Pentecost presents that Someone. At Pentecost the Holy Spirit came as our Provider. The Spirit, who made us children of God at our baptism, now flows through us as a river of "living water." The challenge is not to *seek* something but to *recognize* the Spirit as He holds Jesus Christ before us in the living water of Baptism, in the bread and wine of the Lord's Supper, and in the Good News of God's mercy. The Spirit gives us faith so that we might receive the good gifts of God.

These gifts were purchased at Calvary, where the earth literally shook with the cosmic consequences of Christ's death for us. Faith, forgiveness, and freedom flow from the fountain of Christ's atoning death. If we want "the good life," it is ours in these good gifts and *nowhere* else.

Jesus' imagery echoes several Old Testament descriptions by people who received the good life. The prophet Isaiah promised, "You shall be like a watered garden, like a spring of water, whose waters fail not" (Is. 58:11.)

The psalmist describes the person who delights in God's Word of grace: "He is like a tree planted by streams of water, that yields its fruit in its season, and its leaf does not wither" (Ps. 1:3).

Water — cool, clean water — brought to mind a picture of productivity and peace for the ancient Israelite. Water meant that life could go on in a hot and hostile land. It meant that grass could grow, that fruit trees could blossom, and that man and animal could live. It was the same for Jesus' audience. It is the same for us.

How fitting that Jesus describes the Holy Spirit as the living water within us! All the benefits of His work — forgiveness of sin, fullness of life, victory over death — are bestowed by the Spirit in the life-giving Word and Sacraments. The good life — the full life — is the life in Christ that the Holy Spirit gives and sustains. It is yours and it is mine by virtue of our baptism. It is nourished by the Word of God as we search the Holy Scriptures and attend the Lord's Supper. Now everything, from our greatest triumph at work to our most trivial moment at play, is changed like Luther's water, fire, and rope into a component of the good life in Christ.

That dry and deadly spirit, Satan, despises our baptismal water even as he opposes the living waters of the Holy Spirit within us. They defeat the death that our sinful life deserved and drown it in the atoning life and death of Jesus Christ. No life, however glamorous, can hold a candle to the good life in Christ.

In times as tumultuous as ours a young man from a successful family sensed this truth when he left a promising career as a member of the British Parliament to serve as a parish pastor in Bemerton, England. His name was George Herbert. He speaks of his search for the good life in a poem that includes these lines:

> At length I got unto the gladsome hill,
>   Where lay my hope,
> Where lay my heart; and climbing still,
>   When I had gain'd the brow and top,
> A lake of brackish waters on the ground
>   Was all I found (From *The Pilgrimage*).

Brackish waters — that's all that most people in our day are finding in their quest for the good life. Our quest could have ended at the same stagnant, still pool. But on Pentecost the Spirit of God brings pure streams of water from outside and causes them to gurgle and gush forth within us. Our sin is washed away; our thirst is quenched; our appetites are changed; and our lives, like the Garden of Eden, bear good fruit.

The Fruit of the Good Life

"The fruit of the Spirit is love, joy, peace, patience, kindness, goodness, faithfulness, gentleness, self-control" (Gal. 5:22-23). This is the good life. It is ours by the Spirit's presence, for He holds us to the source of our salvation, Jesus Christ.

The ancient world was rocked by Pentecost. This event resounded throughout the Roman empire through the apostolic proclamation of the Gospel. Those ancient, Pentecost Christians displayed a different life-style. They called others to "the good life' in Christ, and the Spirit turned the tongues of men from brackish to living waters.

The same sequence will follow as we live the good life of the Spirit. How noticeable it is when someone changes in behavior pattern! Changes in mood, in language, in actions — we recognize them quickly in those whom we know well. We worry or rejoice according to the nature of the change.

You, Pentecost pilgrims, are and will continue to be noticed. Those around you will recognize the difference. Your good life in Christ will stand out as sharply as an oasis in the desert. Even more significant will be the discovery that the difference is not in you, but in the Spirit who dwells within you and who invites them to quench their thirst in Christ. There are only two places to drink, only two tables at which to be seated, only two ways to live life.

One caution is necessary. The Holy Spirit did not deliver the apostles or any of us from struggles. The good life in Christ is ours, but the Spirit leads us not to some kind of blissful utopia, but back to the cross where we are to daily drown our sinful self with the living water.

Luther so aptly describes our struggle when he writes:

> For a pious Christian is still flesh and blood, as other people are. He fights against sin and evil lust and feels what he does not want to feel, wheras non-Christians are wholly unconcerned about these things and do not fight against them at all. . . . The Christian should fight against the sins which remain in him and which he feels, should permit the Holy Spirit to work with him, and should sigh without ceasing to be relieved of sin. Such sighing never does cease in believers, but they have an excellent Auditor: The Holy Spirit Himself.

Share your struggles with the Spirit. He will listen every time. The good life will not escape you even in times of trial. O Holy Spirit, hear our prayers.

The Importance of Conversion

THE HOLY TRINITY
FIRST SUNDAY AFTER PENTECOST
JOHN 3:1-17

B. Dale Thomas

How can we awaken the hearts of members who are far from Jesus like Saul, David, Judas, Peter, and Nicodemus? How do we do this and at the same time not stir up doubts in the hearts of members like Grandma Schmidt, who know their lives are far from perfect? We want the penitent members, who will always have weaknesses and shortcomings, to be sure of their salvation because they believe the Good News that Jesus died and rose for them and that Jesus loves, forgives, and saves them. Yet we also want to appeal to those certificate-waving members to repent of their deeds of the flesh (Gal. 5:19-21), for God sees what is in their hearts, and He cannot be deceived (Gal. 6:7). We trust the power of the Holy Spirit working through His Word to comfort the distressed and to disturb those who have taken their conversion for granted.

Taking Conversion for Granted

I assume Nicodemus was not converted when he first came to Jesus by night. His outward appearance would lead us to believe that he was a faithful man of God. He was a devout member of the Jewish church and a leader in the highest court of the church. He believed that Jesus was a great teacher and miracle worker; he was a student of His teachings. It is possible to be all of this and still be unconverted.

We cannot fool Jesus; He can see through the veneer. He knows whether our hearts are in Him or far from Him. In the previous chapter of John's gospel Jesus saw through the business done in the temple in the name of religion. He rejected that unconverted merchandising (John 2:16). At the end of that same chapter He saw through the many who "believed in His name" (John 2:23). He knew their faith was a sign-seeking faith — a fraud.

Now we have another one who could not fool Jesus — Nicodemus. Jesus points out to this upright church leader that he is still lacking what is essential. "I say to you, unless one is born anew, he cannot see the kingdom of God" (John 3:3). Jesus even goes so far as to say that Baptism is the only way he can enter that kingdom. We know from other passages that it is also possible to be born again by hearing the Word (Rom. 10:17), but Jesus may have stressed Baptism for Nicodemus because of the way that the Pharisees had rejected the plea of John the Baptizer to repent and be baptized (cf. Luke 7:29-30). The typical Pharisee trusted his birthright as a Jew and his good works for salvation. He rejected Baptism. Jesus is saying that if Nicodemus wants to enter the kingdom of God, he must be reborn by water and the Spirit.

There is other evidence that Nicodemus was not converted. His cautious nature as he comes to visit Jesus at night may have been a result of his fear of ridicule and rejection by his peers. It may have been the only time these two very busy men could find to get together. His unconverted state is evident as he fails to understand the spiritual answers given by Jesus. "The unspiritual man does not receive the gifts of the Spirit of God, for they are folly to him, and he is not able to understand them" (1 Cor. 2:14). It was not that he actually thought he had to get back into his mother's womb, but it was just as ridiculous for Jesus to expect him to make such a radical change at his age and begin all over again. This was foolishness to an unspiritual mind. As a typical Pharisee he still thought this change was something he had to accomplish for himself. Just as iron can be melted but cannot melt itself, so he needed to be converted but could not convert himself, and it was impossible for his carnal mind to understand how this radical transformation would take place by the Spirit through Baptism.

Reborn for a Fruitful Life

Praise God! Nicodemus was converted! The cautious, curious, carnal church worker was transformed into a born-again, bold believer in Christ by the power of the Holy Spirit. Nicodemus heard the Law, which made him realize his lost condition. He repented, and I believe he was baptized as Jesus taught. He heard the familiar story recorded in Numbers 21:6-9 about the bronze serpent that Moses lifted up in the wilderness so that those who were bitten by the snakes and trusted in God's deliverance were saved.

The Holy Spirit gave Nicodemus a new spiritual understanding. He saw Jesus as the bronze serpent. Just as the serpent was made in the form of evil snakes, so Jesus took on the form of evil men. Just as the bronze serpent had no poison, so Jesus was without sin. When the people who were bitten by the poisonous snakes looked at the bronze serpent and believed, they were delivered. When we, who are bitten by Satan, look on Jesus and believe in Him, who died on a cross for us, we too will not perish but have the forgiveness of sins and the gift of eternal life.

By the power of the Holy Spirit Nicodemus became a new creation (2 Cor. 5:17). He was changed from death to life (Col. 2:12-13). He moved out of darkness into light (1 Peter 2:9). Just as it is impossible to see the wind, so we cannot see this supernatural process of rebirth. But just as we can see the presence of the wind as we watch the limbs of the trees sway back and forth, so we can see the evidence of the Holy Spirit in the lives of the reborn.

Evidence of this change in Nicodemus shows up in John 7:50-52. The Pharisees sent guards to arrest Jesus. The guards were so impressed with Jesus that they returned empty-handed. They were ridiculed by the Pharisees. In this tense setting, when most would hide their faith in Jesus, Nicodemus stood up and defended Him.

After the crucifixion we see more evidence of the change that took place in Nicodemus as a result of his rebirth. Peter had denied Jesus, and the rest of the disciples were hiding behind locked doors. But the reborn, bold believer, Nicodemus, together with a secret believer, Joseph of Arimathea, gave Jesus a proper burial (John 19:38-42). Being born again shows itself in our lives (Gal. 5:22-23).

So what am I to do? First I must look into my heart. I need to examine my heart to see if I am still in the faith, as St. Paul advises: "Examine yourselves, to see whether you are holding to your faith. Test yourselves" (2 Cor. 13:5). I cannot deceive Jesus. He knows if my heart is near or far from Him. It is possible that I have been bitten by that fiery serpent, Satan. His venom can create a paralysis that prevents me from bringing forth the fruits of the Spirit. It can drug my mind so that I am easily deceived. I may think that my relationship with God is adequate, when in reality I am trusting in my own efforts and taking His forgiveness for granted. I need to hear the call of

Jeremiah to repent: "Return, faithless Israel, says the Lord. I will not look on you in anger, for I am merciful, says the Lord; I will not be angry forever" (Jer. 3:12).

That call and gracious invitation leads me to sorrow for my sin. David told Nathan, "I have sinned against the Lord" (2 Sam. 12:13). Peter went out and wept bitterly (Luke 22:62). When I have repented, I can then rejoice in the Good News of forgiveness. Nathan responded to David, "The Lord also has put away your sin; you shall not die" (2 Sam. 12:13). As surely as God's curse fell on the serpent that tempted Eve (Gen. 3:14), so Jesus has become a curse for us (Gal. 3:13). He has taken all of the poison of our sins and has suffered and died in our place. When we, like the children of Israel in the wilderness, look to Him with a childlike, trusting faith (Matt. 18:3), our sins are forgiven, and we have eternal life. Faith in Jesus as our personal Savior is the only antidote against the fatal venom we receive from Satan's bites. Not only should I be baptized, but I must live in daily repentance and trust in Jesus. His promise assures me that I am reborn and alive in the Spirit.

As the conversion of Nicodemus showed itself in his born-again, bold behavior, so our conversion will show itself in our life-style. In the Spirit we will not take that conversion for granted. Daily we will repent of our sins. Daily we trust in Jesus and are assured by His Word that we are forgiven and that eternal life is ours as a free gift. As new creatures in Christ, we can expect to bring forth the fruit of the Spirit in our daily lives.

Be Merciful, Not Judgmental

SECOND SUNDAY AFTER PENTECOST
MARK 2:23-28

B. Dale Thomas

I remember reading about a pastor who would not do things the way everyone else did them. For example, one Sunday there was a note tacked on the church door: "Baptism service down at the lake. Bring hot dogs, and stay for lunch." He was the talk of the town, and the talk was not kind and supportive. He was told to fall in line or get out. He fell in line, and the attendance at this campus church fell by two-thirds. Today's Gospel sets forth a principle about the way we are to treat others, especially those who break man-made rules. Jesus enables us to show mercy instead of harsh and bitter judgments.

The Pharisees' Judgment

This is a story about Jesus and His disciples as they were walking through a wheat field on the Sabbath day. The disciples were eating some grains of wheat, and the Pharisees accused them of breaking the Sabbath.

It was probably late in April or early May. There were no sidewalks in those days. Often people had to travel through a farmer's land. They would not just scurry through a wheat field any way that they wanted. That would ruin the man's harvest. There were paths to walk on, and the wheat was sown right next to the path. It was not unusual for those going through such a field to pluck heads of wheat, rub them in their hands until the chaff would be removed, blow the chaff away, and eat the grains of wheat.

It wasn't that the disciples were famished or starving. As they passed through, they simply reached over and took some grains of wheat to eat. According to Deuteronomy 23:25 this was permissible. It was not stealing; God allowed it.

The Pharisees, however, did not allow it. Their interpretation of Exodus 34:21 caused them to be harsh in their judgment of the disciples. When the disciples plucked the heads of wheat, that was considered to be reaping. When they rubbed the heads together and blew away the chaff, that was threshing. Put is all together and the disciples were guilty of harvesting on the Sabbath.

This all happened in the context of the hostility of the Pharisees against Jesus that was so bad it led them to constantly look for ways to destroy Him (Matt. 12:14). To work on the Sabbath was no small infraction of the rules. In Numbers 15 there is a story about a man who went out and gathered kindling wood on the Sabbath. The Lord said he should be killed. To work on the Sabbath meant to defile that holy day; the offense was punishable by the death. So the Pharisees were making a serious charge. They were looking for the death penalty. They wanted to get rid of Jesus.

But Jesus defended His disciples: "Have you never read what David did, when he was in need and was hungry?" (Mark 2:25). The Pharisees were supposed to be very learned in the Bible, and so Jesus gave them a test. He used a story in which their hero, David, actually broke a ceremonial law, not just a man-made interpretation of the law. David went to the priest when he was being chased by Saul and he and his men were hungry. They asked the priest for food, but the only food available was the holy bread in the tabernacle (1 Sam. 21:1-6). Twelve loaves were made each week and placed on the golden table in front of the Holy of Holies. Each week these were replaced, and the old ones were eaten by the priests. No one else was to eat this bread. But David was hungry, and there is no other food, so the priest allowed David to eat the holy bread. Notice the contrast between the mercy shown in the Old Testament by the priest and the harsh, bitter judgment of the New Testament spiritual leaders, the Pharisees.

Jesus used another illustration, recorded in Matthew 12:5, to defend His disciples. He pointed out that the priests worked on the Sabbath. They circumcized children and cut up animals for sacrifices on the Sabbath. Nowhere is there any condemnation in the Bible against what David did or what the priests did.

The Call to Mercy

What is the point? You can't claim that you love God and religiously keep all the man-made rules and regulations about the church and then be bitter, hostile, and unloving toward other people. The religious attitude that places rules and regulations of the church above a loving relationship with people is just not acceptable to God. The Sabbath was made to help man; man was not made just so he could keep the Sabbath.

The purpose for which God places His people in the world is to show love and mercy in the name of Jesus. We are not to be like the Pharisees who were harsh, judmental, and bitter in their dealings with people who did not do things their way. Jesus ushered in a whole new spirit. His was not a spirit of religious legalism, of a ritual purity that is unloving toward people who do not fit into our particular mold. Instead, it is an attitude of mercy, love, and compassion.

"For God sent the Son into the world, not to condemn the world, but that the world might be saved through Him" (John 3:17). This is a different spirit than that of the Pharisee who comes to judge and condemn. Jesus practiced what He preached as He prayed from the cross, "Father, forgive them; for they know not what they do" (Luke 23:34). He showed mercy and forgiveness toward His murderers. When we become like the Pharisee in our harsh words about others, we join the murderers at the foot of the cross.

Not only does Jesus perfectly keep the law of love for us, but He also pays our debt for being so unloving. He reaches out to us with His mercy and love. He forgives our harsh words. As we personally receive Him as our Lord and Savior, He comes to live within us. He becomes our holy bread. He gives us new life. He enables us to love others as He loved us. Instead of being bitter and judgmental about man-made rules in the church, we are enabled to be kind to one another.

Let me share several examples to illustrate how we can become guilty of the judgmental attitude of the Pharisees. Back in the 1950s coeds from our school were judged by the elders of the local church to be breaking God's Word. They came to church without hats. The girls were admonished by the school administration to wear hats, so they went out and found some of the most ridiculous bonnets you could have ever seen. On the following communion Sunday, they paraded down the center aisle and sat in the front pew. The snake won! Harsh, bitter judgment reigned instead of mercy and tenderhearted kindness.

In the 1970s I went to a bus ministry conference put on by a conservative non-Lutheran group. At the time my hair was down to my collar, a moustache and goatee covered my face, and a large crucifix hung from my neck. Any one of these things was enough to convince my brothers and sisters in Christ that I was not saved. Their interpretation of the Bible did not allow for hair over the ears or images of God to be worn.

I think of unkind judgments made of pastors who change the words of the consecration from "drink ye all of it" to "all of you drink it." Remember how critical people were when the pastor encouraged the members to smile when they come back from Holy Communion? You have just been assured again that your sins are forgiven. It is all right to rejoice. Some still feel this destroys the reverence and dignity of the sacrament. Or how about the reaction to guitars? Some harshly judge a nonliturgical service, the clapping of hands, and the movement to greet one another with the Peace during the service as non-Luthern and improper pandemonium.

At Shepherd's Gate we like our freedom, we like our nonliturgical service, and we like our spontaneity, but we must watch out! We could be guilty of having a harsh, judgmental attitude toward the traditional church. We could easily sit over here and say that those people have dead formalism and mechanical, meaningless, lifeless worship services. We may even feel that those people are not really Christians unless they do it like we do it. You see, that would be the same attitude in reverse, and that is the kind of attitude that Jesus is denouncing.

The point is that we are to show mercy, not judgment, toward people who do not march to the same tune that we do. We know that we do not always show mercy to others. Jesus has a right to condemn us, but He doesn't! He loves us and forgives us and empowers us to love as He loves. David was merciful to Saul who was out to kill him. Jesus was merciful to those who crucified Him. Jesus is merciful to us who often kill Him by harshly judging others.

Instead of judging David, the priest gave him the holy bread. Instead of judging us for our critical attitude, Jesus gives us His body and His blood in the Sacrament of Holy Communion. As a priest, He offered Himself on the cross of Calvary. He suffered and died for our sins — including those of being unmerciful toward others. He loves us and forgives us. Because of His love, we can control our critical and sarcastic tongue.

Once we put our trust in Jesus as our personal Savior, He not only forgives our critical nature, but He lives in us and loves through us. We now can defend others with mercy and kindness. What a joy to share this new spirit from Christ! He has given us a spirit of tenderness, kindness, love and forgiveness toward people who may not look like and act like we do. In Christ we can accept people who break our man-made rules and show them mercy and tenderhearted love.

Dependence or Independence

THIRD SUNDAY AFTER PENTECOST
MARK 3:20-35

Allen P. Kolkman

Soon we'll be celebrating the Fourth of July, remembering the day when we signed the Declaration of Independence from England. It was the day when we cut the ties to the royal crown and the English people and decided to go it alone. I don't know how the English feel about this, but we look back on the event with some pride and generally agree that we benefited from it.

Unfortunately, some people have signed a declaration of independence from God and His people. They've decided to cut the ties and go it alone. Sometimes they look back on this event with some pride, but they never benefit from it. The results are always tragic.

Satan Says "Sell Out!"

The enemies of Jesus had a real problem on their hands. Unlike the fakes they had encountered before, Jesus performed incredible miracles that could not be explained away. He cured the sick, healed the lame, and rescued the possessed from the vise grip of Satan. Even His opponents could not deny it. "But by whose authority?" asked the scribes, "by whose power? This Jesus is possessed by Satan himself! He casts out demons by the power of Satan!"

Perhaps with a smile on His face, Jesus responds, "How can Satan cast out Satan?" The whole thought is absurd, almost laughable. The goal of Satan is not to remove himself from the lives of people like you and me, but to remove God from our lives.

There is a Danish fable that tells of a young spider who lived in a large barn. One day, while crawling about on the ceiling, he looked down and saw a spot that seemed just perfect for a new home. So he came down on a thin filament of web until he reached that wonderful spot, and there he created a huge, beautiful web. He grew slick and prospered. One day, while walking about his domain, he saw that thin filament of web reaching up into the darkness above and thought to himself, I have no need of this, and so he cut it. The whole web (spider and all) came crashing to the ground and a big cow stepped on him! How very much we are like that young spider. We are quick to declare our independence from God — sometimes with pride, but always with tragic results.

We get a lot of encouragement to cut the ties. This is exactly what Satan did so long ago, and now he wants us to follow in his footsteps. "Sell out!" he says. "Declare your independence; cut the ties; go it alone." His goal is to drive a wedge between God and man, to get us to ignore God, or better yet, to rebel against Him. It's been his goal right from the start. In the Garden of Eden he twisted and confused God's Word and appealed to Eve's pride. He asked with lethal innocence, "Don't you want to be wise and experienced? Don't you want to be more like God? When you eat of the fruit, your eyes will be opened to a brand new world." Who doesn't want to be wise? Who doesn't want to be more like God? She took the bait and so rebelled against God, declaring her independence.

Satan even tried it on Jesus. Not even the Son of God incarnate in the flesh was exempt from his attacks. Of course, Satan had to wait for the right time when Jesus was tired and hungry and alone. But when the time came, Satan was ready. He took Jesus to a high mountain and showed Him all of his domain. Satan had a lot of control over a lot of people, but he had a deal for Jesus — oh what a deal! Jesus could have it all — the whole world, lock, stock, and barrel — on a silver platter. Satan would pack up his bags and flee the world and the lives of all its people. What an intoxicating offer! Satan would throw in the towel — for a price: Jesus must bow down and worship him. It didn't work. Jesus realized that would make Him a servant of Satan instead of God. He refused to bite. Instead, He reaffirmed His declaration of dependence on God the Father by stating, "It is written, 'You shall worship the Lord your God and Him only shall you serve'" (Matt. 4:10).

Satan is a master of deceit. He works in ways that are hard to recognize. He always works in disguise, hiding his hooks in the most inconspicuous places. He doesn't appear in a devil's costume, wringing his hands and laughing, "Let me show you this sin." No, he is much too smart for that. He is a seducer, par excellence. He comes offering things that appear to be good and positive. Like any good fisherman, he makes the bait enticing and the hooks deadly. St. Paul wrote: "We are not contending against flesh and blood, but against the principalities, against the powers, against the world ruler of this present age, against the spiritual hosts of wickedness in the heavenly places" (Eph. 6:12). St. Peter advises: "Be sober, be watchful. Your adversary the devil prowls about like a roaring lion, seeking someone to devour" (1 Peter 5:8).

Satan uses that old military strategy of divide and conquer, and he uses it with astounding success, dividing people from God and Christian from Christian. It is not as hard as you might think. He often gets a lot of assistance from us. That is one reason why I'm so concerned with the drop in church attendance and involvement all over the world. I'm concerned because it means there are a lot of sitting ducks out there just waiting for Satan to get around to them. He is like a wolf who attacks the one lamb that has wandered off from the flock. Satan rarely attacks the whole flock, and when he does it's just to stir things up in hopes that some will run off in their own direction and so become easy prey.

Christians are all brothers and sisters in Christ, it's true, but sometimes we act too much like brothers and sisters — the fighting kind of brothers and sisters! A lot of Christian families, congregations, and denominations seem more like a battleground than the body of Christ. Of course, no one enjoys this more than Satan. He loves it when Christians won't talk to one another, or when someone storms away from a voters' assembly, or when people spread rumors around the church. Nothing makes Satan happier than a good old-fashioned church fight. Sometimes Christian families and congregations lack common vision and goals. Many church members are just sitting on the premises instead of acting on the promises. Sometimes members are busy chasing after their own goals instead of working together for the Lord's goals.

Satan appreciates our assistance. Sometimes the battle can be compared to a boxing match. Too often, the scene is something like this: Satan comes into the ring wearing a silk smoking jacket and holding a martini —

up, with an olive in it. Then the Christian walks out with all his armor and shields and swords. The bell rings. Satan steps back a little, and the Christian starts in — on himself! He hits himself on the head, punches himself in the stomach, and clobbers himself on the side. By the time the round ends, the Christian is flat out cold. Satan wins, and he didn't have to do a thing! Jesus said: "If a kingdom is divided against itself, that kingdom cannot stand. And if a house is divided against itself, that house will not be able to stand" (Mark 3:24-25). That's Satan's work; his mission is to divide and conquer.

Christ Says "Hang Tight!"

Christ came to unite and redeem. He came to bring us together, to make us one again. He came to be the Reconciler. Paul wrote: "While we were enemies we were reconciled to God by the death of His Son" (Rom. 5:10). "You, who once were estranged and hostile in mind, doing evil deeds, He has now reconciled in His body of flesh by His death, in order to present you holy and blameless and irreproachable before Him" (Col. 1:21-22). Even though we deserve to be cast off, even though our sins pierce through His soul, God still loves us, reaches out to us, and embraces us.

A team of mountain climbers once braved the mighty Matterhorn in Switzerland. At a particularly difficult point one of the men lost his footing and fell back with a tremendous force. There he hung precariously at the end of his rope. His back was broken, and he was barely maintaining conciousness. One of the other climbers came down the mountainside, being careful of the unstable rock, and lowered himself to the man dangling below. Through the use of special safety lines and pullies, he was able to rescue him from certain death.

That's what Christ did for us. Mankind fell from God with a tremendous force. We hung precariously, our souls broken. Yet Christ left the comfort of heaven to come down to us, lowering Himself to us, reaching out to us, embracing us, and restoring us. In the encounter in the Gospel Jesus said, "No one can enter a strong man's house and plunder his goods, unless he first binds the strong man; then indeed he may plunder his house" (Mark 3:27). That's what Jesus came to do. He came to bind Satan in order to rescue us from his evil rule and to protect us from his venomous bite. He came to unite us with God and one another. That's His purpose and mission. Jesus says to us, "Hang tight. Stay close to God and one another. Declare your dependence."

Paul wrote: "God is faithful, by whom you were called into the fellowship of His Son, Jesus Christ our Lord. I appeal to you, brethren, by the name of our Lord Jesus Christ, that all of you agree and that there by no dissensions among you, but that you be united" (1 Cor. 1:9-10). "I . . . beg you to lead a life worthy of the calling to which you have been called, with all lowliness and meekness, with patience, forbearing one another in love, eager to maintain the unity of the Spirit in the bond of peace" (Eph. 4:1-3).

Christ calls us to be united with God our Father, with all our brothers and sisters in Christ, and with the mission He has left for us to do. He calls us to be loyalists to the King of kings and faithful workers in His kingdom.

Some of you are sports fans. There are only two types of sports enthusiasts — those that don't and those that do. The first type signs up for cable TV or perhaps season tickets for the local professional team. The second type signs up to play for a team! There's a big difference! The first are just observers; the second are athletes. The first sit in the bleachers; the second work on the field. But there are no observers in the kingdom of God. There are no bleachers in heaven. Christ is not offering us tickets to the stadium; He's encouraging us to sign up for the team! His call for loyalty to the King of kings involves active participation in the mission He has given to us.

Yet Christ is not insensitive to the temptations we share. He too felt the full onslaught of Satan. He too knows the difficulties of the work and the lure of the easy way out. In the TV movie "Eric" we watch young Eric struggle with cancer. There is a scene in which he stands on the beach of the family's summer home with his father. "Daddy," he says, "remember how I wanted to swim across the bay with you? We got halfway across, and I said I couldn't make it. Remember how you reached out and helped me? Well, Daddy, I don't think I can make it now." Eric's father quickly spread his arms around him and said, "I'll help you."

That's God's promise to us. He has not promised a rose garden. Satan is alive and real, and he has us on his most wanted list. He is encouraging us to cut our ties with God, to at least ignore Him, if not forsake Him and His church and people. He's encouraging a declaration of independence.

Jesus came on His mission to reconcile us to God the Father and to all our brothers and sisters in Christ. He wants to unite us in the task of the church on earth. He is encouraging a declaration of dependence. And He promises to be an ever present help and constant Savior.

Which will it be? The signing is held anew each day.

Blessed Assurance

FOURTH SUNDAY AFTER PENTECOST
MARK 4:26-34

Allen P. Kolkman

When I was a small guy, my father and I used to play roughhouse. He would hold me upside down and swing me back and forth between his legs. Then with one mighty swing he would toss me high in the air so that I would do a flip, and he would catch me as I came falling down. I loved it. I wanted him to do it over and over. Just about the time he was totally exhausted and ready to collapse on the floor, I would say, "Do it again, Dad! Do it again."

Not everyone approved. Some thought it was too dangerous. They may have had a point. It would have been easy to miss me or to toss me in the wrong way, but that thought never crossed my mind. He was my father. He was big and strong, and he loved me very much. He wouldn't let anything happen to me. What could have caused fear and terror was enjoyed in confidence and assurance because he was my father and I was in his hands.

God wants us to have this kind of assurance in our lives. Jesus brings that out in the two little parables that we heard in the Gospel for today.

God Loves Us

Many people are afraid because they feel so alone. They feel they have been tossed high in the air, and they aren't sure by whom or for what. They also aren't sure there is anyone out there to catch them.

Jesus' parables speak to people now perhaps even more than to the people of His day. Modern man tends to see God as a kind of heavenly watchmaker who created the universe and all the physical laws by which it operates and then stepped out of the picture, leaving everything up in the air. Others see God as too holy, too majestic, or too magnificent to care about the day-to-day concerns of people like you and me.

There was a tourist in New York City who went to the Empire State Building and rode an elevator to the top observation room. As he was looking down at the people on the sidewalks far below, he observed how they looked like little ants running around. He said, "I imagine this is the way the people of the earth look to God."

No way! God does not look down on us from His ivory tower, watching with detached curiosity as we scamper around. His chief characteristic is not passive majesty, but active love. His greatness lies not so much in His sovereignty as in His grace — His undeserved and unending love. This is a love that will not fail. Insurance companies may fold; banks may close; houses may burn down, but the love of God is steadfast and sure. The grace of God lasts forever.

When Commander Scott Carpenter returned from his flight into space, the red carpet was really rolled out for him. All the big shots were there to honor him. Newspaper reporters and TV cameras were all over the place. In the middle of the ceremonies his five-year-old daughter, Candy, tugged at his sleeve. She wanted to show her daddy the scratch on her right elbow that happened while he was away. What did he do? He turned away from all the honors and the cameras and the glory to his little girl. He looked at the scratch and assured her of his love and concern.

That's the way God is concerned for us. Sure He's glorious. Certainly He's powerful and majestic. But above all He's our Father, and we are His children. He's concerned about the bumps and scratches that come our way. What's important to us is important to Him.

There's great assurance in knowing that we are not just cogs in an impersonal machine — that we are not merely dust blown around by the winds of fate. We are children of God, brothers and sisters of Jesus Christ. We are objects of His love and of His concern. We are not alone. We are in the hands of our Father who loves us.

God Saves Us

There's another assurance, too. God's love leads Him to action — loving, personal, involved action. He's a God who reaches into the real world to love and give life to you and me. St John tells it best: "God so loved the world that He gave His only Son, that whoever believes in Him should not perish but have eternal life" (John 3:16). Mankind was stuck in sin like a fly stuck on flypaper, like a bug trapped on a spider web, like an animal caught in quicksand. We were in sin up to our eyeballs and going down for the count. There was nothing we could do; in fact all efforts to save ourselves only made matters worse.

Our end was all too certain, but God's love meant action. He didn't just stand by the edge of the problem and mourn our situation. He didn't give us instructions on how to save ourselves. He jumped right in with us, took hold of us, rescued us, and restored us to safety once again. That's God for you! St. Paul put it this way: "God shows His love for us in that while we were yet sinners Christ died for us" (Rom. 5:8). We can't do it. In fact, all efforts to save ourselves only make matters worse. But God can save us, and He has saved us!

There's real assurance in knowing that our eternal life is in the hands of our all-powerful and all-loving God. The farmer in Jesus' parable could be confident about his crop — even though its life was unseen. Jesus promised, "In My Father's house are many rooms . . . . When I go and prepare a place for you, I will come again and will take you to Myself, that where I am you may be also" (John 14:2-3).

When I was a student at the seminary, I tried to drive home for Christmas and summer vacations. It was a long distance — over 2,000 miles — so it took a few days. I remember making careful plans the first time I made the trip. I knew just how far I expected to go each day and where I would spend the night. Unfortunately I didn't make any reservations. The first night I pulled into the town about 10:00 or 11:00 and couldn't find a single room. I had to drive another hour to the next town. There I found a room in one of those big chain motels. The next morning I made a reservation at my next planned stop so I would be sure to have a room. This time there were unforeseen detours and problems along the road, so I didn't get into that town until about 9:00. I found the hotel and walked up to the desk, all ready for a hot shower and a nice dinner. But the room had been reserved only until 6:00 and had been given to someone else. The clerk was nice enough to get me a room at another hotel and to give me some sound advice. I needed to make reservations days in advance and pay for them at the same time. That would guarantee a room, no matter what.

That's what Jesus Christ did for you and me. He made the reservation for us, and He paid the total cost with His own precious blood shed for us on the cross of Calvary. Our place in heaven has already been reserved and paid for by Jesus Christ Himself, and that guarantees it, no matter what. We may not know when we'll get there or what will happen to us along the way, but one thing we do know: There's a place reserved in heaven for us.

God Raises Us

God's love reaches out to us and embraces us, granting us salvation and eternal life. But He doesn't just save us and then leave us. His love continues to embrace us, drawing us ever closer to Himself. He adopts us as His beloved children and then enables us to grow and mature into adult Christians.

Jesus uses the example of a mustard plant to make this point. Mustard plants start from small seeds, so small that they are barely visible. But God gives the seeds life and growth. Around here mustard plants grow to be three or four feet high, but in Israel they can grow to as much as 15 feet — all from that tiny seed.

It's the same with us. We begin with a tiny faith. It's saving faith, but it can't always be seen by others and doesn't always fill our lives. Yet God makes it grow through the nourishing Word and the energizing sacrament, enabling small beginnings to result in giant ends.

There's certainty here, too. Sometimes we can't see the growth in a loved one. Sometimes nothing seems to be happening. We may be tempted to dig up the seed and look for growth, but like the farmer in the parable, we can be confident. It is God who gives the life and the growth. He promises, "My Word . . . shall not return to Me empty, but it shall accomplish that which I purpose and prosper in the thing for which I sent it. (Is. 55:11). St. Paul wrote that the Gospel is "the power of God for salvation" (Rom. 1:16). Our mission is to baptize and teach. We can rejoice in confidence, knowing that those we reach are in the all-loving and all-powerful hands of God.

These two short parables offer much assurance to people like you and me — people who sometimes feel alone, inadequate, and out of control — people who sometimes worry about our salvation and the salvation of others. In a world in which we often feel alone and afraid, Jesus reminds us of our heavenly Father. He has enveloped us in His love and rescued us in His Son, and He enables us to grow and blossom here and in eternity. There is blessed assurance because we are in the hands of God our Father.

The Man Who Brings Peace

What manner of Man is this? Christ wants His people to discover through His acts and Word that in Him are the very resources of God for bringing peace and calm into turbulent lives and a turbulent world. While He allows the crisis in order that we might wake Him up and discover His power, He also allows the crisis in order that He might wake us up, for in the end it is we who have been asleep.

Jesus wants us to become more and more aware of His presence and dependent on Him. He wants us to discover again and again with people like St. Paul that God's grace is sufficient — all that we need — and that His power will be made perfect in our weakness. He does not ask us to be perfect in order to call out to Him. But in calling out to Him, we shall have our strength renewed.

A young man with cancer realized that his days on earth were quite short. He said to a pastor friend that he was not afraid to die, for he had found Christ, or rather, Christ had found him. This young man believed that his task was to witness to everyone who came through his sickroom door. When the pastor left that day, he found himself in a struggle. He had gone to bring comfort to a dying man and instead found his own faith uplifted. Although he did not like to admit it, when he had first seen his friend, he had questioned God's goodness in the light of such intense suffering. When he left the house of this dying-yet-living man, tears were rolling down his face, and somehow there were words of praise on his lips. Through the faith of the sick he had experienced a God who had so filled that dying life with His power and love that the illness and impending death were but secondary events. The pastor could almost hear Jesus saying, "Peace! Be still! You shall not perish."

The Man Who Saves

What manner of Man is this? "My power is made perfect in your weakness," He says. Now perhaps we can begin to see how the cross, the symbol of suffering and death, can be the very power of God to those who are being saved. In the midst of the storm comes the saving Word.

With awe the disciples looked at Jesus and asked what manner of Man He was. While they did not express it in so many words, the incident reveals that He is none other than the God of heaven and earth. God in Christ enters into the journey of life with us, takes on Himself our rejection, our willingness to let Him sleep, our lack of faith — even our criticism. He goes through the crisis with us, awaits our call, passes over our arrogance and ignorance, gives command that even the wind and waves must obey, and offers to us salvation and deliverance now and forevermore. This is the same Jesus whom the cross of suffering and sin could not defeat and whom the grave could not contain. This is the God/Man, whose love never lets go of us, even when we may have forgotten Him.

This Christ goes with you as you leave here today. He is always present in Word and Sacrament, and by the power of His Spirit He is ready to be called on, able to help, and working toward the end that we might each day all the more entrust to Him every situation of life — even ourselves.

He invites us to call on Him. He wants us to know Him as Lord and Savior, as Author and Giver of faith, as the One who can and will still the winds and calm the waves, as the personal God who loves and who acts on that love for us. With such a One in the boat of life we can indeed sing with the multitude of generations of believers:

Be still, my soul; the Lord is on thy side;
Bear patiently the cross of grief or pain;
Leave to they God to order and provide;
In every change He faithful will remain.
Be still, my soul; thy best, thy heavenly, Friend
Through thorny ways leads to a joyful end.

Be still, my soul; thy God doth undertake
To guide the future as He hath the past.
Thy hope, thy confidence, let nothing shake;
All now mysterious shall be bright at last.
Be still, my soul; the waves and winds still know
His voice who ruled them while He dwelt below. (*TLH* 651:1-2).

What Manner of Man Is This?

FIFTH SUNDAY AFTER PENTECOST
MARK 4:35-41

Rex D. Spicer

Sometimes you can miss out on a special event or hoped-for opportunity. Could you picture yourself not being home when your favorite TV quiz program called to give you a chance at the $100,000 prize? Suppose later you discover that you could have answered the question that was asked? You might just talk to yourself about that missed opportunity! How often we have said, "If only. . ."

Today's Gospel has something to do with not missing out — not missing out on the One who presents Himself as Lord, Ruler of wind and wave and so much more. Rightly we ask with the disciples,

What Manner of Man Is This?

Like the disciples of old, we can take Jesus along with us without a full awareness of who He is, what He can do, and why He is even along for the ride. We can hear the Word about this Jesus but lack the trust that would lead us to bow to Him as Lord and Savior. That is the reason for this story — for the storm, for the rebuke, and for the inspiring quieting of the waves. Let us join the disciples with Jesus and learn anew what manner of Man this is.

The Man Taken for Granted

It had been a busy day. There had been teaching and healing as the people clamored around Him with their many needs. Evening had come, and Jesus was ready to move on. There were other people and other places — always the call of the unreached and the untouched, the need to bring the Word to other areas of distress and ignorance. So Jesus left the crowd. After all, He had not come to live off their adoration but to serve them. So it was time to set out for the "other side."

The disciples were fishermen, at ease with all that was involved in navigation on the lake. They let Jesus fall asleep, probably feeling confident both in their ability to handle the boat and in Jesus' presence. There was no apparent reason to bother Him when all was going right, and everything seemed to be under control.

Isn't this quite typical? As long as we seem to have matters in hand we are willing to let Jesus rest. We don't want Him out of the boat, but we so often fail to remember that everything depends on Him. So the disciples let Him sleep. After all, He had worked hard and deserved some time off. Jesus, however, has a greater purpose than going along for the ride or being a part-time Lord to a half-faithful following.

Then a great storm of wind arose, so intense that the waves beat into the boat, filling it with water. How great the storms of our lives can become, almost to the point that it seems we will perish. In their moment of anguish the disciples recalled that Jesus was with them. That's not a bad thing to recall. It's like knowing the answer to the prize question and having a chance to give it. The disciples called out to Jesus to wake up and save them. Revealing their humanity, they lamented, "Teacher, do You not care if we perish?" Their statement is so natural. Haven't we all at some time raised similar questions to God? "Don't You care, Lord, what happens to us? How could You let this happen? Are You really in control?"

Can He help? Is He willing to help? These are questions asked throughout the ages. We worry because, if we perceive a situation out of control, it must also be out of God's hands. While it is true that God in Christ shares in our terrors, He is not thereby terrified because we are. While the disciples communicated their fear to Jesus, He communicated to them the peace and power of Almighty God.

The Man with Power

Can He help? Is He willing to help? The answer points to the type of Man He really is. Jesus "awoke and rebuked the wind and said to the sea, 'Peace! Be Still!'" (Mark 4:39). And do you know what happened? The wind ceased, and where there had been a great storm, there was now a great calm. Jesus, by the power of His Word, was able to quiet the wind and the waves. That's the power of this One called Jesus. His action also reveals His intent.

What manner of Man is this? Jesus wanted them to know. He wanted them to trust that He could handle the problems and situations disciples confront every day and that His intent for His people is good. They would need to recall in troublesome times — as we too must — what Jesus could do. They needed to trust that He would do what was best according to the will and plan of God the Father. He wanted them to learn that in the midst of the storm He would be there for His own. Perhaps it is hard for us to see a blessing when the winds and waves of crisis are all around us. As the boat rocks, we are more inclined to complain than to praise. Luther reminds us of the blessing of the storm as he relates, "It is well with those who find water breaking into their ship, for this moves them to seek help from God." We might also add that we can discover that God can help.

The Man to Be Trusted

Jesus acts to calm the storm in order that His people might trust Him. He acts to bring about faith — a faith that will hold on to the truth that God acts in our behalf in all situations. He brings it about that we do not perish, but rather turn back to Him. He wants to arouse in us a desire for Him; He wants us to cry out to Him in order that He may hear and answer us. He wants to hear us in order that He may save us. In this way He teaches us to distrust ourselves and put our confidence in Him. This Man Jesus, who acts with the power and intent of the heavenly Father, does not want us to hold back from relying on Him. He knows that if we do not learn to call out to Him, we will end up substituting for Him the mechanics and technology of this age. We will seek in ourselves what can only be found in God. That would be to miss out on what manner of Man this Jesus is.

So Jesus must confront the disciples and us not only with the storm, but also with the question "Why are you afraid? Have you no faith?" Why do we look more to the storm than to Him? To see only the visible rather than the invisible, only the temporary rather than the permanent, only the partial instead of the whole is to look at events through the eyes of fear. Then almost anything can and probably will happen.

Jesus calls us from fear to faith. The two are mutually exclusive. While they may both exist in a person, fear must give way when Christ is present. To have fear is to forget faith; to have faith is to overcome fear. The disciples should have known this, but in the trying situation they lost sight of Jesus, even though He was with them in the boat. Their fear overcame their faith. This can easily happen, for fear blindly dictates when the eyes of faith have closed. It is not less a problem for us today. If out of fear we would strive to subjugate the wills of others and direct events according to our wishes, there is the danger that we too can let Jesus sleep while we attempt to hold everything together.

Faith and Human Boundaries

SIXTH SUNDAY AFTER PENTECOST
MARK 5:21-43

Rex D. Spicer

Boundaries are something we understand well. We are taught that we may go just so far and no further. Trespassing signs limit access. Traffic indicators set speeds and give directions and other warnings. We have scientists who seek to define the bounds of reality and to set limits on divine interventions. In many ways human life is governed by established limitations, by lines we have drawn. To cross them can often bring pain, conflict, or ridicule. These limits are often rigidly set.

Today's Gospel breaks barriers. It crosses the line. It tells of One who dares to transgress our precepts, who ignores our self-imposed realities, who goes beyond what we allow ourselves to hope or permit ourselves to believe. It reveals to us Jesus, who opens doors we had long believed were nailed shut. For our help and health it is important to note the lines He crosses and what such action means for all people. We will look at several boundaries and how Jesus dealt with them.

Boundary 1 – The Kinds of People to Whom Jesus Will Respond

Many church people think that a person must know a lot about Jesus in order to come to Him and relate to Him. They feel that Jesus has something to do only with those who have a close personal relationship with Him, who devoutly believe in Him, who exercise a good understanding of vital doctrine, and who belong to the "correct" church. Thus people tend to set limits on whom Jesus will welcome and to whom He will respond.

However, the Gospel presents us with two people who approach our Lord with very little knowledge of Him, who have mixed feelings about Him, and who apparently come to Him as a last resort. Certainly these are not the kind of people some might think that Jesus would be interested in. Yet He responds positively to both the Jewish synagog leader and to the woman with semimagical ideas about how to be healed.

Why does He respond in this way? Because they come to Him. They seek help from Him. They are people in need. Their coming gives evidence of a spark of faith that perhaps this One can and will do something about their needs. They come with a poor understanding — with their religious medals, their good luck charms, their pious observances — but they come.

And they get what they expect from Jesus. Our Lord's response to them reveals an openness to those who will come regardless of the completeness of their understanding of Him, no matter how shallow their faith, even if they come to Him as a last hope. Unbelievable? I guess it is, especially to those who would impose limits on His love.

Boundary 2 – There Are Limits to His Help

There are those who say we should not expect too much of Jesus. They assert that many problems are beyond His abilities. They question whether He really can help me cope with my troubled marriage, my wayward child, my alcoholic spouse, or my terminal illness. Perhaps I must simply grin and bear it. We tend to think that because a problem is out of our hands, it is thereby out of God's.

The Gospel deals with the question of His ability. The woman came to touch His garment and was healed. While she was wrong about the garment, she was right about the faith. In her trust and hope was saving power, as our Lord revealed to her, "Your faith has made you well." Jairus also realized the outcome of his request as his daughter was graciously restored to life.

When someone asks why Jesus should be troubled with a problem, we should ask, Who else is there who can really help? He alone has the words of life (John 6:68). And He is able to do far more than we ask or imagine (Eph. 3:20).

Boundary 3 – He Is Not to Be Interrupted

Have you ever been interrupted while you were quite busy? You know the feeling that can come over you when there is work to be done and along comes that one person who loves to bend your ear. There never seems to be any concern that we have other things to do.

The disciples were often protective of Jesus' time and sought to limit who could come to Him and when. However, Jesus did not allow Himself to be governed by ideas and standards imposed on Him by others. As He was getting ready to teach, He allowed Jairus to interrupt. On the way to help Jairus' daughter, He allowed the woman with the flow of blood to interrupt.

Perhaps we too have not wanted to bother Jesus. With all the problems in the world, why would He want to hear our little complaints or to deal with our insignificant hurts? But that is just the way it is with Him. The sick woman is given some of His time to experience His healing power, and then Jesus will not go on until she has also come to an increased knowledge of the nature of her Benefactor. He literally invites interruptions as He reminds all generations, "Come to Me, all who labor and are heavy laden, and I will give you rest" (Matt. 11:28). He wants us to come at any time, wherever we may be.

He would also like it if we could govern our lives in a similar way. Can we adjust our schedules to answer the calls of life and meet the needs of others for our service of love? Jesus saw the people who came to Him not as interferences but as opportunities.

Boundary 4 – But He Can't Respond to All

In our story we see Jesus individualize His attention. After the woman had reached out to Jesus, she heard Him ask, "Who touched Me?" The disciples responded in a somewhat sarcastic manner, "You see the crowd pressing around You, and yet You say, 'Who touched Me?'" (Mark 5:31). How could one person be singled out in the crowd? But that is exactly what Jesus proceeded to do! He responded to the shy approach of an individual need as surely and deftly as a compass needle responds to the magnetic North Pole.

It seems preposterous, at least to many, that God could care for one person when there are billions of people in the world. But that is precisely the concern that Jesus demonstrates. He whom the whole world cannot contain makes Himself small enough to enter the loneliness of one single sister. He is there for each of us as though there were only one person in need. Jesus saw in the sick woman — and sees in each of us — one of His Father's children. He wants each of us to know Him personally, to see what faith has really grasped — not the hem of a garment, but the very power of God.

He wants us to know what is happening in this relationship with Him. So He called out to the woman. Perhaps she was scared. Will Jesus punish me for what I have done? In touching Him, she had contaminated Him. That was the rule of that day. If a person was ill and declared socially unclean, anyone the person touched also bore that stigma. And that is just the point! Our uncleanness is traded for His healing and restoration. We who are sick with sin can transfer that illness to Jesus for His healing through forgiveness. He came so that each and every person might be blessed through Him. The people of all ages are to learn that there is no other name under heaven by which we must be saved.

Boundary 5 – To Be a Witness Is of Little Use

How often is it said, "I don't know enough about Jesus to speak of Him. Besides, that's what we pay a preacher for." People also fail to testify because they forget how the Lord has been with them through some very difficult times. I recall a farmer who was seriously injured in a tractor accident. He promised his pastor that if God saved him, he would be in church every Sunday. Well, the miracle occurred, but the every-Sunday attendance did not.

As Christians we must ask what happens to people in trouble when we forget what God has done for us and thus fail to tell others. People sometimes need to hear how God has delivered us. It was that kind of report that the woman in our text had heard, and it brought her to the Savior — to increased faith and fulfilled hope. May our lives and actions carry reports of Jesus that would make those who see and hear us eager to begin a journey to Him!

Boundary 6 – The Point Beyond Which No One Can Go

There is a point, many say, beyond which no one can go. A group of mourners came out to Jesus and told Him He need not bother to come to the house of Jairus, for the young girl had died. They implied that this was a boundary that not even this Teacher could cross. But Jesus ignored what they had to say. The art of ignoring, as here illustrated by our Lord, can be one of the fine arts of faith. We need to learn this also, for we can get caught up in the fear that Jesus cannot go beyond a certain point. We can pay too much attention to the limiters. Jesus reveals that the last word never belongs to His detractors.

But people do not give up easily when someone crosses the line. The mourners laughed at the coming of Jesus. They laughed at Him for thinking there could be something on the other side of death, for believing that He could venture beyond the fixed limits of life. So Jesus threw them out of the house. When faith arrives, doubt must go. Faith must always ignore the rumor that hope has died.

Jesus proceeded to the child's bedside, and by the power of the Word that resides outside the realm of human bounds He commanded the little girl to arise. And she did — just as though she had been asleep. "O grave, where is thy victory?" Those who come to Christ — who take Him seriously enough to cross the line of doubt, peer pressure, personal opinions, and shame — who fear not, but only believe — shall hear the healing word of Jesus, "Your faith has saved you!" This Great Physician is not just some poetic soul, kind and good. This is God reconciling the world to Himself. The last laugh shall be His.

There are no boundaries that Jesus will not cross in our behalf. We have seen His power and compassion triumph over hopelessness, fear, ignorance, and death. He comes into the limits of our world and opens up the possibilities beyond those limits. He goes with us, blazes the trail ahead of us, and reaches back to draw us to Himself. He heals along the way and bears the taunts of cynicism and disbelief even to the point of His own death on a cross.

His constant support, encouragement, and forgiveness enable us to break through to the Father and overcome sin, guilt, and self. He is the One at our deathbed whose words of great promise shall bring forth joy beyond all imagination as we hear Him command us to awake from the sleep of death and eat in the house of the heavenly Father forevermore. He crosses all barriers and carries us safely through hell and death to where the best is yet to be.

A View from the Inside

SEVENTH SUNDAY AFTER PENTECOST
MARK 6:1-6

Frederick W. Kemper

The little Boy was born in Bethlehem one eventful night. Apart from a hurried trip to Egypt to escape the fearful wrath of King Herod, His life was much like any baby's. He cried when He was hungry or wet; He gurgled and cooed when the neighbor women made over Him. When the family returned from Egypt, He became the darling of Nazareth, the town where they settled.

He kept His father company in the carpenter shop. (Joseph was a carpenter, probably fashioning yokes for oxen and furniture for homes.) He played with the shavings and learned to use the mallet — just like any normal child. As He grew, He became a help to His father, first probably cleaning the shop, later handling the lumber, and finally actually working with the wood. He loved His brothers and sisters, and they in turn loved Him. The family was typical of all families, weathering the ups and downs of relationships. Being the oldest, He was often arbiter in disputes among His siblings.

He was a favorite in the village and among His aunts and uncles. "Why can't you be more like your cousin Jesus," His aunts would say to their children. "My, He's a fine lad," the townspeople said to Mary and Joseph, who accepted such praise humbly and gratefully.

When Joseph died (according to tradition), Jesus assumed the role of provider and head of the house. By that time He was as proficient with the tools as His father had been. People didn't flock to His workshop, but there was enough business to keep the family in food and clothing. According to custom, He trained His brothers in the woodworking arts, so that the mother's future was assured, should anything happen to Him.

It was all very normal, very average, very conventional. The years passed. Mary, who had nourished and nurtured her children, was proud of each of them. Most of all she watched her firstborn, marveling again and again at the kindness, patience, and love He had. She still pondered the events of His birth, wondering whether to tell her Son how it had all happened, how there had been one miracle after another — the conception, the angel's appearance to shepherds, the star leading the Wise Men to Bethlehem, and a vision that necessitated their flight to Egypt. She locked all these things in her heart, knowing that in His good time the Lord would reveal His purposes for her — and His — Son.

His Mission

Word came that Cousin John, son of Elizabeth, had become a prophet and that he was baptizing at the Jordan River. Jesus went hear His cousin preach. Thus it was that He was baptized, and the Lord's voice was heard: "Thou art My beloved Son; with Thee I am well pleased" (Mark 1:11). And the Spirit appeared in the form of a dove, hovering over Him.

Jesus went was led from His baptism by the Spirit into the wilderness to be alone — to try to comprehend the meaning of Sonship and to determine His course based on the baptismal announcement. Satan came seeking to seduce Him from that course. "If You are the Son of God. . ." Three seduction attempts are recorded in the Gospel According to St. Matthew, although St. Mark suggests that there may have been many more. So convinced is Jesus of His identity and His mission that He will not be seduced. He will not change stones into bread, jump from the temple parapet, or bend His knee to Satan for the sake of a shortcut to kingship.

He emerged from the wilderness prepared to fulfill of His destiny. He began to take up where John had left off, preaching to all who would listen. He told His incomparable stories about the Kingdom. He touched and spoke words that healed all manner of diseases. A woman touched the hem of His garment; power went out from Him; and she was healed. The number of witnesses to His compassion, His power to heal, and His message grew.

Inevitably He came to His own country, to the place where He had grown up. Here were the same familiar houses, the same streets and alleys, the same people. "Hi, Jesus!" many of them called as He walked into town. "Where have you been?" they asked. It was old home week. That delightful kid down the block, who took such good care of His mother, had come home. It was about time, too.

His Mission Rejected

On the Sabbath He preached in the synagog according to the custom of the Jews. What He said that day astounded them. He healed some of the old neighbors. Something had happened to Him; some sort of change had come over Him. They didn't trust Him. "Where did this man get all this? What is the wisdom given to Him? What mighty works are wrought by His hands!" (Mark 6:2). By what right does the carpenter's son speak with such authority or do miracles? Who does He think He is?

These were Jesus' old friends, mind you. They were the people He had grown up with. They were His family and His neighbors. They were people He had played with as a boy, run errands for, listened to stories with, worshiped with in the local synagog. They couldn't comprehend this new Jesus, who came with a message and a power.

Jesus looked at them sadly when they came to Him and said they didn't appreciate the new Jesus. Familiarity breeds contempt, the old adage goes. Jesus saw it another way: "A prophet is not without honor, except in His own country" (v. 4). Those words have entered the ranks of the great quotations. They are used by mothers whose children cite their teacher at school as the ultimate authority and by politicians whose words of wisdom sound trite to their constituents. So Jesus, the new Jesus, who came back to His hometown after the baptism experience and the wilderness struggle, was not accepted.

Hindsight sees with 20/20 vision, foresight with myopia. The townspeople could only see the little boy, the carpenter; that Jesus was the Son of God they could not see. That He spoke with authority they could appreciate; that He performed mighty works they could also appreciate but not comprehend. Not seeing or comprehending, they took offense at Him.

Jesus was patient with them. He understood their dilemma and their perplexity. He looked at them with compassion and chose to give them time to react to the new Jesus. He would do no miracles in His home city. He would wait until they had heard the news of His travels through the country, of His message, and of His power. One day, He prayed, they would understand. Some day they would believe and accept Him for who He was. They would understand the purpose for which He had been called. Whether or not His prayer was answered we have no way of knowing, but we can hope it was, for the sake of the good people of Nazareth.

His Mission Completed

The incident in Nazareth became history. Jesus moved on along the dusty roads and paved highways — along the path to His destiny. He had come into the world to redeem it from the wrath and judgment of God. In due time He set His face toward Jerusalem, there in public places to be condemned by the church, the state, and the empire. He was crucified between two thieves. He suffered the terrors of abandonment by His Father. He died. He was laid to rest in a newly hewn grave.

He rose again from the dead. He ascended into glory. He had accomplished what He set out to do. He came preaching repentance and the imminence of the kingdom of God. He established the Kingdom. He made it available by the outpouring of the Holy Spirit. Repentance — turning around and leaving false gods behind — is still the call of the Holy Spirit. He wants all people to enter the kingdom of the living God and to "live under Him in His kingdom and serve Him in everlasting righteousness, innocence, and blessedness."

His Mission Accepted

Christians see Jesus with 20/20 vision. He is the very Son of God, the King of kings and Lord of lords. He is our warm, compassionate, loving Savior — our dearest friend. We have made the leap of faith, overcome the obstacles of reason, and accepted the mysteries of God and of His Christ. Though we cannot understand all the vicissitudes that life thrusts at us, we trust. Though we cannot comprehend the vastness of God, we know we have been apprehended by Him. Though we cannot fully fathom the hope of the glory to come, we believe it.

His Mission Rejected Again

The world (that is, the non-Christian people) sees Jesus, at best, the way the people of Nazareth saw Him. At worst, He is met with derision. It doesn't matter that Chrisitanity has spread across the continents, or that the Bible that proclaims the story of Jesus has been and is being translated for all the tongues and dialects of the world. It is of no significance that churches are the hubs of countless communities, or that radio and television proclaim the Good News. It isn't noticed that Christians provide the impetus for charity, education, democracy, and love for fellow human beings. Who needs Christianity? Who needs Christ?

Within the church the number of those who have been exposed to

Jesus — by Baptism, in Sunday school, through confirmation — fall out the back door when they get out from under their parents' influence is awesome. Have they been offended by Him like the good people of Nazareth?

So many contemporary life-styles have no room for Jesus and His church. One-night stands, shacking up, homosexuality and lesbianism, adultery, sexual harassment — the dubious pleasures of this world exclude Christ. When Joseph was being seduced by Mrs. Potiphar, his strength to refuse her came from his faithfulness to his God. "How then can I do this great wickedness and sin against God?" he said to her — and also to himself. So many people don't say that anymore. Rather, they have abandoned God for will-o'-the-wispish pleasures.

When Jesus approached Jerusalem, the whole city with its teeming population was spread out before Him. The long history of that city came to His mind — the prophets God had sent to it, the kings God had placed over it, and the lack of faith that had so often characterized it. He wept. He said, "How often would I have gathered your children together as a hen gathers her brood under her wings, and you would not!" (Matt. 23:37). He then went into the city to redeem it — and all the world besides.

He still must weep over the city and the world. He was the last of the great prophets to visit it, and the people crucified Him outside its walls. He had come as the King above all its kings. Through His apostles and evangelists the Good News of His sacrificial and vicarious death for its sin and the sin of the whole world has been proclaimed. He has tried to gather the world under His wings, but it would not be gathered. His tears on that first occasion must surely have been copious, but He dried them at last and went into the city to tragedy and triumph.

Now with the salvation of the world accomplished in the darkness on Calvary, with the prison of the tomb opened by His resurrection, with His message of forgiveness won and hope reborn shared throughout the world, does He still weep as He sits at the Father's right hand and sees humanity and the church from His perfect vantage point? I cannot help but think He does — more copious tears than He ever wept over Jerusalem.

His Mission Continued

But the tears give way to joy. In one of His parables Jesus said, "There will be more joy in heaven over one sinner who repents than over ninety-nine righteous persons who need no repentance" (Luke 15:7). But don't be misled. There is also joy in heaven if each of those 99 repent in his or her turn. The joy in heaven is ongoing as people make the leap of faith, turn from their evil ways, and cast their lot with Jesus and His unshakable promises.

Jesus, the Christ and the Son of God, continues to call each person right up to the moment of death. The thief on the cross is evidence enough for that. I don't think He gave up on Nazareth. He may have marveled at their unbleief (we do, too), but He refused to take offense. Surely some of His prayer time in the mountains alone and apart must have been spent on the friends and neighbors of His early years, even as He now prays for all the world with groaning.

How much better it would have been if the Nazarenes could have recognized the Christ in that address in the synagog by their hometown boy or seen the Son of God in the healings that took place after the encounter. How much better it would be if all who hear the Word of God would really keep it. But we can answer for no one but ourselves. It is our own faith that saves us, not that of a member of our family or our neighbor.

I pray that we have all seen God in Jesus, have not taken offense at Him, and will not let the pleasures of this world get between us and Him. Thus we will keep the tears from Jesus' eyes and a twinkle born of our faith and trust in Him in our own.

Disciples of the Christ

EIGHTH SUNDAY AFTER PENTECOST
MARK 6:7-13

Frederick W. Kemper

Technical jobs have required apprenticeships through the ages. One still has to learn to lay bricks before he can command a bricklayer's salary. One must receive computer science training to become proficient in that rapidly developing field. Nurses practice their art while they study. Doctors must undergo a rigorous internship before they are granted a license to practice medicine.

Even pastors, at least in our church, are required to take a year of internship (which we call vicarage), in addition to their seminary training, to equip them for their ministry. The year before their final year, all students are sent to a congregation to work with an experienced pastor in a congregational environment. During that year they preach, visit the sick, run the mimeograph, make evangelism calls, work with the youth — all in order to develop and hone skills needed for the ministry. Some find that they are not suited for the work and turn to other pursuits. The majority of them return to their final seminary year with questions about the ministry raised by their experiences on their vicarage and with determination to make the last year count as they look toward graduation and ordination. The experience is invaluable as an introduction to the office of the ministry. The new pastors can begin their work with a better understanding of its demands and with a real concern for the congregation that they will serve for the Lord.

The Internship of the Disciples

The disciples were in a learning situation as they moved about the countryside with Jesus. They entered the course of study as He called them to be His disciples. He talked to them as they walked the roads of Palestine and as they ate together. They heard Him preach in synagogs and on street corners. They saw how He dealt with people. They witnessed His miracles. They were privy to explanations of His parables. When He thought they were ready, He sent them on internships, of which the story in today's Gospel is the first. If they were to carry on His mission, they must experience the work firsthand.

Jesus sent His disciples out in pairs. Even though they had their credentials, He must have felt that traveling and working with someone would reinforce the weaker member of the team. Each could offer the other encouragement and criticism. They could talk over strategy. Having a companion would help overcome loneliness. I wonder whether they had a choice of partners of whether Jesus assigned them to a team — strong, self-reliant Peter with doubting Thomas, perhaps; educated Nathanael with James the Less; or mystical John with rational and calculating Judas of Kerioth. It is not important to the cause. The lessons to be learned would be gained regardless of the partner.

Their instructions were to take only a staff, no extra cloak, one pair of sandals, no food or money. They were to trust God completely and unconditionally — for everything. Social work students are sometimes put through such an exercise. They are assigned a few blocks of the inner city, given very little money, and put on their own for three days. They are forced to sleep in doorways, to scrounge food where they can, and to check every telephone and coin-operated machine for coins returned but not picked up. It is a harrowing experience, but it teaches reliance on God, self-reliance, and a great deal about the plight of the destitute. Being a disciple after Jesus was gone would require great fortitude, great trust. It would mean imprisonment, harassment, and, for all but John (according to traditions), an untimely death. They must learn to trust — now.

The disciple-students were given two charges. The first was to preach repentance and, by implication, that the kingdom of God was at hand. That was the message Jesus had come to bring: Repent; turn 180 degrees; leave evil; forsake other gods; move beyond the old covenant; turn around and look for the kingdom of God. The kingdom of God has been variously interpreted. Some have said it meant obedience to the laws of God, but that is hardly consistent with the Good News of forgiveness and grace. Others have said the clue is in the Lord's Prayer, which does seem to connect the kingdom with the will of God in the third and fourth petitions. Some have defined it as the rule of God, and if that means living under the dominion of a gracious God, it is more nearly compatible with the Gospel message. Still others have described the kingdom of God, in conformity with the Gospels, as the trouble to which God has gone to woo and win people back to His care, which certainly includes the redemptive work of Jesus, since the incarnation and crucifixion of the Son of God was a lot of trouble. Repent, they preached, for the kingdom of God, the Good News, is at hand.

The second charge Jesus gave the disciples was to cast out unclean spirits from the demon-possessed. He gave them the power to make this possible. Demon-possessed people were certainly a reality in Jesus' day. These were people in an abnormal state of mind (not at all like insanity), on whom only religion seemed to have an effect. The unclean spirits have personalities, for they recognized Jesus and spoke audibly through the persons they inhabited. The disciples were given the power to exorcise them. St. Mark mentions only this one power as given to the disciples on this occasion, but since it is the most demanding power, it probably also stands for the power to heal diseases, which the disciples also did.

No report is given in St. Mark's account of the success of the internship. We can only assume that the disciples handled themselves well, learned to trust God for their daily provision, began to understand the power of God over unclean spirits and man's infirmities, and grew a great deal in their discipling. They surely came back with varying reports. Some experiences must have been harrowing others exhilarating. God had nurtured them through people the whole time. Not one of them was so discouraged by the experience that he elected to quit the band and go back to the safer, less demanding fishing industry. They were indeed catching the spirit of Christ and wanted to know more about this strangely wonderful Man before they made a decision like that.

Discipleship Today

The dividing line between internship and discipleship is ill-defined. Were the disciples less disciples because they interned? Were they more than interns because they were disciples? The answer to both is no. Nor are we, as we test the waters of a disciple in mission, less than disciples. We are committed to the Christ. Like the disciples we are sent into the world to call it to repentance and to faith. The church's mission, its vocabulary, and its liturgy remind us of that.

During the last decade our church reexamined its priorities. It asked itself some searching questions about its purpose in the world. It came up with a number of answers that were gathered into several propositions. None of them were new; all found their source in the Scriptures; all had been set forth by Jesus. They dealt with the mission of the church in the world.

To be in mission means to be carrying out orders. A reconnaissance patrol is a group of men sent out to survey the conditions of the territory into which a general would like to lead his troops. The patrol is on a mission. An ambassador is sent to a foreign land to represent the United States (or his country) in that place. Ambassadors are people on a mission for their nation or its leaders.

The Christians and the whole church in the world are on a mission. The mission is *God's*, not the church's. The church can only implement the mission, always with much prayer that it is doing God's will. Its mission is first to the church. Christians are to minister to Christians. In the continual search for better understanding of God's truth, Christians of differing persuasion have an ethical and moral responsibility for each other. The mission is to the whole person, not just to the soul. The church's medical mission addresses itself to the sick, the weak, and the dying. It's social arm addresses poverty, abortion, nuclear threats, food pantries, economy stores, slum conditions, prisons. Its mission is to preach the Gospel to all the world, so it sends missionaries to foreign lands, does Braille work, provides missionaries to the deaf, and conducts radio and television missions.

Have you ever noticed how many of the words we use in the vocabulary of the church have a discipleship dimension to them? Take a simple word like *worship*. Worship is our response to God. We usually think of that response as something we do in divine worship, but actually and in a broader sense it is our response in every corner of the vineyard in which God has placed us. In response to the blessings of God in our lives, we concern ourselves with our neighbors and our community. Cups of cool water given in the name of Christ are worship acts.

The word *liturgy* contains the fullness of that response, at least in its original sense. It derives from a word that means a person's voluntary contribution to the state. In our usage it describes our voluntary contributions to the world for the sake of the kingdom. We are baptized not only to receive the forgiveness of sins, but also to be made members of the royal priesthood. Through it we become ambassadors for Jesus. The word *laity* also includes the idea of service to God; so does the word *clergy*. The priesthood of believers is made up of people who are at the service of the King.

If this is not enough, the liturgy — in the narrow sense of what we do in a worship service — is constantly sending us back into the world. When we pray the General Prayer, for instance, we pray for all sorts and condition of men. It is hardly possible that we can let it go at that. As we bring all these needs to the attention of God, we also bring them to our attention before Him. We are committing ourselves before God to go out and to do good to all people. When we pray the Lord's Prayer, we are covenanting with God to carry out the mission of evangelism in the first three petitions.

Songs and hymns of praise are not only something between ourselves and God. They are a witness to one another and to the world. The recitation of the Creed raises the banner of the faith to which we are committed. It restates the Good News, which gives us life and which we are to carry to the world. When the Benediction is pronounced at the close of the worship hour, it is filled with great meaning, for it is placing the stamp of God on the soldiers of Christ, who go out to the trenches to be the Church Militant. There can be no doubt that if we are truly committed to our Lord, we are to be in mission to the world.

There is a theology of the worship hour that sees the worshipers coming to church battered and bruised by the battles they have or have not fought for Christ during the week. They have encountered people who are without faith, who do not know or appreciate the love of God in Christ. They have encountered such people and have failed to speak or minister to them. They have had the responsibility to offer cool water to the thirsty, food to the hungry, clothing to the naked and they have failed as they passed by on the other side. They should have been reading and meditating on the Scriptures. They should have been praying. But the week got too filled with other things to allow time for that. They come to the service on a Sunday morning in need of healing, rest, and recuperation.

Jesus is there where several are gathered in His name. He is there with healing in the absolution, with reassurance in the Gospel, with His divine presence in the Sacrament. They are refreshed, restored, and healed. They take their stand with the blessed Trinity again in the words of the Creed. They are sent out to the parapets and trenches again under the Benediction, to serve the Lord in mission to the world.

Discipleship

We come at last to you, friends of Christ, soldiers of the cross, ambassadors of the King. You have been baptized and therefore ordained priests at the disposal of God. You have been confirmed in the Christian faith and are therefore in covenant with the Almighty. You have heard again and again of our great forgiveness from a merciful God. The hope and the assurance that heavenly glory is in store for you at the end of your allotted days is strong within you. The King has work for you to do.

When you hear of needs in the community, are you sure that this is not a call to be in mission at that point? When the church establishes a mission like an economy store, a helping hand to the poor, or a hospital, are you sure that your hands and head are not needed? When you hear that missionaries to foreign lands and Bible translators are dependent on your generosity, do you hear a call to help with your substance? When you hear the command to love, to forgive, and to have compassion, do you hear it as the word of the sending God? When you hear again from your reading of Scripture, from the pulpit, or from your Sunday school teacher the call to be an evangelist, do you hear it sending you to someone whose soul is in darkness and despair?

You have all the credentials you need. You have served your internship. You have the authority of the King of kings behind you. You have the power of the Holy Spirit with you. You have the message of God's love in Jesus Christ burning inside you. You have a mandate from the very Son of God to go forth into the world to preach repentance and the Kingdom. Grasp your credentials, trust in God, and, like the disciples of old, carry the message of a crucified, risen, and reigning Savior to the world.

Give Me Eyes to See

NINTH SUNDAY AFTER PENTECOST
MARK 6:30-34

William B. Knippa

An aged mother, who had known little else than toil and care in this life, was about to pass into eternity. Her pastor spoke comforting and assuring words to her. He spoke glowingly of heaven with its many mansions, banquet feasts, angelic choirs, and joyful reunions. A twinge of concern clouded wrinkled face as she asked, "Pastor, do you think the Lord will just let me rest a while?"

Jesus had planned a rest for Himself and His disciples as they gathered around Him. How wonderful His invitation must have sounded to those men, wearied as they were by the intensity of their activity. Sent two-by-two, they had journeyed from village to village. They had preached repentance, cast out devils, and healed many. What exhausting work it had been! A rest would be most welcome.

But that was not to be. Jesus and His disciples reached the planned place of leisure only to be met by a multitude of people. The multitude had hurried a number of miles. They did not do so in order to join in the planned rest. Rather, they wanted to see Jesus. They pressed on Him. They were not about to let Him rest.

We too desire and seek rest in the midst of the busyness, demands, and confusion of our daily lives. "Just leave me alone! I've done enough! I'm not going to do one more thing!" But plans change. And often those plans are changed as a result of needs arising from those nearest us. The single and the married, parents and children, young and old alike are called on to deal with the weighty demands of relationships, responsibilities, and reality even when they don't feel like it. We are called to respond when we would much rather rest. How are we to respond? Where are we to receive the power to act, to love, to care?

Let us see how Jesus dealt with this situation in His life. How does He respond? What does He do? Let us also be strengthened by the Scripture's promise that our risen Lord lives in His people and empowers us with His love.

Jesus Sees the Needs

We begin by asking the question, What does Jesus see as the multitude gathers around Him?

> Two men looked out from prison bars.
> One saw mud, the other stars.

Two people can witness the same event or person and disagree markedly about what they saw. What does Jesus see as He climbs from the boat? Yes, He sees many people. But He sees more than just a faceless crowd of exhausted, bone-weary, hurting men, women, and children. He sees more than a blurred conglomeration of bodies, colors, and shapes. He sees more than a pulsating mob of nameless humanity. Though they may appear to be a field of grain, Jesus sees each stalk. The crowd is composed of individuals. And Jesus sees them in their human need. Each is seeking a word of hope, a word of power, a word of life.

What do we see when we look within ourselves and at people around us? So often we see only what we want to see. Seeing, we do not really see. We have an uncanny ability to overlook the most obvious of truths about ourselves and others. We are adept at filtering out those things that might threaten our security, move us to make a sacrifice we have judged to be too costly, or challenge an inflated view of ourselves.

Our drive to see only what we want to see affects not only ourselves but also our relationships. We can work with people, live with them, face them eyeball to eyeball, and yet fail to see what is of central importance and significance in their lives. A parent may see a child only as a drain on the family resources and a limit to certain freedoms, instead of a gift entrusted by the Father of all. The teacher may see a young person as a nuisance or social misfit and fail to see the profound need for love and understanding that lies beneath the external behavior. We may see our spouse or employer as an antagonist or foe and fail to see the eternal truth that this person is loved by God and precious to Him. We may see the poor or oppressed as in some way deserving their affliction and forget that we too stand in constant need of the grace and mercy of a God whose love in Jesus Christ washes away our sin and imperfection.

Jesus looks and sees more than merely a group of people gathered along a lakeshore. He sees people in their need. Instead of retreating to the solitude of a desert place, He stays where He is. He stands in the midst of the people. There is a time to rest, but this is not the time. The needs of these people are too great. Seeing their needs, Jesus responds. Those people — no less than you, me, and all others around us — are precious to the Father.

Jesus Is Moved with Compassion

Jesus is moved with compassion in the presence of the multitude. He cannot see the needs of those surrounding Him without being profoundly moved by that experience. He is drawn to these people. He feels a deep, loving concern for them. He is filled with compassion. Compassion — what a deep and powerful emotion! The word describes Jesus' feeling as He encountered the widow of Nain (Luke 7:13), a leper (Mark 1:41), two blind men (Matt. 20:34), and the city of Jerusalem (Matt. 23:37). Compassion was not a new emotion for Jesus. He feels it again as He looks on the multitude.

What had they done to earn or elicit such deep love and concern? Absolutely nothing! As a matter of fact they were crowding around Jesus on a day He had planned to be relaxing with His disciples. For some, that alone would be grounds for refusing to care! But Jesus does care. He is moved with compassion because the people are like sheep without a shepherd. And sheep without a shepherd, like sinners without a Savior, are lost.

Jesus perceives that the people have no focus to their lives, no direction, no protection. They are unable to find food for their bodies or hope for their souls. They have no one to lead them through doubt or despair, fear or frustration, pain or pressures. They are separated from God, who created their world and breathed into them the very breath of life. Most assuredly, they are sinners, for "all have sinned" (Rom. 3:23).

This striking scene before Jesus' eyes is exactly like that described by God through the prophet Jeremiah: "My people have been lost sheep. . . from mountain to hill they have gone; they have forgotten their fold" (Jer. 50:6). Through Ezekiel our God says, "My sheep were scattered; they wandered over all the mountains and on every high hill; My sheep were scattered over all the face of the earth, with none to search or seek for them" (Ezek. 34:6).

But all that is changed now! The time of God's decisive gathering of His flock has arrived. Jesus, the Good Shepherd, who came "to seek and to save the lost" (Luke 19:10), is doing exactly that. His motivation is a love and concern arising from the very depths of His being. God is love, and God, enfleshed in Jesus Christ, is moved with compassion. That compassion is extended to those who stumble through life burdened by their sin. The Shepherd calls the sheep to Himself.

Jesus' Compassion Results in Action

Jesus' compassion results in action. It is not an idle sentiment or detached romanticism. His inner emotion expresses itself in outward, visible action. Henry Ward Beecher said, "People may excite in themselves a glow of compassion, not by toasting their feet at the fire saying, 'Lord, teach me more compassion,' but by going and seeking an object that requires compassion."

Compassion in action — what a concise description of Jesus' life! He does something. He teaches those people who have come to Him. He gives them what they are seeking. He reveals Himself. He proclaims the Good News of the Kingdom with authority and power as He did in the temple (John 7:14), on the mountain (Matt. 5:2), from Simon's boat (Luke 5:3), in the synagogs (Matt. 4:23), or wherever He went.

In this case His compassion is demonstrated by His teaching the people who came to Him. We know, of course, that our Lord's compassion was not limited to His teaching, as powerful as that was. Moved with compassion, He cured diseases (Matt. 14:14), fed the multitudes (Matt. 15:32), gave sight to the blind (Matt. 20:34), healed a leper (Mark 1:41), and many other deeds.

As great and mighty as these compassionate acts were, Jesus' ultimate act of compassion was His death. To shepherd the sheep through the dangers of life only to abandon them in their darkest, gravest hour, when the debt of sin is called and its wages are to be paid, would be unthinkable. The Good Shepherd "lays down His life for the sheep" (John 10:11). Yes, and even as He hangs on the cross, His abiding love is evident: "Father, forgive them" (Luke 23:34); "Behold, your son! . . . Behold, your mother" (John 19:26-27); "Today you will be with Me in paradise" (Luke 23:43).

Jesus' compassion goes the limit. We can ask no more of anyone. We receive no less from our Lord. "Jesus, Thou art all compassion," wrote the hymnist. How true! How marvelously true! In His compassion He took our sin, our guilt, and our punishment on Himself. And even as He has had compassion on us, so did the Father have compassion on the Son. On the third day the love planted in the ground on that dark Friday blossomed forth in the light of God's glory that endures to this day.

So today we stand in the presence of our Lord as did our distant cousins almost two thousand years ago Our needs are the same. We stumble and fall in attempts to find our own way in the world. We are burdened with fears. Our faith is often weak. We have sinned. We cannot save ourselves. But our Lord is the same, too. He sees us in our need. We are no longer sheep without a shepherd. Our sins are forgiven. We are now "in Christ." Through our baptism we are united with Him — in time and through eternity.

Our Lord now calls us to see brother and sister, parent and child, friend and enemy as an individual whom Christ has loved. Pray for eyes to see. Look closely and see that person's needs. Look past external behavior, appearance, and unpleasantness, and see the person Jesus does. He sees someone precious and worth dying for. By the grace of God, see the presence of Christ in that other person.

Then, confident of Jesus' all-embracing love for you and that He will indeed give you strength, peace, and rest, be moved with compassion. Respond! By the power of the Holy Spirit act in a way that the need is met. In so doing, you will serve your Lord and Savior, for "as you did it to one of the least of these My brethren, you did it to Me" (Matt. 25:40). Do so today, beginning with those nearest you. Do it to the glory of the Father.

> O give us eyes to see the needs
> Of those around us placed.
> Your Spirit grant, so that we might,
> In them see Jesus' face.
>
> Your love and grace have made us whole;
> We are Your very own.
> Compassion may we freely show
> Until You call us home. Amen.

A Feast That Does Not Cease

TENTH SUNDAY AFTER PENTECOST
JOHN 6:1-15

William B. Knippa

There is a hunger deep within the heart and soul of all people that can only be satisfied by the presence of the living God. As Augustine said many years ago, "Thou hast made us for Thyself, and the heart of man is restless until it finds its rest in Thee."

The marvel of God's love and grace is that He has sought us out in the person of His son Jesus Christ. Through Jesus' life, death, and resurrection God feeds us and thereby satisfies that great hunger of heart and soul for His saving presence. In a letter to his friend Philip Melanchthon, Martin Luther described both his need and the grace that filled that need: "I am seeking and thirsting for nothing else than a gracious God. And He earnestly offers Himself as such and urges even those who spurn Him and are His enemies to accept Him as such" (Ewald M. Plass, ed., *What Luther Says: An Anthology* [St. Louis: Concordia Publishing House, 1959], II, 602).

In St. John's account of the feeding of the 5,000, we see a striking picture of the magnificent way in which God draws His people to Himself and feeds them. This event was undoubtedly of special significance in the life of the early church. It is the only miracle recorded in all four gospels. Let us look more closely and see the power and message of this familiar passage.

Jesus Is the Host

The central figure in the feeding of the 5,000 is, if course, Jesus. To see fish and bread multiplying without seeing the One whose power made that happen is to miss the point. Yet how often do we not focus on the gifts, the goods, and the glory in our lives without recognizing the Giver. What would the people gathered on the mountains have seen as this miraculous event unfolded before their eyes? Those who were waiting for the promised Messiah would surely have seen something significant and exciting. According to Jewish tradition and expectations, the Messiah would perform many great acts. In a miraculous way He was to prepare a banquet feast for His people. The miraculous feeding of the wandering Israelites in the Sinai desert would be reenacted and reexperienced in the presence of the Messiah. Jesus claims His messiahship.

Jesus is in charge. The host prepares the meal. He silences the pragmatic and earthbound voices of Philip and Andrew. They, like us, are inclined to doubt in the face of what appears to be an impossible situation. "Where will we get what we need? Our resources are insufficient." Jesus proceeds undaunted. He will feed His people, and even if they fail to see or misunderstand the nature of the food He offers, He will still provide it. He will provide it in abundance. Only He can do that.

Jesus Can Feed Us

Only Jesus can feed and satisfy the hunger of the heart and soul. The food we find and choose for ourselves is spoiled and of no lasting value. We prefer to choose our own diet, find our own way, make our own rules, live our own lives The garden fruit still looks good, because eating it will make us like God, or so we think.

But such a meal does not sustain us. We remain hungry, under-nourished, and bound for death. Our hunger cannot be satisfied by fish and bread, steak and potatoes, or burgers and fries. It is rooted deeper than the lining of our stomach walls. We hunger for the relationship that God first established in the garden and we destroyed. God has placed that hunger within us. And He has revealed the means by which it will be satisfied. There on that mountain Jesus shows that He will indeed satisfy His people's hunger.

Jesus Satisfies Our Hunger for Forgiveness

For what do we hunger? We hunger for forgiveness. The weight of sin and guilt hangs mercilessly around our necks. To say we have no sin is to play a foolish, deadly game with our eternal future. Washing our hands, accomplishing great deeds, walking the straight and narrow, cleaning up our acts, being nice to our spouse, buying gifts for our children, doing our best at work or at home — all these have no effect on our sin. At best, such works are appreciated by others and temporarily salve troubled consciences.

But the soul that sins will indeed die unless it is nourished by the life-giving forgiveness of God. As the hunger pangs of repentance rumble within, we are fed and satisfied with the assurance that forgiveness is ours. Relying on the grace of God, we are nourished and strengthened through the forgiveness of our sins.

Jesus Satisfies Our Hunger for Fellowship

We hunger for fellowship. We want a sense of belonging and acceptance. To be abandoned and isolated in this world is to be enveloped in terror and fear. Broken homes, refugee camps, separated families, runaway teenagers, drug abuse, and a multitude of similar tragedies attest to the fragmentation of our society. The outcast, the hurting, the unattractive, the poor, the rich, the popular, the successful, and the powerful all yearn for a place where they can be accepted and openly received. "All I have really wanted," recounted the troubled young woman to her counselor, "is to be accepted, to have a place."

Jesus, aware of our need for a place and a sense of belonging, calls us to Himself even as He drew the multitude to Himself. It doesn't matter where we have been or what we have been up to. Jesus is the friend of sinners. He eats with us. He joins us. He identifies with us. He feeds us. He changes us.

He gives us a reason to live, for we are now in fellowship with Him, the promised One.

In Jesus' day the meal was a symbol of unity acceptance, and celebration. The sharing of a meal is an outward sign that a personal relationship exists. Jesus proclaims through His feeding of the 5,000 that, "I am one with you." He satisfies a hunger for fellowship that no one else can fill.

Jesus Satisfies Our Hunger for a Future

We hunger for a future, and so we attempt to build our own. But the foundation is sinking sand. In our wisdom we calculate what we need and how we will get it. Though our intentions might have been honorable initially, the quest for future security becomes a fevered race to accumulate money, material goods, and position. Consumed with a quest for a future good, we ignore our present relationships. Obsessed with financial gain, we lose sight of the meaning of our work and the precious gifts of spouse and children.

We finally get what we had for so long deemed essential, only to find that we are neither happy nor satisfied. Only God, breaking into our lives in Jesus Christ can show us our folly in such a way that we place our cares and our futures into His loving hands. We hunger for a future, and Jesus offers Himself as the Bread of life. Such bread will never run out or be found lacking in any way.

Jesus Feeds Us Daily

We pray, "Give us this day our daily bread." What are you hungry for today? Forgiveness? direction? fellowship? hope? faith? strength? May our prayer be, "Lord Jesus, feed me today as You did the multitudes long ago. Fill me with Your loving presence and satisfy my hunger." Be assured that our Lord hears our cry. Though we are slowed and weakened by sin and often seek only what fills the belly, Jesus' presence will lift and nourish us. Just as He fed the 5,000, so also will He feed us.

The location of the feeding has changed, but Jesus remains the same yesterday, today, and forever. Once He fed His people on a mountainside. Today He feeds us in the middle of crowded cities, noisy factories, lonely hospital rooms, tension-filled offices, mortgaged homes, decaying apartments, mobile homes, and family farms. Jesus feeds us in our world of rapid transport, fast foods, synthetic fibers, instant communication, and home computers. He feeds us in times of personal distress, spiritual darkness, impending danger, disrupted plans, failing health, and political unrest.

And we will be fed eternally. Jesus Christ has seen to that. He guaranteed this when He took on Himself our sin, our pain, our guilt, our hatred, our afflictions, and all manner of spiritual hunger. Everything that would crush us, destroy us, and plunge us into despair and death was heaped on Him. And it broke Him. On the cross His body was broken. The Bread of life was broken and laid in a tomb. But that Bread did not decay. Rather, the life-giving Bread, our Lord Jesus Christ, was resurrected. Sin could not hold Him. Death could not hold Him. Satan could not hold Him. He lives and continues to feed the hungry.

The hungry gather around the Lord, drawn by His love. They gather around Word and Sacrament to be fed. And we are fed. We are fed with forgiveness, with fellowship, and with the assurance that the ultimate victory is ours.

Let's eat! Let us again today savor the goodness and grace of a Savior whose presence is real, whose love is unconditional, and whose acceptance of us will culminate in a heavenly feast that will have no end!

Do We Have Our Work Priorities Straight?

ELEVENTH SUNDAY AFTER PENTECOST
JOHN 6:24-35

Otto C. Hintze

Think of the hours, days, months, and years of our lives that we spend at our jobs to earn a livelihood. A major part of our efforts and time goes to provide the food we consume, so our work is a very important activity in our lives. From the beginning God has intended for us creatures to work (Gen. 2:15). He wants us to do with might whatever our hands find to do (Eccl. 9:10) and to enjoy our work (Eccl. 3:22), and He admonishes that if anyone does not work, he should not eat (2 Thess. 3:10).

Now we hear the astonishing words that Jesus spoke to those who had participated in His miraculous feeding of the 5,000. When they found Jesus the next day on the other side of the Sea of Galilee, He told them *not* to work for "the food which perishes" (John 6:27). On the surface it appears that Jesus is opposing what we just said about work. However, He added that they should rather work "for the food which endures to eternal life." So He does not mean for us to stop working for food to eat. Instead, He is helping us to answer the question:

Do We Have
Our Work Priorities Straight?

In other words, what is the most important, most valuable kind of work that we should be doing?

The Work That Some Value Above All Else

Jesus was prompted to make a value judgment about the work that people do by the thoughts of those who sought Him after He had fed them on the Galilean hillside in a miraculous way with five loaves of barley bread and two fish. He purposely allowed them to find Him on the other side of the lake. Out of concern and love for them He pointed out that they looked for Him "not because you saw signs, but because you ate your fill of the loaves" (v. 26). The people had come to make Him a "bread king" by force. So He confronted them with the shocking warning: "Do not labor for the food which perishes" (v. 27). They had been making the pursuit of food their number one priority in life. They had their eyes and hearts fixed on a present but passing goal.

Translated into present-day terms, their chief concern in life was to work day after day to put food on the table and groceries in the pantry. We should include with food for the stomach also the many other material things that people strive to obtain. They work for money, clothing, furnishings for the house, new cars and the many new high tech products. Others pursue health, education, sex, positions of influence and honor, membership in social organizations, family relationships, and so on. These things can so easily become obsessions for which we may labor hard and long. We may place top value on them and strive for them to the exclusion of all other things in life.

Why should we think twice about working for these kinds of things? Jesus reminds us that they are perishable in nature. Food is consumed and passes on into waste. It easily rots and does not last forever. Clothing wears out and is thrown away. Relationships change. People are here today and gone tomorrow. Influence and honor are evasive and fickle. Money is spent, lost, or inherited by others. Cars end up in the junkyard. In the words of Jesus on another occasion: "Moth and rust consume and . . . thieves break in and steal" (Matt. 6:19).

All our possessions or other desires in this world are of limited duration. Sooner or later they all perish. What lasting good can be gained from working all our lives only for things like these? The man in one of Jesus' parables (Luke 12:16-21) planned to tear down his barns to build bigger and better ones to store all his food and possessions after his land had produced plentifully. He assured himself, "You have ample goods laid up for many years; take your ease, eat, drink, be merry" (v. 19). But when God required his soul that night before he could accomplish any of the thing on which he had placed the highest priority, all his plans were in vain. Jesus called him a fool for laying up treasure only for himself not being rich toward God.

The Work That Jesus Values Most Highly

Jesus not only warns against setting up work priorities for things that will perish, but He also strongly urges us to work "for the food which endures to eternal life" (John 6:27). This food is quite different from bread for the table. The bread that endures to eternal life is none other than Jesus Christ Himself. Later in His words to the people He referred to Himself as the "Bread of life" (v. 35).

Jesus used one of the most common foods in the world to communicate one of the most profound truths. Yet the crowd could not understand what He was trying to say. The previous day they had all eaten from a few loaves of bread and a couple of fish and had participated in gathering 12 baskets of leftover pieces. As Jesus went on to explain what He meant, the people asked Him, "What sign do you do, that we may see, and believe you?" (v. 30). They thought that Jesus should do some great wonder, like Moses did when their fathers received manna from heaven, before they would believe Him.

Jesus corrected them by pointing out that it was not Moses who had given them the manna, but God. Now in Jesus God is giving them true bread from heaven. Manna was never in heaven, but Jesus was. He is the "Bread of God" (v. 33), coming directly from God Himself. Jesus is God. In Him God comes down and "gives life to the world" (v. 33). As a genuine human being He became the source of life by His perfect obedience to the will of His Father. He became the perfect Bread, from which people may receive life, by substituting His sinless life for their sinful and death-deserving lives. As bread satisfies hunger, so the death of Jesus satisfied God's just sentence of death for every sinner in the world. Furthermore, there is life for the world in Jesus' death, for He rose from the dead and now lives forever. That is why He can claim that He is the Bread of life. He is living. He is full of life and able to give life to any in the world who will eat the Bread.

"This is the work of God, that you believe in Him whom He has sent" (v. 29). That was Jesus' answer to the question, "What must we do, to be doing the works of God?" (v. 28). Believe, have faith in Jesus, put your whole confidence in what He has done as the Bread of life for the whole world. That is what He wants us to do above all else. The work that we do cannot be exactly the same as the work Jesus did. *Work* here signifies an activity of our intellect and will that appropriates and trusts in Christ's work. It does not mean that we do something to achieve our own salvation. Luther said of this work: "Christ is speaking of the work which we should do, namely, believe. For faith is a work that must be done by man ... But where this faith comes from (for no one has faith of himself) Christ teaches us later on when He says, 'No one can come to Me [believe in Me, cf. v. 35] unless the Father who sent Me draws him'" (v. 44). Another great man of God (Franz Pieper) once said, "It is not the Holy Spirit, but man who believes through the operation of the Holy Spirit." Jesus Himself pointed out to the people that it is *He* who gives us the food that endures to eternal life through faith (v. 27).

Work for that food of faith in Jesus Christ that endures to eternal life, rather than for the food that merely goes into our stomachs. Jesus does not mean to say that the one work excludes the other. He is saying that working for this spiritual food of faith is top priority with Him. He values that work as first above all. He wants us to spend time — a good amount of prime time — all through our lives in pursuit of spiritual food, the Bread of life, which will produce and nourish eternal life, beginning right now. Only a few minutes or hours of days of our total lives is not enough. Putting the effort to feed our faith in Christ first means that we shall spend a great deal of our time, as did the early Christians, devoting ourselves "to the apostles' teaching and fellowship, to the breaking of bread and the prayers" (Acts 2:42). Jesus said, "Man shall not live by bread alone, but by every word that proceeds from the mouth of God" (Matt. 4:4).

Jesus values that kind of work so highly that He would have us share with others what He worked for all His life, so that they too will be able to labor for the food that endures to eternal life. He is the true Bread "which comes down from heaven and gives life to the world" (John 6:33). His work was for the whole world. We need to spend lots of time and money to bring that true Bread to everyone in the world so that they will never hunger but have eternal life.

Why Make Jesus' Priority Ours?

Why should we value so highly and work so diligently for the food that endures to eternal life? First, what profit is there if a person "gains the whole world and forfeits his life" (Matt 16:26)? The loss of eternal life, ending up in eternal separation from God, is the frightful result of placing our values wrongly. On the other hand, going with Jesus will result in possessing eternal life now and being with God forever. Our eternal destiny lies in the balance. That is why we want to make Jesus' priority ours.

We all know of people who have all the food and other things that they want but still are not satisfied. They are still searching. They are restless and are still hungering and thirsting after something that they can't quite achieve or even define. There is no deep, lasting satisfaction in the things of this world. "Never satisfied are the eyes of man," says the inspired writer of Proverbs (27:20). But Jesus promises that all who come to Him, who believe in Him, will never hunger or thirst (John 6:35). Deep in our spirits the Holy Spirit will give us complete satisfaction and peace that surpasses all understanding because "there is therefore now no condemnation for those who are in Christ Jesus" (Rom. 8:1). There is perfect peace for those whose minds are stayed on Christ — no fear, no restlessness. Are not these blessings worth making Jesus' priority ours?

The value that the Father has set on Him is another reason why we should establish our priorities in accord with those of Jesus. Jesus said we should work for the food that endures to eternal life — the food that the Son of Man will give us — because "on Him has God the Father set His seal" (John 6:27). In other words, God the Father has certified Him. He has given Him power from heaven. He was well pleased with what the Son was doing, as He said at Jesus' baptism and transfiguration. Jesus has the seal of the Father's authority. therefore, what Jesus has said and done for us is worthy of our acceptance and trust.

Henry Ford once said, "He who would really benefit mankind must reach them through their work." This is exactly what the Savior did in reaching people through the message of His work for the entire world and of the work that we should do for the food that endures to eternal life. He turned everyday values upside down and made laboring for the food that endures of greater importance and value. How tragic are the consequences of not having our work priorities straight! And how deeply and eternally rewarding it is to have them right!

Who Has Eternal Life?

TWELFTH SUNDAY AFTER PENTECOST
JOHN 6:41-51

Otto C. Hintze

We would surely want to know in time if a dreadful cancer were developing within our bodies. Knowing the truth in time to respond would be extremely important to our well-being. Even more crucial is to know the truth about our spiritual condition. Since that is a matter of *external* life or death, wouldn't we want to know before it was too late?

This raises a tantalizing spiritual question that each of us may very well ask ourselves: Who has eternal life? We have a personal, vested interest in the answer to that question. It concerns our eternal well-being. The answer will determine our attitude and response both to ourselves and to others in the world.

Who has eternal life? How can we tell? There's no chance to find out unless God tells us. Fortunately, He has clearly informed us in His Word.

Some Reject Jesus and Eternal Life

In the Gospel that we just read we are told, "The Jews then murmured at Him because He said, 'I am the bread which came down from heaven'" (John 6:41). There was hostility against Jesus because of what He had said. To claim that He originated in heaven—in other words, was equal with God—would be blasphemy. Some of his hearers could not consent to that. He appeared simply to be one of them, born in the same place, born of earthly parents. He was merely human, and that was it. And so they said, "Is not this Jesus, the son of Joseph, whose father and mother we know? How does He now say, 'I have come down from heaven'?" (v. 42).

Jesus' obvious humanity kept them from perceiving His being, understanding His claims, and seeing the connection between His miracles and those claims. These were some of the same people who had just been fed with two fish and five barley loaves, but Christ's humanity became a rock of offense over which they stumbled. As a result, they did not possess eternal life because they could not see Him as heavenly, divine Life personified.

That He was truly human has always been a vital point. If He were a real human person, Jesus would not have been able to put Himself under the Law. Nor would He have been able to become sin for the whole human race—past, present, and future. Nor would He have been able to suffer death, the consequences of sin. But that is exactly what He did. He was sent by the Father for that purpose. "When the time had fully come, God sent forth His Son, born of woman, born under the Law, to redeem those who were under the Law, so that we might receive adoption as sons" (Gal. 4:4-5). Because Jesus carried out His mission as a real human being, it is possible for every human being to have eternal life.

Many people today follow those who murmured at Jesus. They are blinded by an impenetrable veil that covers their perception and insight. They cannot see Jesus for what He truly is—*God* in the flesh. They can see only the human side. This is true of Jews who are unable to receive Him as the promised Messiah and also of those who see Jesus only as a good example, a great human being who realized His human potential more than most others have—someone on the same level as Gandhi or Buddha, for example. Some see Him only as *a* god or as a human being who somehow achieved a kind of divinity. But anyone who perceives Jesus *only* in these terms does not have eternal life. Rejection of Jesus as true God and true Man who came into the world to win salvation for us by His suffering, death, and resurrection destroys the basis for eternal life.

Eternal Life Is Found in Jesus

Jesus has eternal life. "He has seen the Father" (John 6:46). He is from God. He is God. God the Father lives forever; He is the Source of life. Thus, Jesus has eternal life in His very Being. St. Paul described it for the Colossians: "In Him all the fullness of God was pleased to dwell" (Col. 1:19). Furthermore, the apostle John gives us the testimony of God the Father concerning Jesus: "This is the testimony, that God gave us eternal life, and this life is in His Son" (1 John 5:11). Having eternal life, Jesus can then rightfully make the claim: "I am the Bread of life" (John 6:48).

In common, understandable words Jesus refers to Himself as consumable food—bread—that any person is able to internalize. But He distinguishes between ordinary bread and Himself. "Your fathers," He said, excluding Himself, "ate the manna in the wilderness, and they died" (v. 49). That bread sustained life only for a relatively short time. But Jesus said that He is the living Bread that gives and sustains life so that "a man may eat of it and not die" (v. 50). "If anyone eats of this Bread, he will live forever," Jesus continued (v. 51). Jesus therefore is that Bread full of life, life that continues forever, and is able to impart eternal life to everyone who "eats" it.

As the One who is eternal life, it is Jesus' mission to make that life available to everyone in the world. Using the same figure of speech, Jesus made it clear that He gave His human flesh in death for the life of the world (v. 51). As the Father gave His Son to the world, so Jesus gave Himself up as a sacrifice (Eph. 5:2). He laid down His life as a ransom for us (John 10:17; Matt. 20:28). The wrath of God consumed that Bread instead of us, enabling us to escape the horrible consequences of His wrath against our sins. He gave

His own flesh for our fleshly sins when He sacrified Himself on the cross in our stead.

And then Jesus conquered death with His return to life. He thereby brought life and immortality to light for the entire world. If He were not alive, not one could receive a new life here on earth or possess eternal life here or in heaven. Jesus promised that at the Last Day He would raise up those who come to Him (John 6:44). How could He make such a promise trustworthy if He Himself did not rise from the dead? But He did. He died on the cross, and now He lives victorious over death, able also to raise the lifeless bodies of those who believe in Him.

If a person possesses nothing and promises us a fortune, he will be able to deliver nothing, no matter how convincingly he might say it. But it's different with Jesus. He is Life. He possesses eternal life because of who He is and what He has accomplished. He is able to give it and will come through on His promise.

Eternal Life Is Given to Believers

His promise is that "he who believes has eternal life" (v. 47). One who merely believes? "Even the demons believe—and shudder" (James 2:19). The mere words, "I believe," no matter how well or how many times they are repeated, are not sufficient to have eternal life. "Not everyone who says to Me, 'Lord, Lord' shall enter the kingdom of heaven" (Matt. 7:21).

Jesus means more than mere words or head knowledge by the word *believe*. He spoke of *eating* that living Bread from heaven. His words were understood by some who heard Him to mean some sort of crude consumption —cannibalism— of Jesus, and so they drew back and no longer went about with Him (John 6:66). However, what Jesus means by "eating" is to appropriate Him into our inner, spiritual selves through our intellect and wills. It means genuinely trusting in Jesus personally as the Bread who is able to give us eternal life. It means having faith in Jesus (not just anything or anybody) and by that faith appropriating what He has done for us. So everyone who has Jesus, the Son of God, through that faith has eternal life (1 John 5:12).

That kind of faith does not come naturally or automatically. Jesus said, "No one can come to Me unless the Father who sent Me draws him. . . . Everyone who has heard and learned from the Father comes to Me" (John 6:44-45). "Coming" to Jesus is another way of saying "believing" in Him. It is impossible to conjure up that kind of faith by our own strength or reason. The Father must draw us.

He draws us "with the cords of compassion, with the bonds of love," as the prophet Hosea put it with reference to Israel (11:4). He draws us by means of the Good News of what Jesus did on the cross. Once Jesus said about His death on the cross: "I, when I am lifted up from the earth, will draw all men to Myself" (John 12:32). All who have heard and learned of —that is, who have believed in—Jesus' death, resurrection, and life for us from the Father come to Jesus. In coming to Jesus we have eternal life.

At the moment we believe by the grace of God and the operation of the

Holy Spirit, we have eternal life. We have it now, fully, in this life—yet not completely. In its final phase, its consummation, we shall be with God in heaven to live with Him forever and ever. As long as we believe while here, we shall always have it. Having it means living this life, surrounded by all its problems, pains, and fears, with a firm, sure base from which we are able to cope and overcome. We can meet life with a smile and real rejoicing, even in suffering and in the face of death, because we possess the zing of eternal life. Unshakable is our peace because our hearts are set on the living God who has given us the down payment and guarantee of the life that is to come. We who have eternal life have a deep conviction and a strong inner compulsion to respond to those who do not have it by sharing the Good News of Jesus with them wherever they are, so that they may be drawn by the Father to faith in Christ and given eternal life.

Thus, we have answered the vitally important question with which we began: Who has eternal life? It should be clear that it is the person who has been drawn, taught, comes to, eats, and internalizes through faith—who believes in—Jesus Christ as His own Savior, the living Bread from heaven. God grant that we continue to have it, live with it, and share it!

The Faultless Food for Faith

THIRTEENTH SUNDAY AFTER PENTECOST
JOHN 6:51-58

Curtis R. Moermond

Perhaps one of television's greatest appeals is that it allows us to see, rather than just hear, the speakers or characters portrayed. However, that can also deprive us of some of the mystery and imagination that we can use when we listen to the radio. Imagine listening to a radio program in which someone is being interviewed. The host asks the question, "What one decision have you made that has contributed to your happiness?" The next thing you hear is a lady's voice saying, "It was when I resolved that would never again go on a diet." She then goes on to say, "I think that it's absurd for everybody to think they have to get into the same size dress. To say that everybody has to wear the same size shoe or to have the same size nose or ears—that we all have to look the same—is ridiculous. God didn't make us that way." I'm not certain how you might picture the lady, but there is fun in using your imagination.

What adds to the interest of such an interview is that most of us are diet-conscious people. Not only do we count calories (or maybe we should), but we are also aware of foods that are not considered good for us. We are told we should think about the nutritional value of the foods we eat, and so we resolve to eat more salads. We may be told that we should eat certain things to keep our iron or potassium levels up, and we should plan our diets accordingly. We are also told that certain foods may produce cancer, and we should avoid them. We can become almost like that ancient mariner who said, "Water, water everywhere and not a drop to drink." We look at food, and because we are concerned about our physical well-being and the effects it may have on our bodies, we wonder if we should eat it — or eat anything at all!

The Faultless Food Offered to the Jews

As concerned as we are about our physical well-being, today's Gospel tells us about an even more important food. This is food that supplies spiritual nourishment. In fact, it gives us the faultless food for faith.

Now you may be saying, "Oh, yes, I remember the story just read. It was something about eating and drinking the flesh and blood of Jesus." You may also be adding, "This morning is the Lord's Supper, and I didn't go last time, so I'll go." Now you are all ready to nod off to sleep. But wait! There is far more in this text than a mere reference to the Lord's Supper. In fact, to see it only as a reference to the Lord's Supper robs the text of its full meaning. So it is well that we spend our minutes this morning looking at what Jesus is saying to the Jews who disputed with Him when He said, "My flesh is food indeed, and My blood is drink indeed" (John 6:55) and "He who eats My flesh and drinks My blood has eternal life" (v. 54).

Perhaps the best way to find out what Jesus is talking about is to look at the context. When we read the rest of St. John's sixth chapter, we find that this discussion takes place the day after Jesus fed 5,000 people in the wilderness. Immediately after they had eaten, some of the people decided, "This guy's got something! We have a good thing here. Let's make him our king. Today it's bread and fish, and tomorrow — well, who knows what?"

We know what happened, Jesus told the disciples to go across the lake while He took off in another direction. But the crowd wasn't ready to give up so easily. Many stayed, camping out that night, and resumed looking for Him the next morning. Not only did they look for Him, but others came across the lake from Tiberias seeking Him. But they couldn't find Him. Then the word came that He was at Capernaum. So they went there.

When they finally did find Him, Jesus looked at them and said, "I know why you're here. You're interested in bread — but that's not why I came. I didn't just come to keep your stomachs full. I didn't come so you could make me a king. I didn't come to attract you by what I could provide for you physically. I come with a different and a far more important message." Then He told them: "I am the living Bread which came down from heaven; if anyone eats of this Bread, he will live forever, and the bread which I give for the life of the world is My flesh" (v. 52). That boggled the minds of the Jews. "How can this Man give us His flesh to eat?" they asked (v. 52).

If they had stopped to think about what the prophets had said, they might have been more ready to understand. The prophets had often used the imagery of eating and drinking the Word of God. Jeremiah wrote: "Thy words were found, and I ate them" (Jer. 15:16). The psalmist wrote: "How sweet are Thy words to my taste, sweeter than honey to my mouth!" (Ps. 119:103).

Now when the Word incarnate stood in front of His contemporaries and said, "I am for you to eat and drink," they missed the message. They questioned, perhaps not daring to understand what He was saying. Jesus wasn't speaking to them about a physical eating and drinking. He offered them nourishment for faith. That nourishment was Himself. He was the foundation for faith, the source of confidence, and the basis for the hope of salvation. He came to give them the Word of life.

He didn't want them to look to Him as a second Moses who would provide them with physical food. The food Moses provided in the wilderness didn't keep the Israelite fathers from dying. He was referring not only to a physical death, but to a spiritual death as well. Any number of those who had complained and murmured against Moses out in the wilderness went their own way and died outside the faith. Jesus was now saying that they should look to Him for spiritual nourishment. He came in flesh and blood so that they might have life in all of its abundance. It was through believing in Him that they could live forever.

You may ask why the Jews didn't comprehend what Jesus was saying? Perhaps to help us understand, it would be wise to go back and pick up some earlier things out of the ministry of Jesus. Go back to the temptation. One of the things Satan tempted Jesus to do was to jump down from the pinnacle of the temple. "Land safely and the people will flock around You" is what Satan was saying. Jesus would really make an impression.

Take another example — the calling of one of the disciples. Nathanael was told, "We have found the Savior, the Messiah, the One promised of old. It's Jesus of Nazareth." His response was "Nazareth? There isn't anything that can come out of Nazareth worth two cents, let alone a Messiah!"

Or just consider this sixth chapter of St. John's gospel. When Jesus met these Jews in Capernaum and said, "I am the Bread which came down from heaven," they said, "Isn't this Jesus, the son of Joseph, whose father and mother we know?" (John 6:41-42).

Jesus wasn't that impressive. He didn't stand a head taller than everybody in Israel like Saul had. He didn't have red hair like it is supposed King David had. There was nothing to look at that made Him outstanding. Isaiah had said that this would be the case: "He had no form or comeliness that we should look at Him, and no beauty that we should desire Him" (Is. 53:2). Jesus was common. You could have rubbed shoulders with Him, and it would never have impressed you.

A couple of years ago there was the story of Jesus on television. One of the things that impressed many was that Jesus had greasy hair. But why wouldn't He? Everybody had greasy hair at that time. They had no special formula shampoos. He was just like everybody else.

That's the way God intended it to be. Jesus came to be a man. One thing never questioned by those critics who dogged His ministry was whether or not He was a man. It wasn't only an appearance. God didn't depend on appearances, just as He isn't impressed by appearances now. In every respect Jesus was man as God created man to be. He took on the consequences of man's sin without becoming sinful. When He was tired, it was a real weariness. When He was sad, it was a sincere sorrow. His birth, His growth in wisdom and stature, the enjoyment of the wine at the wedding at Cana, the tears shed when Lazarus died, His own death on Calvary — through it all He was a man.

But He was also never less than completely God. As He stood in front of the people at Capernaum, that was His message. "Here in the flesh — right here, right now — is God incarnate. I am the promised Messiah; I am Immanuel. If you believe in Me, you will have eternal life." And He went one step further: "The blood that is goind to be poured out on Calvary is the final sacrificial death for your sins. That is the way God hasplanned your salvation. Believe that, and you will have eternal life."

The Faultless Food Offered to Us

There's a more important question to ask than why the Jews had a difficult time comprehending what Jesus said. That question is, How about us today? Are we ready to listen when Jesus says, "My flesh is food indeed, and My blood is drink indeed. He who eats My flesh and drinks My blood has eternal life. Believe in me and I give you the life that lasts forever"?

Luther wrote in one of his sermons on this chapter, "I know not where to find God, either in heaven or on earth, except in the flesh of Christ." Then he went on to speak about how works are of no avail in a search for God (*Sermons on the Gospel of St. John, Chapters 6-8*, trans. Martin H. Bertram, ed. Jaroslav Pelikan, *Luther's Works*, American Edition, Vol. 23 [St. Louis: Concordia Publishing House, 1959], p. 123.)

Today many still seek other routes to God. They go from Transcendental Meditation to the Moonies. Some seek their god in materialism or in any number of other philosophies of life. Each of them provides an answer that some feel is right. Each has a particular type of worship, and most demand a great deal of sacrifice. But those roads are all dead ends. There is now, as there always has been, only one way to find God, and that is through Jesus Christ, who came to be our Savior. Believing in Him, we have eternal life.

But many have the same problem the Jews had. Jesus still is not impressive enough. He's not impressive when He comes in something as common as the water of Baptism. They fail to see God working in this water. They are not impressed with something so common as bread and wine. They don't hear our Lord say, "This is My body; this is My blood, given and shed for you for the remission of sins." For them there is no strengthening and preserving for life everlasting.

And how commonly is the Word treated? Talk to members of an evangelism committee. They might tell you about some of their calls — calls made not only on the unchurched, but also on inactive members. The major concern of many people is so often something like a nursery program or what the church is doing to the elderly. There may be complaints about the preacher or about the shock they get from the static electricity in the carpet when they receive Communion. But nobody says anything about Jesus Christ. Nobody says anything about His Word. Why? They take that for granted. It's too common. The result is that they take Jesus for granted, and He is lost! We know what happened at Capernaum. The Jews who looked for Jesus because of the bread and fish He served missed the spiritual food He offered in Himself.

We know Him. But let's make certain we are seeking Him for the right reason. Let's not take Him for granted. More important, let's not let Him become so common that we pass right by and never even notice Him. Let's be concerned about our spiritual nourishment. Let's eat greedily of that flesh and drink of that blood of our Lord Jesus Christ, believing that Word He shares with us. He promises He will bless us, not only now, but also eternally. He is the only faultless food for faith.

Your Most Important Decision

FOURTEENTH SUNDAY AFTER PENTECOST
JOHN 6:60-69

Curtis R. Moermond

According to the encyclopedia, the term is originally from an Indian language. It became famous, or least common, during the presidential campaign of 1884. A newspaper editor picked it up, and soon everybody was using it. But it was Teddy Roosevelt who gave it a definition that is perhaps most easily remembered. "A *mugwump*," he said, "is a bird that sits on a fence with its mug on one side and its wump on the other." It's someone who can't make up his mind. Maybe that's where we get the expression of someone who's sitting on the fence.

Decisions especially important ones, are not easily made. We know that. We readily understand anyone who says, "I'm really having a hard time making up my mind." Usually that means the person is trying to work out the facts, get all the data, and then come up with the right conclusions or make the right decision.

The disciples in today's Gospel were making decisions. Individually, they each made a decision. It was a decision that affected their spiritual life and their eternal welfare. Because you and I are concerned about our spiritual and eternal welfare, it is important to look carefully at the facts presented for us this morning in this word from the Scriptures.

The Reality of the Decision
We don't know how many people were involved in the incident that St.

John reports for us. They were people who had listened to Jesus present the message of salvation. In the preceding verses we heard Him say, "You are to eat My flesh and drink My blood." He was referring to the incarnation — that He was the Son of God in the flesh, who had come as the Savior of the world. He had taken the form of one of the creatures of creation in order to pour out His blood for the salvation of mankind. Those who heard Him responded, "This is hard saying; who can listen to it?"

Perhaps our first reaction to those words is much the same. We may agree that it's hard to understand and comprehend what Jesus is talking about. But what follows demonstrates that understanding wasn't really the problem for those people. Slowly, one after another, they began to realize something else. Jesus' saying was hard because this Man standing in front of them was claiming, "I am the Messiah." They also realized that they had to respond to His claim. They had to answer the question, Is He really the Messiah, or isn't He?

This meant that they would have to make a decision. It was an either/or situation. As long as Jesus fed 5,000 people and performed other miracles that drew the attention of the crowd, they were intrigued by Him. As long as they could wonder how He got from one side of the lake to the other in the middle of the night without a boat, their imagination was tickled. He was unique. He had a new way of presenting things. He offered them a change from the rather monotonous routines of daily life.

But now He was presenting them with a choice. If He really was who He said He was, if the only way to eternal life was to accept Him as true God in the flesh, and if they were going to continue to follow Him, they were going to have to change a lot of their ideas. They were going to have to change their lives. They understood what He was saying, probably far more clearly than they wanted to understand it. For them, as for all people ever since, the decision had to be made on the basis of what they knew and understood.

There are far more people who leave Jesus Christ because they understand what He is saying than leave because they don't understand Him. There are far more people who have left the church and are no more seen in the church because they *understand* what is being preached than because they are confused about the message from God.

The disciples who left made a decision. Jesus knew what was going on. He knew that some were having problems deciding. In order to make it all crystal clear, He presented another situation: "What if you were to see the Son of Man ascending where He was before?" What if suddenly He would have opened their minds so that they could see, as St. John was later to see on the isle of Patmos, the vision recorded for us the Book of Revelation. He could have done it. Instead He said to them, "My friends, that's not the important thing. My words give life and spirit."

Jesus knew that a faith that is fed on miracles and depends on visions is always going to be hungry for more and will never be satisfied. He offers not miracles or visions, but Himself. "Eat My flesh and never hunger, drink of the living water that I give and never thirst." That is what He comes to give. The people heard and were considering what He was saying. They were making their decisions.

Finally, Jesus looked at all the company of His disciples, some of whom had probably been walking with Him for some time. He knew that some would continue to walk with Him for a while longer. One would go all the way to the upper room. He would still be there, keeping up an appearance, before he would go his separate way. Jesus knew that some followed Him for the wrong reasons. He also knew that the time was coming when they would have to make their decision. That decision would be either to turn and go their own way or to trust in Him as the Messiah, the Savior of the world, and the Lord of their lives. And St. John reports, "Many of His disciples drew back and no longer went about with Him" (John 6:66).

Their departure was no mass exodus, like a flock of birds that suddenly leaves a bush or a tree. It was probably more often that Jesus would look at the people who were following Him and notice that one more was missing. Perhaps He would say something, and it was the type of remark that He knew a particular individual would enjoy. But now there was silence because that individual was no longer there. Or maybe He would hear a question, and as He explained the answer, His eyes would search for someone who had asked something similar before. But He would look in vain. The person had left. Perhaps in the evening one or two would be with Him, and the next morning they were gone. They hadn't bothered to explain why or to say thank you or even good-bye. They had simply chosen to go their own way.

A Decision Is Still Required

We don't have to go much further in imagining how the people may have left Him, do we? Who of us has not noted that the place where a particular family or individual always seemed to sit in church has been vacant for the last few Sundays? At a planning committee meeting the question is asked, "Where has so-and-so been lately?" At voters meeting the roll is called, and we realize it's been two or three years since we've last seen someone at the meetings. Perhaps you have heard by the grapevine that a person was offended because someone did something or something happened, and now you no longer see that person around.

It still goes on today, doesn't it? People make a decision, and that decision is to go their own way. They reach the point where it's either Jesus and all that He means or it's taking a path other than the path of discipleship. That other path may not appear to be all bad. It may be good, clean, and moral. But, it's not dedicated to the Lord. It's not a path that's ready to make the sacrifices and commitments that the life of discipleship requires. When the choice is between Jesus and the work-righteousness of some other system, between Jesus and the popularity of the friends that I run around with, between Jesus and success in my business that may come more easily with a couple of shady deals, a decision has to be made. When people seek the pleasures of the physical life and excuse themselves with, "I'm only young once; who's going to condemn me if I sow my wild oats?" they have come to the point of that decision. Regrettably, for many the decision is to go their own way.

There were some, of course, who stayed. Jesus turned to them (perhaps it was a few days later; St. John doesn't give us any time reference) and asked them a question: "Do you also wish to go away?" (v. 67). He was asking, "Have I lost My attraction with you, too? Are My words falling on deaf ears? Were you also only seeking to have your stomach filled, your intellect teased, and your eyes amazed?" St. Peter gave the answer: "Lord, to whom shall we go? You have the words of eternal life; and we have believed and have come to know that You are the Holy One of God" (vv. 68-69).

"Ah," you say, "that's a good answer." But, I'd like to correct you on that. That's the *only* answer that can be given by a disciple of Jesus Christ. "You have the words of eternal life." If there was ever a reason for following Jesus, it isn't the popularity, the ease, the pleasures, the social position, or the profit that some may seek in material things. Believe in Jesus Christ because He is this Word of eternal life. As St. Paul wrote to the Philippians: "I count everything as loss because of the surpassing worth of knowing Christ Jesus my Lord" (Phil. 3:8).

Decisions are not easy to make, and we would grant that. Pascal, the 17th-century French philosopher, hit on a real truth when he said, "Men despise religion, they hate it, and they fear it may be true." Many know what the Gospel teaches. They have made a decision, and they have reached the point where they realize that Christianity can never be a both/ and religion. It can never be both the pleasures of this world — living and looking at things the way this world looks at them and having this world's values — and having Jesus Christ as Lord of your life. It's always a matter of either/or. Jesus Christ is either the Lord of all your life, or He is not Lord at all.

That's the same decision the followers of Jesus made in the Gospel. Some "no longer went about with Him." Others, with St. Peter as their spokesman, asked the simple question, "Lord, to whom shall we go?" They knew the answer. There is no one else. Jesus Christ alone has the words of eternal life. Those who stand with St. Peter have the joy of the assurance of eternal life. Those who choose to walk the other way will inevitably bear the consequences of their decision sooner or later.

I don't know about you. I can't look into your heart. Your relationship with the Lord is just that — your relationship, no one else's. But I can tell you this: If you are troubled by being confronted with the decision to follow the call from Jesus through the Gospel, and if some other call than our Lord's is causing you to turn your gaze and look in another direction, then before you lies the most important decision you will ever make. Today the Lord looks at you and says, 'Do you also wish to go away?" Before you turn away, I pray sincerely that you weigh the facts very carefully.

Cleanliness in God's Eyes

FIFTEENTH SUNDAY AFTER PENTECOST
MARK 7:1-8, 14-15, 21-23

Ronald H. Goodsman

"Cleanliness is next to godliness." Cleanliness is certainly something that we all like to see in one way or another. A housewife might envision it as a house where the children keep their rooms neat. A salesman might think of it in terms of appearance — clothes freshly laundered, pants pressed, shoes shined, and a face aglow with healthiness. We might even think of cleanliness as a desirable quality for the whole nation. We picture Holland with its whitewashed houses gleaming in the sun and its sidewalks and streets swept so clean that one can eat off them. Cleanliness is certainly next to godliness. There is something almost divine about getting rid of all the spots and stains and making something pure.

Our personal standard of cleanliness or purity is very important to each of us. But by our nature we are also concerned about another standard — God's standard. What does it take to be clean before God? What does it mean to be pure in His eyes? How can we sinful humans hope to measure up? To find an answer, today's Gospel from Mark 7 can help. Some Jews were discussing the same question with Jesus. He tells us, just as He told them, what cleanliness in God's eyes really means.

Coming for the Right Reason

"The Pharisees gathered together to Him, with some of the scribes, who had come from Jerusalem" (Mark 7:1). The story that deals with cleanliness in God's eyes begins with people coming to see Jesus. Of course, the gospels are full of stories about people coming to see Jesus. What is important here, however, is not just *that* they came to see Jesus, but *why* they came. We might say that cleanliness in God's eyes begins with coming for the right reason.

Why did these Pharisees and scribes come to see Jesus? We read that "they saw that some of His disciples ate with hands defiled, that is, unwashed" (v. 2). Clearly, when these Pharisees and scribes sought Jesus out, they were not looking for help or comfort or a Savior. They were looking for a chance to accuse. To their evil joy, they witnessed the disciples break a Jewish tradition. They didn't wash their hands according to the Jewish ritual. Never mind that the washing of hands wasn't required by the Bible but by tradition. The Pharisees and scribes had come to Jesus to find fault, and they were pleased with their apparent success.

Before we point a self-righteous finger at these religious hypocrites, however, we need to examine our own cleanliness in God's eyes. Do we come to God for the right reason, or do we also, like the Pharisees and scribes, sometimes come to God in order to find fault? When we come to worship Him in church, do we look for an opportunity to be offended by another member, an usher, or a greeter? Do we scrutinize the liturgy or the hymns to find something to which we may object? Do we listen to a sermon to judge its delivery? Do we look for distractions to justify our lack of attention? All too often we *are* just like the Pharisees and scribes — we come to God in order to find fault with His people!

But there is another way. Cleanliness in God's eyes means, first of all, coming for the right reason. Ironically, just prior to this story in which people come to Jesus to find fault, St. Mark tells of people who came to Jesus for the right reason — to find help. They "began to bring sick people on their pallets to any place where they heard he was. And wherever He came. . . they laid the sick in the market places, and besought Him that they might touch even the fringe of His garment; and as many as touched it were made well" (6:55-56).

People were coming to Jesus for the right reason — to find help and comfort. And it was not just physical help that they sought, but, more important, spiritual help. That's why Jesus offers the greatest help to the paralytic in Mark 2 when He says, "My son, your sins are forgiven" (v. 5), and only later commands, "Rise, take up your pallet and go home" (v. 11). If we want to be clean in God's eyes, we must also come to God for the right reason — to find help. It is really strange how we can carry a problem around for days, somehow forgetting that God is always there to help! As we come for asking for His help, He promises to answer us. The psalmist proclaims, "O Lord, Thou wilt hear the desire of the meek; . . . Thou wilt incline Thy ear" (10:17).

Coming to the Right Source

Unfortunately, just as people can come to God for the wrong reason, people can also listen to the wrong source. We see an example in the Gospel: "The Pharisees and the scribes asked Him, 'Why do Your disciples not live according to the *tradition of the elders* but eat with hands defiled?'" (Mark 7:5 — emphasis added). These Jews really wanted to be pure in God's eyes, but they were listening to the wrong source — the tradition of men.

Many Jews thought that their heritage would make them clean in God's sight. They looked down on all non-Jews as impure. They had even developed this self-righteous attitude into a formal tradition. As St. Mark notes, "The Pharisees, and all the Jews, do not eat unless they wash their hands, observing the tradition of the elders; and when they come from the market place, they do not eat unless they purify themselves; and there are many other traditions which they observe, the washing of cups and pots and vessels of bronze" (vv. 3-4). Whatever was touched by a Gentile — clothes, food, furniture, anything bought at the market — had to be washed according to a special ritual. Otherwise a Jew could become defiled in God's sight. This concern developed into a complicated man-made procedure for washing almost everything, lest they become impure or unclean.

Although that kind of man-made tradition sounds pretty strange today, we are also guilty of the very same thing. That tradition of ritual washings was basically saying, "Jews are better, cleaner, and purer than Gentiles. Stay away from those poor, wretched sinners." We can often see that same attitude of superiority within the walls of Christian churches today. Christ also speaks to us when He says, "You leave the commandment of God, and hold fast the tradition of men" (v. 8). We're a bit uncomfortable with having "sinners" in our midst. After hearing something bad about someone, Christians too often would rather gossip about or ostracize them.

The truth is that anyone who listens to all that gossip is also a "poor, filthy sinner." For cleanliness in God's eyes includes listening to the right source — the Word of God. There we read about our true condition: "We have all become like one who is unclean, and all our righteous deeds are like a polluted garment" (Is. 64:6). Our tendency to find fault and look down on others in itself reflects the fact that we are impure and defiled before God. In that state our future is bleak. The Word of God warns, "Woe to her that is... defiled" (Zeph. 3:1). Borrowing a word from the old Jewish dirges, God pictures us as unclean souls marching to the grave — a pathetic procession passing into the pit.

Listening to the Right Message

We cannot, however, stop our reading of the Word with that fearful message. Cleanliness in God's eyes means not only listening to the right source — God's Word — but listening to its entire message. St. Mark records Jesus' words as the theme of His gospel: "The Son of Man also came not to be served but to serve, and to give His life as a ransom for many" (10:45). He did not come to be served — to be made clean in God's sight. He was already pure, for He was true God. Instead He came "to serve, and to give His life as a ransom for many." Paraphrasing this in our context, we might say that Jesus came to pay the laundry bill — the price necessary to wash us and make us clean in God's eyes.

The price for our cleanliness was quite high. It was death. The Good News is that Jesus Christ has paid the price for you and me on the cross. With His holy precious blood He washes away the stains from our soul. Now we can live in purity and cleanliness before God. That's the Good News of His resurrection from the dead. He died so that we might not die in our filthiness, and He rose so that we might live in cleanliness now before God.

How did those in our text respond to God's Word? Jesus has an unpleasant judgment to make of them: "Well did Isaiah prophesy of you hypocrites, as it is written, 'This people honors Me with their lips, but their heart is far from Me'" (Mark 7:6). He condemned them for giving mere lip service without trusting God in their hearts. He said, "In vain do they worship Me, teaching as doctrines the precepts of men" (v. 7). Although they had heard the Word of God — that Jesus had come to wash away their filthy sin and make them clean again — they rejected it. They responded to the Word with legalistic actions, still trying to make themselves outwardly clean apart from Christ. They resorted to man-made laws pertaining to the outside of man, but not to his inside. They abstained from certain foods and beverages. What they did eat, they washed thoroughly. But they responded only with external actions, never with the heart.

Today Jesus would say to us, "Hear Me, all of you, and understand: There is nothing outside a man which by going into him can defile him" (vv. 14-15). We are not unclean in God's sight because of what we eat or drink. And on the same count, we cannot be made pure before God based on the external things we say or do. Jesus says, "What comes *out* of a man is what defiles a man. For from within, out of the heart of man, come evil thoughts, fornication, theft, murder, adultery, coveting, wickedness, deceit, licentiousness, envy, slander, pride, foolishness. All these evil things come from within, and they defile a man" (vv. 20-23 — emphasis added).

Trusting with the Heart

The heart is the heart of the matter. As goes the heart, so goes our cleanliness. Purity in God's eyes therefore must involve a trusting heart. Cleanliness before God means clinging to the promises of the Word with our heart. Those promises stand firm. Jesus has suffered death to wash away the stain of sin from our souls. Jesus has risen from the dead that we might live in purity before God.

If cleanliness is next to godliness, then Jesus has brought us next to God. He has cleansed us so that we may listen to the right source — not to the snobbery of men, but to the Good News of God. He has cleansed us so that we might come to Him for the right reason — not to find fault with His people, but to find help. He has cleansed us so that we might respond, not in outward legalism, but with a trusting heart. He has cleansed us — forgiven all our sins — so that we might live with Him as our Savior forever in heaven.

Cling to the purity that we have in Jesus! "Come now, let us reason together, says the Lord: through your sins are like scarlet, they shall be white as snow; though they are red like crimson, they shall become as wool" (Is. 1:18).

I Hear and I Speak

SIXTEENTH SUNDAY AFTER PENTECOST
MARK 7:31-37

Ronald H. Goodsman

St. Matthew tells us in general terms that when the Lord Jesus returned from the region of Tyre and Sidon to the Sea of Galilee, "great crowds came to Him, bringing with them the lame, the maimed, the blind, the dumb, and many others, and they put them at His feet, and He healed them" Matt. 15:30). From this multitude of cures St. Mark selects one to relate in detail. It was a deaf man who also had an impediment in his speech, probably being incapable of making articulate or intelligible sounds. Friends brought the man to the Great Physician and "besought Him," as the evangelist tells us, "to lay His hand upon him" (Mark 7:32). But it was not exactly in the way they had imagined that Jesus willed to heal him. He first took the man aside from the multitude and led him out of the village.

Before performing the miracle, the Savior lifted up His eyes to heaven and prayed to His heavenly Father. Then He put His fingers into the man's ears, spit, touched his tongue, and said to him, "Ephphatha," which means "be opened." The man was able to hear, and he spoke plainly. Not only were the powers of hearing and speach restored, but the full use of those powers seems to have been instantaneously conferred. Well might the people say, "He has done all things well" (v. 37).

Whether those who watched drew any further inference as to the character of the One who had worked this strange and complex cure, we are not told. Yet from the silence of the evangelist about any deeper feeling than one of astonishment, we may probably conclude that no deeper feeling or conviction was excited. The real character of Jesus dawned slowly on His contemporaries. Repeated miracles were necessary to gain any hearing whatever for the claims of the Nazarene, and after all His miracles — except the last and most stupendous, His resurrection from the dead — there was always a residue of doubt that showed in the people's desire to see some sign of their own choosing, different from any that He had done.

The people of the Decapolis were really astonished. They were overcome with genuine admiration, but they did not surrender themselves to Him. They did not accept Him as Lord.

An Amazing Miracle

Yes, the people "were astonished beyond measure" (v. 37). They went home talking about what they had seen. They shared with their neighbors the news about the healing powers of Jesus of Nazareth. "He has done all things well," they said. "He even makes the deaf hear and the dumb speak."

I am sure that the man who was healed went home thinking that the greatest miracle in his life had just happened and that nothing could be greater. On that he would be wrong. Our Lord and Savior still had not performed the greatest miracle. That would happen on Easter Sunday when He rose from the dead.

Jesus left the Decapolis and continued His ministry, and His great fame went before Him wherever He went. His ministry contained so many miracles — making the blind to see, the deaf to hear, the dumb to speak, the lame to walk; raising the dead; ministering to all those who came His way;

always reaching out with love and compassion; always having time to stop and listen, to touch and heal, to comfort, and just to be there. "He has done all things well."

He came to the Decapolis, and the man who had been unable to hear could now hear. His tongue was loosed so that he could now speak. At that point he could only hear the general news of the day; the Good News was yet to be proclaimed and heard.

When Jesus healed the man who was paralyzed, He first forgave his sins. Then He healed him. Jesus did this to show what was really important—that a healed body was nothing without a healed soul. This is something we can easily lose sight of. If we go to a hospital or to a sick room, it is so easy to think that the most important thing is to have the disease cured so that the person can again lead a healthy life. That is important, but there is a greater truth, a greater need. The most important thing is that the man be spiritually healed, that his sins be forgiven, that he stand right before God. It was for this purpose that Jesus came. He came that we might have life.

His ministry continued, and His name was known throughout the land. His ministry of healing drew many followers—and many enemies. On Palm Sunday He entered Jerusalem, knowing that His death was ahead of Him. On Maundy Thursday, after praying in Gethsemane, He was betrayed and taken away to be tried and executed. On Good Friday He died on a cross. He had done nothing wrong. He was innocent. He bowed His head and became obedient unto death. even death on a cross. He died as punishment for sin—your sin and mine. He died on a cross so that you and I would not have to. He took my place. He died for me.

He was in the grave for three days, and then the greatest event in the history of the world took place. Jesus Christ rose from the dead! He who was dead is now alive. He lives! He is Risen! He is Risen indeed! This miracle dwarfs all of His other miracles.

The Greatest Miracle

The miracle in the Decapolis region was great, but this one was greater—beyond comparison. In the Decapolis region Jesus healed a man's body; on Calvary He healed the man's soul. The man with a healed body would still have to die. After Calvary the man with a healed soul would live forever.

Once in a hospital a nurse said, "Won't it be great when we find a cure for cancer?" A pastor replied, "Yes, it really will. But then the patient will die from heart trouble or some other disease." The nurse looked a little stunned, but she knew that his statement was true. Then he continued, "But we are part of a group—the holy Christian church—whose leader has given us the cure for death itself. The cure does not come in a bottle of medicine, in a tablet, or in a hypodermic needle. The cure is to be found in the cross where He shed His holy precious blood in innocent suffering and death."

When the Good News of the resurrection of our Savior Jesus Christ was first preached in the area of the Decapolis, imagine the joy of the man who was healed as he heard it. He was now hearing the greatest message an ear can hear because of the miracle of healing performed by Jesus that day. Now he also knew why the Savior had unloosed his tongue: so that he could speak of the things that he had heard, so that he could tell and witness of those things that had been told to him.

The marvel, the wonder, the beauty of all this is that God reaches out to *me* — even to me! He makes *me* to see. He gives *me* the ability to hear. He makes *me* speak. He died, He rose again; He is coming back — all for *me*! As the little hymn says:

> I am so glad that Jesus loves me
> Jesus loves me, Jesus loves me.
> I am so glad that Jesus loves me,
> Jesus loves even me.

That's the neat thing about all of this — He even loves a sinner like me. He "loves even me." I am able to say with the men of the Decapolis, "He has done all things well."

If all of the people in this world were perfect, and I was the only one who was sinful and lost, Jesus Christ would still have gone through all of the suffering and agony of the cross that He did. He would do it for me. He *did* it for me! He even did it for *me*! This is why I follow Him and call Him my Lord and my Savior.

In Jesus Christ I have received forgiveness for all my sins. In Him I have peace with God. It is a gift to me from the gracious hand of a God who loves me. He called me by the Gospel. He enlightened me with His gifts. He keeps me in the faith. "He does all thing well."

I hear the voice of my Savior in His Holy Word. I speak of the things I have heard and seen. I tell of the greatest miracle that has ever happened to me — when He saved my soul by dying to make me whole. That was a true miracle of love and grace.

The Way of the Cross

SEVENTEENTH SUNDAY AFTER PENTECOST
MARK 8:27-35

Hubert F. Beck

Once upon a time there was a Man who laid claim to no possessions. He laid claim to nothing whatever, in fact — not even His life. He was a Man with many enemies who were determined to "put Him in His place," even if that meant putting Him in a grave.

His big advantage over them, though, was simply this: He laid claim to nothing, not even the power to keep them from killing Him, and that simple act really gave Him all power. How could they threaten Him if they could find no handle with which to do so, no way to make Him afraid? No matter what they threatened to do to Him, He brushed it aside as of no consequence. If they threatened to take something away from Him, it was no threat at all, for He didn't claim to possess His life as something valuable in itself. It was His unwillingness to speak of anything as His own that made Him so invulnerable. Where there can be no threat, there is no power.

You recognize the Man of whom we speak. It is Jesus, who holds the center of the Gospel. And He urges us to follow Him on this path of possessing nothing so that we might possess all things. Or, to use His words in today's Gospel, "If any man would come after Me, let him deny himself and take up his cross and follow Me. For whoever would save his life will lose it; and whoever loses his life for My sake and the Gospel's will save it" (Mark 8:34).

Our Problem in Hearing Jesus' Exhortation

Most will agree that those are beautiful words. Christians are united in taking them seriously — at least in theory. But what happens when we are put to the test? Is it not in the hardness of the everyday world that all this seems to turn to dust? How can we claim nothing when our children are hungry or when the poor cry out for bread and we have little more than enough to feed ourselves?

If we could be like Jesus, turning a few loaves into several basketfuls and multiplying a few fish into the feeding of thousands, then we would not need to claim anything for ourselves. So we speak to ourselves when we hear words like these, admiring the beauty of their intent, but denying the possibility of their achievement in the world of our realities.

Yet there the words are, as plain as can be: "If any man would come after Me, let him deny himself and take up his cross and follow Me."

A little thought will clearly tell us that if we were able to follow these words as they are given to us, we would have some major advantages in our everyday living. For example, we would no longer need to be defensive. If we could literally claim nothing, then we would have nothing to defend. That is where Jesus' power lay, as we suggested earlier, and we can see that we too could lay aside all our defensiveness if we claimed nothing to defend! We could give much more willingly to the needy, for we would say that it is as much theirs as it is ours. We would not need to defend it as though our own substance had to be protected from these beggars. Instead, we would see it as a joint possession, to be used for their good as well as our own.

But this simple suggestion already cuts deeply into our consciousness, does it not? We realize that we are a long way from being able to renounce our possessions that easily. If Jesus is our model, He is also our Judge at this point. For He who gave up all things, renouncing even the claim to His life, asks us to follow in the same fashion — and we falter at the very first steps of the journey! We cannot even take our first steps to the cross on which our life is to be given in service to God before we stumble and fall.

Ah, no, there is nothing simple about all this — not in envisioning that Christ calls us to give away our lives and all that is involved in them in service to God and our fellow human beings. It is almost impossible to even comprehend such a total renunciation of all earthly claims in the name of God, who alone has a right to claim our life and our possessions. It seems on the very face of it to be an impossibility, for the moment we did that, we would no longer quite know how to live in a world that seems to *require* us to have food and drink and housing and clothing as possessions if we are to be able to serve others.

Is Jesus misleading us in this command to deny ourselves and follow Him? The world, after all, will press quite another word on us — that it is not merely *desirable* to possess things, but actually *necessary*. So we must at this point decide who speaks truth and who speaks deceit; we must decide between the Word of Jesus and the word of the world.

Let us examine still further the Word of Jesus. (We know the word of the world quite well, do we not? It calls us to obtain possessions and guard them most carefully!) He urges us to "lose our life" for His sake and the Gospel's in order to save it. Is there anything else that our life could gain if we lay claim to nothing? It has been suggested that we could — in fact, we *must* — stop being defensive about our life and goods, thus freeing them up for the use of those around us instead of guarding them only for our own use. What else might we learn from this exhortation?

Does this urging of Jesus not help us also to clarify considerably the most important thing in life? If one is to give up all things in order to follow Jesus, one must clearly know what *is* worth possessing and what needs to be given up, lest it get in the way. Perhaps we can turn that inside out and ask the question this way: What in life would you like to control *you*? Our possessions seem to have this peculiar power to suddenly turn on us and possess us when we think that we possess them. Many people who have a great deal of money have found themselves actually possessed by their money, and those who have possessed great reputations or power have become possessed by the reputation or power that they thought they controlled.

Is this not the very root of our sinfulness — that we do not guard against the idols that would possess us because we are all too willing to let them run our lives so long as they give us ease, pleasure, or whatever it is that we think is important to the fullness of life?

But that is the point of sorting through our lives under the impact of Jesus' exhortation. Are all the things that we have permitted — and even invited — to rule our lives so important that they now claim us? When we must deny ourselves and take up our cross and follow Jesus, do these same possessions chain us to themselves, refuse to turn loose of us, and rule our lives with a frighteningly iron hand from which we cannot gain release?

That is the crux of the matter — a fundamental reason why we must take these words of Jesus with such earnest seriousness. If we do not take them seriously, then the word of the world rules us, and our lives are enslaved to those very things that Jesus calls us away from in order to follow Him.

Jesus, the Crossbearer

Where, then, shall we turn? When the Word of Jesus comes to us in all its power, it calls us from those things that the world has imposed on us as necessary. We hear that Word, but we are held immobile by the needs that the world, which has trapped us in our idolatries, has imposed on us. It seems such a simple thing to just shrug our shoulders and spring free from them when Jesus calls, but instead we find ourselves bound and restrained from the very thing that now sounds to us like the Word of life.

When Jesus indicates the direction that His free renunciation of all things — even life itself — will take *Him*, Peter tries to intervene. Anywhere but Jerusalem, Peter insists, as Jesus turns His face in that direction. Jesus must rebuke Peter forcefully, for this very one, who has just spoken the great confession of Jesus as the Christ, the Anointed One of God, has now become the spokesman for Satan. He wants to stop Jesus from suffering many things, and being rejected by the elders and the chief priests and the scribes, and being killed, and after three days rising again. Jesus' clear vision of His path is the only way that He will travel, and anyone who is a disciple of Jesus must travel it with Him. Anyone who holds back from Jerusalem and the cross can no longer be a disciple of Jesus.

And so the little band of men, now rather dejected — save for Jesus — turns toward the place where the cross will be raised. They see no rhyme or reason in it, for they can see only the way in which the world will lay claim to Jesus and His life. They cannot see at this point how Jesus, in the selfsame moment that the world claims Him on the cross, will claim power over sin and death!

With clear vision Jesus now renounces not only possessions and fame and reputation, but also His very life. But He knows with equal clarity that in this way of the cross He will clear out the idols and false gods that have chained the world to death. It will be a mortal combat, a battle to the death. But if death will die, it must be through the death of the Lord of life, who now sets Himself on the path to where the combat must take place. There is only one path that Jesus will follow, and it will be the path to Golgotha. All who would be His disciples must come there to be with Him.

Our Path Is Now Determined by Jesus

And that brings us full circle back to where we started. If Jesus is our model, He is also our Judge. How can we, caught up by these words and promises of the world and chained to all the idols that make such great promises for our life in the world, gain our freedom?

It is precisely to find this freedom that we must go with Jesus to Golgotha. There we must see Him dying on the cross, not as victim of the world's crassness, but as the carrier of God's grace, the willing offering for the sins of the world. There we must look on Him and see in Him the greatness of God's love, the means by which our chains are snapped free from the idols of this world and we are set before God as forgiven and beloved children of the heavenly Father. There we must see Him not only as model and Judge, but also and above all, as Savior.

Our baptism is this trip to Jerusalem and Golgotha. There the Crucified One, risen again from the dead, names us by His name in the waters. There He claims us as His own, snatching us from the idols that try so hard to hold us, and makes it possible for us again to know God as "Abba — Father." Jesus' Father reveals Himself as *our* gracious Father when we take up the name of Jesus. Our way is the way of the cross, for we are called to it in our baptism. It is the way of renouncing the devil, the world, and our flesh — of renouncing our possessions and even our life itself in the name of and in service to the Father. It is the Spirit's call.

The same Spirit has given us guidance and direction in the Word of grace. How can we, sprung free from the enslaving chains of sin and death in Christ, remain firmly planted on the way of life? The Spirit's Word of life calls to us, and in and through this Word of life, along with the regular feeding at the altar of our Lord on His body and blood, we are kept bonded to the divine presence. We possess all things now as though in possessing them they belong to God and we are merely temporary holders of these earthly things. Whether it be treasures or fame or life itself, all is handled with care, for it all belongs, in the final analysis, to the Giver.

So we hear the Word that binds us to God with His promises, bringing nothing but the confession of our sins, to which is now joined His Word of grace. We come to His altar where we bring nothing of our own except our sins and needs, and He comes into the barrenness of our life with the wealth of His grace and mercy.

Would we be like Jesus? Can we — dare we — take His words seriously about denying ourselves and taking up His cross and following Him? Are they mere visionary words, designed for people stronger than we? Or are they the words for us at this moment, at this point in our path of life?

Go with Jesus to the cross. See there the man who alone among all people renounced all things. In His gracious death see the world's forgiveness offered, and in your baptism and the faith there engendered know again your participation in a dying to the old and a rising to a new way of life. It is yours, for Jesus Himself claims you for His own through the sending of His Spirit. The week stretches before you, a week in which you are called to walk the way of the cross, the way of self-renunciation in the name of Jesus Christ.

It won't be an easy way. It never has been. It wasn't for Jesus, although He willingly went that way. Why should we expect it to be easier for us? Yet in walking it we will find, remarkably enough and quite contrary to all outward appearance, that, hard though it may be, the way of the cross is also the way of life.

The Way of Strength

EIGHTEENTH SUNDAY AFTER PENTECOST
MARK 9:30-37

Hubert F. Beck

One must be prepared for some very strange contrasts with ordinary thinking when one walks the way of Jesus. Last week the Gospel made plain that we must lose our life, give it away, lay no claim to it, be made a pauper over against life and all its treasures, if we would find our life and be saved. That is a hard thing for the ordinary person to swallow. Its truth can be known only by faith.

Today's Gospel does the same thing, but on a different level. It turns everything we would normally think, all our ordinary ways of life, inside out and upside down, telling us that what seems quite apparent is all wrong, and that what does not seem true at all is the deepest kind of truth. Today we are taught that the way of strength is the way of servanthood (Mark 9:35), while the way of seeking power is a way of weakness. How strange a truth can we find? Everything seems turned upside down when we listen to Jesus, and when we follow Him, we see that truth played out in the most unlikely ways. How can weakness be strength — or how can strength be weakness?

The Way of Weakness

Most of us recognize that when people bluster through life, it is rarely a sign of strength. Those who talk big and push people around are often trying to cover up some deep inner insecurities. They are afraid that their weaknesses will become apparent in some humiliating way unless they put on a big show, act tough, and in general make a play for power.

While such blusterers are often quite obvious, it is astonishing to discover how many ways we all play that game. We learn to disguise it so well, however, that we not only fool others much of the time, but we even begin to fool ourselves — which may be the worst part of the whole game. We not only learn to cover up the many little ways we have of pushing people around, of getting our way at the expense of others, and of being sure that we aren't the ones stepped on by the world, but we even learn to justify them.

We have an excuse for every one of our pushes and shoves in life. Sometimes it is plainly set forth as "getting even." At other times it is as simple as "I couldn't help it." But the greatest excuse or justification comes when we say, "That's just human nature," or "Everybody does it, so why shouldn't I?"

Of course, there is truth in that, but that does not excuse such life-styles. It only recognizes and confesses the way sin has ensnarled the whole human race. The truth of the matter is that we do indeed have a strong sense of wanting to gain our own advantage, even if it be at the expense of others. We all search for a place in life from which we can exercise a measure of power, whether that be through accumulating wealth, attaining certain authoritarian positions, or entertaining ambitions regardless of the cost. That makes us all sound ruthless, of course, and we know better than to tip our hand that plainly. For that matter, we are decent enough for the most part to keep undue ruthlessness subdued. We aren't trying to be mean. We just need to get along in life.

All this, of course, is part of trying to make a place for ourselves in life. It is hard enough to get along, and we have to make our own niche, or we soon get left in the dust. We must determine how we fit into life and fight to maintain that place. If it is not harmless, it is at least necessary if we are to survive. Can something so necessary be evil and destructive?

The disciples had fallen into the same trap. "On the way they had discussed with one another who was the greatest" (Mark 9:34). They were trying to find their niche in the hierarchy of people surrounding Jesus. If that sounds strange, it is only because we sometimes try to make the disciples a cut above the average human. Here we find them in our shoes, vying for a place in what they understood to be "the kingdom of God" that Jesus was bringing among them. They also have ambitions and jockey for position.

The Way of Weakness — The Way of Chaos

The problem is that this way does not lead to high position, but to chaos. It creates a jungle within which we must survive instead of a garden where we can live with dignity. The Epistle for today puts it well: "If you have bitter jealousy and selfish ambition in your hearts, do not boast and be false to the truth. This wisdom is not such as comes down from above, but is earthly, unspiritual, devilish. For where jealousy and selfish ambition exist, there will be disorder and every vile practice" (James 3:14-16).

Words like these must be taken seriously. This way of life pits us against one another. It makes the world a battlefield and throws everything into turmoil, even though the battlefield may be gaily decorated, and bright music may cover the sound of the combat. Quite far removed from what God intended, the world has lost its way and swallowed us up in its blindness and self-deceit. How easily we fall into this trap, for to the naked eye it all seems so right even while we recognize that something is wrong about the whole thing.

The Way of Strength

So what is the alternative? "If anyone would be first, he must be last of all and servant of all," Jesus tells us in today's Gospel (v. 35). He takes a child in His arms, telling the disciples that greatness consists in serving the weak and helpless — such as this child. "Whoever receives one such child in My name receives Me; and whoever receives Me, receives not Me but Him who sent Me" (v. 37).

We stop our blustering long enough to nod our heads in agreement —

who would want to argue with Jesus? — and even to pat the child on the head in passing tribute to the wisdom of Jesus' statement. But in our heart of hearts we know that this doesn't sit well with us. It is the way of weakness by every standard of the world. How can a servant be first of all? We know where servants belong, and we know who comes in first in every contest in the world. The words have such a nice ring to them, and we don't really care to tangle with Jesus, but when all is said and done, His words are best ignored if we want to get ahead in the world.

And that, of course, is true. If we want to get ahead *in the world*, we have to disregard these words. But we are not talking about getting ahead *in the world* right now. We are talking about the *kingdom of God* and about the way things *really* are — not the way they seem to be to the naked — the worldly — eye.

So what do we make of Jesus' words if we take them seriously enough to turn them into a life-style? First of all, they do not suggest that we become the great doormats of the world! They have nothing to do with putting yourself down and telling yourself that you are nothing, a nobody, a worthless person who belongs hidden away in a corner, wearing a slave's chains and groveling before the lords of the earth. That kind of picture had no place in the life of the Chief Servant, whose own ministry determines the meaning of His assertion. When He says earlier, "The Son of Man will be delivered into the hands of men, and they will kill Him," He is not telling His disciples that He is a weak and spineless man who knows nothing about defending Himself and that all the lords of Jerusalem will be able to destroy Him mercilessly because of His weakness. That would be a terrible distortion of the words.

Those are words of power and strength. They are the words of a person who knows Himself very well and has set a path for Himself to walk. They are the words of a man who has decided in His strength to give Himself into death for the sins of the world. No person will be able to force Him to do what He does not want to do, but He undertakes His mission because His will is in conformity with the will of the Father, who has bidden Him come to die. That is His task and He will do it with strength.

He came to be the Chief Servant so that the orders of the world could be overturned and men and women could find their strength in Him from whom they came and to whom they must return. In this singular act Christ made possible freedom from everything that enslaves God's fallen world so that it can again know and serve the Father. That is not an act of weakness, but of strength — by no means an act of seeking His own glory, but of giving it up that He might take on Himself the weakness of our mortality and become a participant in our death. It was for this that He came into the world, and He did what was given Him with all the strength at His command.

To this clear-cut statement of Jesus' anticipation of His death and resurrection St. Mark adds, "But they did not understand the saying, and they were afraid to ask Him" (v. 32). Perhaps he added that for our comfort, for we also have a hard time grasping how one can make a strength out of weakness, how a cross can be turned into the salvation of mankind, and how the resurrection can be God's affirmation of the strength that issues from self-imposed weakness and service.

The way to which Jesus points us, however, is a way of self-knowledge and strength. It requires — as does the way of the world — that we have a reasonable knowledge of our capabilities — a self-inventory, so to speak. For if we try to do what God has not made us capable of doing, it is like beating air. We may exert a lot of energy, but not much of anything results. The way of strength in humility lies in knowing the gifts that have been given us by the heavenly Father and sizing up how they fit in with the opportunities that surround us. All these things are not strange to the world, and if we are serious about understanding our place in life, we will not find the way strange to this point.

But now comes the strange crook in the road — the place where we choose the way of weakness or the way of strength. The question is simple: Will these gifts, given us within the basic framework of the opportunities that surround us, be used in our own behalf or in behalf of others? If we decide that they are to be used basically and primarily in our own behalf, we start creating the corpses of those over whom we will climb in the ascent to that pinnacle to which the world beckons us. That is really the way of weakness, for it is in many respects the easiest way, the way to which we are bidden by others who climb the same way and with whom we must engage in feverish competition. That is what makes the way *seem* difficult, for it knows nothing of love or compassion but must struggle so much to get nowhere.

Why is the other way, the way of using our gifts in behalf of others, the way of strength? Because it means bending all gifts away from ourselves toward those who are as weak and helpless and in need like the little child whom Jesus sets in the midst of them. "Whoever receives one such child in My name receives Me" (v. 37). These are the words with which Jesus impresses on us the need to receive the needy and helpless and to serve them, for *this* is the way to greatness. If the disciples want to discuss who is greatest among them, they must discuss who is most willing to serve this child and others like it. This means that we must lay aside any goal of personal ambition or self-aggrandizement and seek the welfare of others.

Three things stand out, then, if we are to be serious about hearing Jesus' words to the disciples and to us: "If anyone would be first, he must be last of all and servant of all" (v. 35). Servants who follow Jesus are ready to *give* themselves away to those who are like this little child. To give is very different from having ourselves wrestled away from us, for if that happened, strength would be to keep what we have, and weakness would be to have it wrestled away. But to *give* ourselves to others implies that we have moved from the very real possibility of using our gifts for our own good to the position of freely giving them away to others. That is an act of strength, not weakness.

Servants who follow Jesus are ready to give *themselves* away to those who are like this child. We know that we do not really own our lives, for we have received them from God and will return to Him. If this is true in the sense of creation (we have been made by God and thus belong to Him), it is doubly true in the work of Christ, who clearly says, "The Son of man will be delivered into the hands of men, and they will kill Him; and when He is killed, after three days He will rise" (v. 31). Not only have we been created by God, but we have been redeemed in the gracious work of Jesus Christ. God has descended into the fire that would devour us and has rescued us in His Son so that we are His twice over. And having rescued us, He gave us back to ourselves, so to speak, that we might freely serve Him. He has no shackles on us — no strings to make us dance like puppets. We give ourselves into His service gladly, and He gives us to our neighbors like the child He set in their midst, saying, "Whoever receives one such child in My name receives Me; and whoever receives Me, receives not Me but Him who sent Me" (v. 37).

Servants who follow Jesus are ready to give their *whole* selves away to those who are like this little child. We do not merely give small tokens — the small change of our lives — to the neighbor while we climb the great mountain of success ourselves. We are not called to give just a few moments, a hand or a foot, a passing word of concern. What Jesus calls for in today's Gospel is the commitment of our entire person — body, soul and spirit, all that we are and possess — to the welfare of those around us. When Jesus gave His very *self* for humankind, He went with everything given Him to the cross. No merely spiritual cross will ever do to save mankind. Here we must behold the Man, Jesus, dying with the burden of the world's sins to understand the magnitude of the sacrifice — or to understand the strength of the gift. And we are called to give in the same way.

The Way of Jesus

When Jesus gave Himself as a gift of strength, He knew full well how immense the cost would be. Like Jeremiah of old, whose words of horror at the plot directed against his life as a prophet of God were the Old Testament Reading today, Jesus went this difficult road in the spirit that says, "To Thee have I committed my cause" (Jer. 11:20).

In the same spirit we commit our cause to the Lord. We take up the strength of our life and submit it to those around us simply because in our baptism we "put on" the Lord Jesus Christ. The strength and encouragement and renewal of His Word has surrounded us, and His body and blood feed our bodies and spirits with that food by which we are enabled to move from strength into the weakness that is the strength of God. For this is the way of Jesus Christ.

Dealing with Disunity in the Church

NINETEENTH SUNDAY AFTER PENTECOST
MARK 9:38-50

Bruce J. Lieske

A Christian leader described a sad event that happened between two Christian friends. One friend claimed that she had been defrauded by the other in a business deal. The Christian leader wrote to the woman, agreed that she had apparently been defrauded, but advised her that according to 1 Cor. 6 Christians are not to take fellow Christians to court. He suggested that she withdraw her civil suit and settle the matter through Christian mediation.

But the woman was influenced by her non-Christian lawyer and went to court. The judge ruled in her favor, granting her a $30,000 settlement. The defendant was unable to pay and went into bankruptcy. The woman received absolutely nothing except unfavorable publicity and a bill from her lawyer for $24,000.

How do we deal with disunity in the church in order to avoid the tragic consequences that occur when a quarrel runs its course? First of all let us consider some *causes* of disunity.

Causes of Disunity in the Church

There are many causes for disunity in the church. Among them are the three deadly *D*s: differences of opinion, disputes about words, and disobedience to God.

In today's Gospel the disciples had a *difference of opinion* with the man who was casting out demons in the name of Jesus. John speaks for the rest of the disciples when he tells the Lord, "We forbade him, because he was not following us" (Mark 9:38). Obviously the unknown exorcist was a Christian, because he cast out demons in Jesus' name. But he was not doing it their way. The disciples had a firm opinion as to how exorcisms should be done. So they forbade him to do any more exorcisms.

Frequently Christians find themselves in a dilemma. There are two different opinions about how something should be done. How do you reconcile them? Maybe you can't! There is a story about a hippopotamus that fell in love with a butterfly. The hippo related his problem to an oracle. The oracle thought about it for an hour or so and then told the hippo to turn himself into a butterfly. The hippo went off deliriously happy—until he discovered he didn't know how to turn himself into a butterfly. So he rushed back to the oracle and said, "I don't know how to turn myself into a butterfly." The oracle replied, "Well, that's your problem. I just make policy; I don't carry it out." The point is, not all differences of opinion can be reconciled, any more than a hippopotamus can turn himself into a butterfly.

The answer is *tolerance*. Jesus replied to John, "Do not forbid him; for no one who does a mighty work in My name will be able soon after to speak evil of Me" (v. 39). Jesus asks us to tolerate those of different opinions when no sin is involved. Paul challenges us to be' forbearing one another in love, eager to maintain the unity of the Spirit in the bond of peace" (Eph. 4:2-3).

The second deadly *D* is *disputing about words*. We read frequently that negotiations between labor and management break down because of disagreements about the language in the contract. Church history abounds with examples of Christians who argued themselves apart — even though their doctrinal beliefs were identical. Paul counsels Timothy: "Charge them before the Lord to avoid disputing about words, which does no good, but only ruins the hearers" (2 Tim. 2:14). When a dispute gets going, our human tendency is to run around (or telephone around) and tell everybody why we take a certain position. That is not God's wisdom. God says: "Let every man be quick to hear, slow to speak, slow to anger" (James 1:19).

The third deadly *D* is *disobedience to God*. Sin causes disunity in the church. The call document that a congregation gives to its pastor says: "We authorize and obligate our called minister. . . to admonish the indifferent and the erring." That is difficult work.

Actually, every Christian is responsible to admonish those who fall into sin. *How* you do that is crucial. You can do it self-righteously, or you can do it in love. "Brethren, if a man is overtaken in any trespass, you who are spiritual should restore him in a spirit of gentleness" (Gal. 6:1). Our purpose is to *restore* the erring brother or sister, not to posture ourselves as righteous. We are to "be kind to one another, tenderhearted, forgiving one another, as God in Christ forgave you" (Eph. 4:32).

The apostle John was *not* tolerant of the unknown exorcist, nor did he attempt to correct him in a spirit of gentleness. That may well describe our own improper approach to troubled relationships.

Take the Problem to Jesus

We pray for good weather, for health, and for the safety of our children. But we often neglect to take those painful disputes to Jesus in prayer. John took the dispute to Jesus, and the hymn writer urges us to do the same:

> What a Friend we have in Jesus, All our sins and griefs to bear!
> What a privilege to carry Everything to God in prayer!
> Oh, what peace we often forfeit, Oh, what needless pain we bear,
> All because we do not carry Everything to God in prayer! (*TLH* 457:1)

As we stand before the cross of Jesus, knowing that He died for all our sins, we no longer need to rationalize about who was right and who was wrong. Our self-justifying arguments must disappear. Jesus knows us as we really are. He died for us while we were yet arguing with somebody, even though we were intolerant, and before we forgave anybody anything. What a friend we have in Jesus! Even though we have destroyed a friendship or injected disharmony into the church by careless speech, He is still our friend. The arms of the crucified Savior reach out in love to forgive those who hold angry clenched fists.

Place yourself— and your dispute— in the presence of Jesus. He loved His enemies, talked constantly with them, wept for them, and eventually died for them. He is not only your Lord and Savior, He is Lord of the church. He bought the church with His own precious blood. He has more of a vested interested in the church than we do. Let Him be Lord of His own church. Let Him— by the power of the Holy Spirit— mediate disputes when they arise.

Do Something Positive!

Jesus next gives us an unusual example: "For truly, I say to you, whoever gives you a cup of water to drink because you bear the name of Christ, will by no means lose his reward" (Mark 9:41). What does this mean in the context of dealing with disunity in the church?

A cup of cold water given to another Christian with whom you have a dispute isn't much, but it is a step forward. That "cup of cold water" might be as complex as agreeing to Christian mediation, or as simple as talking person-to-person with the one with whom you disagree.

God expects us to talk to those people with whom we have disputes. How many times have we heard people say, "So-and-so is not on speaking terms with so-and-so"? Maybe you have been in that situation. God says, "If your brother sins against you, go and tell him his fault, between you and him alone" (Matt. 18:15). That type of communication is painful, un-natural, and difficult, but it is a way of giving "a cup of water" to your brother who bears the name of Jesus Christ.

Rather than do something positive to heal a dispute within the church, we may be tempted to do nothing— to let the quarrel run its course. Consider from God's perspective the scandal of disputes in the church. First of all, they confuse and damage the faith of the "little ones"— whether those little ones be children or adults who are weak in their faith. That is why Jesus said, "Whoever causes one of these little ones who believe in Me to sin, it would be better for him if a great millstone were hung round his neck and he were thrown into the sea" (Mark 9:42).

When I was a young teenager, my congregation became involved in a dispute over whether the ladies guild should buy an electric potato masher for the church kitchen. Our normally peaceful congregation became polarized into the pro-potato masher group and the anti-potato masher group. As a young man just learning the things of God, I became dis-illusioned with the people who were to be my guides in Christ. Fortunately, the dispute was resolved quickly.

The offensiveness of sin, especially the sin of disputing in the church, is vividly portrayed by Jesus. Hands, feet, or eyes that cause sin are to be *removed* rather than have sin continue. Jesus is here utilizing a rhetorical device called *hyperbole*— purposeful exaggeration— in order to make a point. The point is that sin offends God and harms others and must be dealt with by positive action.

God has acted in a positive way toward the sin of the world. His justice demands a punishment for sin. But His love gives protection and care — even for the sinner. And so He sent His Son, Jesus, to die on the cross, to bear the burden of our guilt. God could not remain silent. He could not let sin just take its course. Because of His love for us He intervened in the dispute between Him and us. He did something positive. The Father sent the Son; the Son was obedient; and the Son "bore our sins in His body on the tree" (1 Peter 2:24).

The world finds it impossible to get along with itself. Wars, lawsuits, slander, and revenge are the unhappy norm. God has called us out of such darkness into the light of Jesus. He wants us to be different, unique — to be *salt*. He says, "Salt is good; but if the salt has lost its saltness, how will you season it? Have salt in yourselves, and be at peace with one another" (Mark 9:50).

Christians do not always get along perfectly this side of heaven. Is there disunity between you and some other Christian — or perhaps within our own congregation? First consider whether it is a difference of opinion, a dispute about words, or disobedience to God. Second, like the apostle John, take the problem to Jesus. Then, standing in His presence, decide to do something positive — to take that cup of water to the person who has offended you.

Brothers and sisters in Christ, God gives us the right to choose our friends. But *He* chooses our brothers and sisters in Christ. We will spend eternity together. There will be no tears and no pain in heaven. But there are tears, pain, and thirst here. *Now* is the time to give that cup of cold water to the person with whom you have the dispute. Now is the time to dry his tears. Now is the time to ease his pain.

Dealing with Disunity in Marriage

TWENTIETH SUNDAY AFTER PENTECOST
MARK 10:2-16

Bruce J. Lieske

Most policemen would agree that one of the most dangerous calls they can respond to is a domestic quarrel. Policemen, ambulance drivers, or friends who try to resolve such quarrels sometimes place their lives in danger. Many of the Christmas cards that we will be receiving in a few weeks will say "Peace on earth." That makes us think of the wars we have known — the Vietnam War, the Middle East, and others. But the real wars that affect everybody are found in homes — in marriages.

Disunity in Marriage Offends God

Disunity in marriage offends God. The ultimate disunity in marriage is divorce. Not only are the emotional pain, guilt, and financial cost of divorce heavy burdens to bear, but God condemns divorce when He says, "What therefore God has joined together, let not man put asunder" (Mark 10:9).

The problem of marital disunity — and divorce — is ancient. Even in the time of Moses over 3,000 years ago provision was made for divorce, although it was not in God's original plan. People have tried to justify and rationalize it theologically, as did the Pharisees, but God's Word is clear: "Whoever divorces his wife and marries another, commits adultery against her; and if she divorces her husband and marries another, she commits adultery" (vv. 11-12). Divorce is contrary to the will of God; it is sin.

Divorce — all disunity in marriage — harms the children of that marriage. Jesus said, "Let the children come to Me, *do not hinder them*; for to such belongs the kingdom of God" (v. 14 — emphasis added). Sociological studies of children from divorced families consistently show that the children are harmed — *hindered* — in many ways by broken homes.

Quarreling, looks of hatred, and the sulking that come with marital disunity confuse children and harm them emotionally. These things are unrighteousness. They are bad news for everybody. But there is also Good News in God's Word: "If we confess our sins, He is faithful and just, and will forgive our sins and cleanse us from all unrighteousness" (1 John 1:9). Although marital disunity harms our children and offends God, what sweet comfort it is to know that the shed blood of Jesus on Calvary's cross has taken away our guilt in the eyes of God. Forgiven by God and enabled by His Spirit, we can begin to deal with the disunity that we find in our marriages.

Male and Female

First we need to note the differences between men and women. Those differences are the Creator's design. Attempts to blur them through any kind of unisex philosophy or legitimization of homosexuality are rank criticisms of God Almighty. Men and women are different physically and emotionally — by design. And we must praise God for His wisdom. "God made them male and female" (v. 6).

We can joyfully affirm maleness and femaleness in marriage. A husband pleases God by doing and saying things that make his wife feel like a woman. That might mean a positive comment on her appearance or purchasing an item of clothing of the right size, style, and color for her. A wife pleases God when she does and says things that make her husband feel like a man. That might mean complimenting him for making a good decision or being responsive to his sexual needs. Jesus reaffirmed that "God made them male and female." Let us also affirm that!

Commitment to One Another

Marriage means commitment. "For this reason a man shall leave his father and mother and be joined to his wife" (v. 7). Marriage can be defined as a public, total, lifelong commitment to a person of the opposite sex. A living-together arrangement is not the same as marriage. It may be public, and it may have many similarities to marriage—even some kind of commitment—but it does not involve the same measure of commitment—and risk—that marriage has. Living-together arrangements with limited commitments stand condemned by God: "Let marriage be held in honor among all, and let the marriage bed be undefiled; for God will judge the immoral and adulterous" (Heb. 13:4).

Commitment to your spouse means *leaving* your father and mother. Jesus quoted Genesis 2 when he said, "For this reason a man shall leave his father and mother and be joined to his wife' (v. 7). Marriage, according to God's design, entails leaving your parents, both physically and psychologically. What do we mean by a psychological leaving of your parents? It does not mean that Mom and Dad are never consulted for advice. It means that a husband should not expect his wife to be like his mother, or a wife expect that her husband be like her father.

For example, if my mother always packed my father's suitcase before a trip, I might expect my wife to do the same. But what if my wife's father always packed his own bags? In no way will she think she must do this for me. In marriage there must be a psychological leaving of the parents as well as a physical leaving. Marriage is the creation of a unique, new family unit, independent of the two sets of parents.

The Two Shall Become One

God said of marriage, "The two shall become one flesh" (v. 8). This means there must be communication in marriage—speaking precisely and listening carefully to one another. The classic example of imprecise speaking is the pastor who stood before the young couple he had just married and said: "It is kisstomary to cuss the bride."

Imagine this scene: Two days before Thanksgiving the wife rushes off to work and tells her husband to "get the turkey out of the freezer." But suppose he does not listen carefully and hears her say, "Get moving, you turkey!" On Thanksgiving eve when it is time to prepare the turkey, there will be both a frozen bird and a frigid relationship.

Oneness in marriage means much more than good general communication. It means intimacy. Adam and Eve were naked in the Garden of Eden. It was only after they had sinned that they felt the need to cover themselves. Sinful human nature wants to hide from God, cover up from Him, get away from Him because it does not want Him to discover sin. God understands our shame and He provides. Our hearts are warmed when we read that "the Lord God made for Adam and for his wife garments of skins, and clothed them" (Gen. 3:21). Blood was shed; an animal was killed; and Adam and Eve had clothing to cover their nakedness.

Jesus, the Lamb of God, was sacrificed on the cross; His blood was shed for us; and as a result we can wear His righteousness. "For as many of you as were baptized into Christ have put on Christ" (Gal. 3:27). God knows you intimately, understands the shame of your sin, and has provided a covering for your sin—Jesus!

The intimacy that we can have with God in Christ has its human counterpart in marriage. Deep within each one of us is the need to be open, to be honest, to share. But in this world of sin that is almost impossible. Marriage is God's provision to meet that need— the opportunity for a person to be completely known by another person and *still be loved*.

Marriage is patterned after God's love for mankind. Jesus Christ is the Bridegroom and the church is the bride. The church, the bride of Christ, is not perfect. The remarkable thing is that Christ chose her even though He knew she was not pure. She was chosen because He loved her. She was purchased by the death of her husband-to-be on the cross. Jesus Christ loved her with an infinite love before she ever loved Him. "While we were yet sinners Christ died for us" (Rom. 5:8). God's design for marriage is that a husband love his wife the same way that Christ loved the church. Love like this builds unity. But love that perfect is rare, perhaps impossible on this earth.

So many issues can divide marriages. The two greatest problem areas are money and sex. It may sound chauvinistic but a wife needs financial security. A husband should manage the family resources so that he can give his wife that financial security. Every marriage needs a budget, a planned financial program. That budget should not express the selfishness of the man, but rather the love of a husband for his wife. A family budget that generously provides adult toys for him but does not provide for her needs is not what God intended.

Sexual problems can divide a marriage. God says: "The husband should give to his wife her conjugal rights, and likewise the wife to her husband" (1 Cor. 7:3). That is not happening in many marriages the way God planned it. You may ask yourself, How does he know? Everything else in God's plan gets disrupted by the devil and human sin, so why not sexuality in marriage—the very thing that should most beautifully express marital intimacy?

Television comedians joke about wives who are frigid. There is no humor in this. Why *are* some married women frigid? We can suggest two reasons, and in both instances the sexual life needs to come under the forgiving, redeeming love of Jesus Christ. A wife may be frigid because she has unresolved guilt about sexual experiences before marriage. She may attempt to resolve that guilt by *denying* her sexuality— an improper resolution of the problem. We cannot solve our problems of guilt by what we do. There must be repentance for what was done before marriage. All sins of sex can be placed under the shed blood of Christ. Claim God's promises of forgiveness! "There is therefore now no condemnation for those who are in Christ Jesus" (Rom. 8:1).

A wife may be frigid not because of her guilt, but because of fear — fear that her husband will once again use her as an object rather than love her as a person. If this is the case, it is not the wife but *the husband* who should repent for treating his wife like a prostitute. And again, God in His Word promises total forgiveness. "Do not be deceived; neither the immoral, nor idolaters, nor adulterers ... will inherit the kingdom of God. *And such were some of you.* But you were washed, you were sanctified, you were justified in the name of the Lord Jesus Christ and in the Spirit of our God" (1 Cor. 6:9-11 — emphasis added).

We are living in the last days. St. Paul, writing to Timothy, describes the last days as "times of stress." He says, "Men will be lovers of self, lovers of money, proud, arrogant, abusive, disobedient to their parents, ungrateful, unholy, inhuman" (2 Tim. 3:1-3). We do live in unholy and inhuman times. Television soap operas preach adultery and easy divorce. Pornographic movies feed lust and make of women mere objects, rather than persons to be loved. That is inhuman.

All of these things pour their poison into marriages. But Christians are working hard at marriage today, trusting God, claiming His promises of forgiveness and help — and they are succeeding! God joins man and woman together in marriage. And He can rejoin them when marital unity disintegrates. God, who raises the dead, can not only heal a sick marriage, but He can resurrect a dead marriage — in the name of Jesus.

Impossibilities Made Possible

TWENTY-FIRST SUNDAY AFTER PENTECOST
MARK 10:17-27 (28-30)

Steven H. Albers

To take a passage of Scripture out of the context in which it is written is to play fast and loose with what God wants to reveal to us through His Word. That is a most dangerous game to play. Yet many people do it with abandon.

An Impossible Word

Jesus' promise in today's Gospel that "all things are possible with God" (Mark 10:27) is a primary victim. People have used that verse of Scripture for virtually every desire imaginable. They use it in the hope of having one of their loved ones healed from an incurable (from human perspective) disease. They use it in the hope for additional material blessings. A TV preacher sent out the call to gather $1,000,000 per day for seven days and then put the burden squarely on the shoulders of the almighty God, because "with God all things are possible." Incredibly, one of the four men who assassinated Anwar Sadat in 1981 said in an interview,

"We knew it would be difficult to pull off, but we believed in what we were doing, and 'with God all things are possible.'"

No! A thousand times no! Resist every temptation to list our material and emotional desires and demands for happiness and wholeness and then believe that God will respond accordingly because "with Him all things are possible." No wonder that we are so often disappointed and even disillusioned in matters of faith when we don't get what we want. Quite frankly, most of what we want and think we need *is* impossible for God to give to us because *He* knows better than we do what we need for happiness and wholeness.

Let's make a further observation on the nature and use of this text before getting into it *in its context*. Some people resist the study of Scripture because, among other reasons, they fear being grasped by the call and claims of God. They approach His Word cautiously and suspiciously, desperately trying to keep it at arm's length. Such a person would approach this particular one and suggest, "Well, Jesus is not talking about me; I'm not rich!" Aren't we wealthy? Who says? And by whose standards? Ours? That's not fair. Let the Third World nations set the criteria for wealth, or people in the ghettos, or those out of work, or people whose stomachs growl not just for a midmorning snack but as they lie in bed at night, too.

No! A thousand times no! Resist also the temptation to keep this Word of our Lord at arm's length, as if He were not talking to us when He says, "How hard it will be for those who have riches to enter the kingdom of God!" (v. 23). For surely He is.

An Impossible Demand

Jesus continues: "It is easier for a camel to go through the eye of a needle than for a rich man to enter the kingdom of God" (v. 25). Wealth is involved here; we certainly cannot deny that. Perhaps this is His way of telling us in absolute terms that money, especially large sums of it, is no key to happiness and certainly no guarantee of problem-free living. Rather, it is often the greatest stumbling block to a rich faith and trust in the Savior of us all.

Trust is so important — that is, an absolute and unwavering *dependence* on the Father, who gives us all that we ever need for daily life. But those who have so much at their fingertips, those who — with some restraints, I suppose — are capable of getting what they want when they want it, have trouble with such things as humble trust and dependence.

When Jesus Christ tried to push the rich young man past the obvious and superficial implications of the Law into full discipleship, which consistently trusts God for strength and sustenance, the man couldn't be budged. His life-style was simply too compelling. "Sell what you have," Jesus says, "and give to the poor, and you will have treasure in heaven; and come, follow Me" (v. 21). Was this only a flair for the dramatic? Could Jesus be serious? Should we take Him at His word?

Why not? Is this Word any different from any other Word of the Lord? If a message like this is necessary for us to switch gears regarding matters spiritual, then so be it. There's an urgency of dependence involved here. The young man sensed it, but he didn't have the spiritual fortitude and faith to say, "My Lord and my God!"

"Sell what you have, and give to the poor. . . . and come, and follow Me." But that's impossible, we counter. And it is — just as impossible as it is for people of means (and remember by whose standards we determine wealth) whose heart and soul is tied to the material to enter the kingdom of God. The enticement of the world's treasures is so powerful that it is impossible for all of us to resist all of the time. We just can't do it.

But sin is still sin, including the sin of having too much and wanting still more or the sin of having so much and giving away so little of it. And sin makes being saved also impossible.

God's Impossible Salvation

Now we can use today's Gospel in its rightful perspective. For with people it is impossible to be saved from sinful preoccupation with self, but not with God. As a *free* — how ironic — and loving gift, our gracious God has focused our eyes and hearts away from ourselves and our presumed needs toward the cross of Christ.

To behold the matchless love made real through the suffering, sacrificial Savior, Jesus, is a humbling experience. To imagine that God would care for us *that* much is unfathomable — but real. And just as we would not be able to believe this impossibility made possible, were it not for the Spirit of God who dwells within us, neither did the disciples.

Faith has never been one of humankind's greatest qualities. The most beautiful scenario is acted out in the verses immediately following the conversation and confrontation between Jesus and the rich young man. Repeated often throughout Scripture, Jesus tells His disciples, "Behold, we are going up to Jerusalem; and the Son of Man will be delivered to the chief priests and the scribes, and they will condemn Him to death, and deliver Him to the Gentiles, and they will mock Him, and spit upon Him, and scourge Him, and kill Him, and after three days He will rise" (vv. 33-34).

Such love! The impossible has been made possible! We are forgiven, and we are free! We are forgiven for our lives of self-service. We are free for lives of service to people whom God places before us and around us. We are forgiven for our desperate efforts to depend on ourselves for happiness and wholeness. We are free to depend on the God of might and mercy. We are forgiven for shallow, superficial expressions of discipleship. We are free for humble obedience to the call and claims of Christ. Forgiveness and freedom — impossible for *us* to achieve or attain — are ours as precious gifts from God, with whom all things are possible.

The great Festival of the Reformation is not far hence. The fourth stanza of Luther's mighty hymn of the Reformation powerfully expresses the faithful determination to follow our Savior, whatever that may involve:

> The Word they still shall let remain
> Nor any thanks have for it;

He's by our side upon the plain
With His good gifts and Spirit.
And take they our life,
Goods, fame, child, and wife,
Though these all be gone,
Our victory has been won;
The Kingdom ours remaineth (*LW* 298:4).

The Art of Followership

TWENTY-SECOND SUNDAY AFTER PENTECOST
MARK 10:35-45

Steven H. Albers

When it is said that an organization has "too many chiefs and not enough Indians," the inference is that there are too many people standing around and advising how a certain project should be done and not enough people willing to do the sometimes thankless tasks that are necessary for that project to be successfully completed. How effective would a quarterback be if he had a flabby front line? What stature would the president of the United States hold if there were no people to govern? Such an organization — including the organized church — would be wise to prepare for an early demise. Today's Gospel calls us to follow — to roll up our sleeves and assume the anonymous but necessary tasks of ministry in the name and to the glory of our Lord Jesus Christ.

The Desire to Be First

James and John wanted to be chiefs. They said to Jesus, "Teacher, we want You to do for us whatever we ask of You" (Mark 10:35). How presumptuous! Yet they were sincere in their request. They were also way out of line. What a horrible misconception of the situation! What a dreadful relationship they wanted with their Master! They were asking Jesus to fit into *their* plans. They had no thought at all of fitting into His.

Still, Jesus played along. "What do you want Me to do for you?" He asked them (v. 36). And so they came out with it: "Grant us to sit, one at Your right hand and one at Your left, in Your glory" (v. 37). Incredibly arrogant, wouldn't you say? Can we imagine the unmitigated gall of those two supposed friends of Jesus? It's amazing what human nature comes up with when it turns a deaf ear to the Word of Christ. Just a few verses earlier in this chapter Jesus had told the disciples, "Many that are first will be last, and the last first" (v. 31). The disciples missed the point then, and they miss it here again.

So Jesus must pursue the matter further: "Are you able? Are you able to pay the price for that degree of glory? Are you able to drink the cup that I drink — the cup of agony, of suffering and death? Are you able to be baptized with the baptism of conflict, crisis, and confrontation with evil?"

Although they didn't know it at the time, their response, "We are able" (v. 39), would prove prophetic. Both were destined to become martyrs for the faith. They are part of that great procession of the faithful who drank of the cup of suffering and death. But Jesus had something more immediate in mind. For they were about to shrink from an imminent crisis, namely, the crisis of the cross, from which they would flee in fear for their lives.

The other 10 were indignant. But one wonders whether their anger was righteous or the result of envy. Their real fear may have been that they were being outwitted. They didn't want to be maneuvered out of something that they coveted for their own possession.

Jesus, who reads the hearts of all people, knew that none of the disciples had yet learned the art of followership. And so He said it again — patiently, perceptively, and lovingly: "Whoever would be great among you must be your servant, and whoever would be first among you must be slave of all. For the Son of Man also came not to be served but to serve, and to give His life as a ransom for many" (vv. 43-45).

The Gospel Relationship

To learn what the art of followership is and what it is not, we must first look inward. There we see attitudes and actions, behaviors and life-styles that are often narrowly focused on getting out of life what we want and getting it when we want it. God must fit into our schedules, not we into His.

The blatant demand of James and John has a familiar ring to it: "Jesus, we want You to do for us whatever we ask of You." We want prosperity and prominence, satisfaction and security. And, Lord, don't put any roadblocks or setbacks in our way. Don't get us upset. Don't throw our lives into a turmoil. Don't make us suffer. Don't interrupt our schedules.

Incredibly, we've inverted the order of our relationship with God. The proper situation is that we are the followers, and God is the leader; we are the Indians, and God is the chief.

It's ironic that James and John wanted something for nothing when in reality the Kingdom that they wanted was theirs for nothing all along. It is a free gift of God through Jesus Christ. The Son of Man came not to be served but to serve and to give His life as a ransom for many. That's the Gospel, purely and simply. Not only did Jesus Christ willingly and freely give up His rights as God, forfeiting His pomp and power, but He also rolled up His sleeves and became involved in the business of meeting the needs of people. He even gave up His very life as a ransom for us all. He became captive to suffering and death in our place He did it for you and for me.

The life, death, and resurrection of Jesus Christ has given us the silver platter we've always wanted — happiness, fulfillment. peace. His Gospel words flow so beautifully and become such a breath of fresh air in this world of demands and rights and desires: "The Son of Man also came not to be served but to serve, and to give His life as a ransom for many" (v. 45).

Becoming Followers

The art of followership begins with Jesus Christ's own selfless love and life. That's a tough act to follow. And yet that is precisely His challenge to us. He is calling us out of the passive into the active. Passively, we are loved before we love. We are served before we serve. But to remain passive, Jesus warns, is the surest way to miss life's greatest possibilities and opportunities. That's what those who seek greatness do; they remain passive; they like to be waited on and served. Real greatness is the direct opposite. Real greatness is service — humble and willing ministry to people's needs, whatever they may be.

Before the week is over, All Saints Day will have come and gone. That is a day to remember all those men and women who have preceded us in faith and who now enjoy the lasting reward of their faithfulness — life forever in heaven. When we join them, it will be interesting to see who really will be sitting at the right hand of the Father. This text suggests that not only will Martin Luther and the apostles — Paul and Peter and James and John and all the rest — be there, but also those countless people who lived their lives on this earth without notice by anyone but God — people who ungrudgingly, faithfully, patiently, and actively served others without fanfare, without fuss, and without any guarantee of acknowledgement or gratitude. These are the people who rolled up their sleeves and did the thankless tasks simply and solely because they dared to care about others.

Such people are also a tough act to follow. But if we couldn't, God would never have said that we must. So He has given us those lovely saints as examples, just as He has given us this Word — and just as He has given us His Son to be our Savior. He has given us all of this for one reason: that we may learn and do the art of followership.

The Reformation — A Celebration of Freedom

REFORMATION DAY
JOHN 8:31-36

Walter W. Stuenkel

It was perhaps sometime in the afternoon of October 31, 1517, that Professor Martin Luther walked down the main street of Wittenberg in Saxony, Germany, from the university to the Castle Church to post 95 statements, or theses, that he was ready to debate with any responsible individual. What prompted him to do this? A Dominican monk by the name of John Tetzel was selling indulgences — certificates of forgiveness — to people in the province of Mainz, just south of Wittenberg.

Although this indulgence traffic was not permitted in Saxony, people were traveling from Wittenberg to Mainz to purchase some of these indulgence letters. They believed what Tetzel claimed, namely, that through the purchase of such indulgences people could gain freedom from the guilt and punishment of their sin. Because they trusted in such a false freedom, the people saw no further necessity for confession. This angered Martin Luther and compelled him to testify publicly against the practice. The 95 Theses were part of his testimony. The very first of the theses emphasized that the entire life of a disciple of Jesus must be a life of repentance.

But why did Luther pick October 31 as the day to post the theses? The next day, November 1, was All Saints Day. Luther knew that a large crowd of worshipers would come to the Castle Church on that day since the duke of Saxony had an unusually large collection of relics, and these would be on display for veneration. Luther thought that as people came to view the relics, his theses would also come to the attention of scholars with whom he wanted to engage in a discussion.

His plan proved to be successful — in fact, far more successful than he had expected. People began to copy the theses, and priests and laymen debated them in lively discussions. This was the first real breakthrough in the movement to correct some of the false doctrines and practices of the church at that time. For that reason this particular day is celebrated as the birthday of the Reformation. It marks the breaking of the bonds and chains that had bound the church for hundreds of years. We want to emphasize that in our celebration today. Therefore we have chosen as our theme:

The Reformation – A Celebration of Freedom

To make this a truly meaningful celebration, we pray that on the basis of the Gospel reading we can gain a new appreciation of three significant words: *freedom, truth,* and *disciples.*

Freedom

No man has ever been more free than Jesus was while He was here on earth in human form. It is inspiringly refreshing to watch Him live and act in His freedom. The circumstances of today's Gospel are a good example. Jesus had spent the night on the Mount of Olives and in the morning had walked to Jerusalem. He sat down in the temple area and quietly taught the people. Suddenly there was a disturbance. A mob of Jewish leaders had caught a woman in the very act of adultery. They grabbed her and dragged her into the presence of Jesus. Very excitedly they asked Him, "Now in the Law Moses commanded us to stone such. What do You say about her?" (John 8:5).

Here we see the freedom of Jesus. He calmly bent down and wrote with

His finger on the ground. When they kept on pestering Him for an answer, He told them, "Let him who is without sin among you be the first to throw a stone at her" (v. 7). Thereupon the Jewish leaders, bound in the chains of their own tradition and insecurity, slowly walked away. Then Jesus showed the woman the path of freedom by telling her, "Neither do I condemn you; go, and do not sin again" (v. 11).

Thereafter Jesus was challenged once more by the Pharisees — this time about His own identity. He demonstrated His freedom again by telling them that He came from heaven. Then He warned them, "You will die in your sins unless you believe that I am He" (v. 24).

Some of the Jews who were present in the temple area heard all of this and became convinced that Jesus was really the Messiah. John speaks of them as "the Jews who had believed in Him" (v. 31). Jesus now promised them that they could be free just as He was. That is the precious gift that Jesus imparts to His own. What He is and what He accomplished in becoming our perfect Substitute, completely fulfilling all the demands of God's law in our behalf and paying the complete penalty for our sin by His suffering and death, He imparts to us. We have not earned it and do not deserve it, and yet it is ours as a free gift of His grace. That gives us freedom — freedom from the punishment and also from the power of sin, freedom to live our lives in His service — freedom to "go, and do not sin again." He guarantees His promise by stating categorically, "So if the Son makes you free, you will be free indeed" (v. 36).

How sad it is that many do not recognize the necessity of Jesus' work and sacrifice to make this marvelous gift of freedom possible for them. Even the Jews who believed in Jesus demonstrated their lack of appreciation because of their false pride in their Jewish genealogy. They answered Jesus: "We are descendants of Abraham, and have never been in bondage to anyone" (v. 33). Their childhood prayer, "Hear, O Israel: The Lord our God is one Lord" (Deut. 6:4), caused them to maintain that they were free because they were subject to no one but the God of Israel.

In sincere patience and love Jesus emphasized to them, "Truly, truly, I say to you, everyone who commits sin is a slave to sin" (John 8:34). Every person who commits any sin thereby lives in the service of sin and is spiritually bound in its chains. And these chains of sin come in all kinds of forms — lust, anger, fear, doubt, brooding in guilt, the conviction and compulsion to save oneself. Those who are controlled by these are not free. And Jesus adds, "The slave does not continue in the house forever; the son continues forever" (v. 35). It is, therefore, only through Christ and His redeeming love that we are the free sons and daughters of God with full claim to the Father's house.

Martin Luther knew all about the chains of sin and bonds of slavery from personal experience. He was a very conscientious young man, but he was bound with the terrible chains of guilt and the compulsion to save himself during all the years of his youth and early manhood. He tried all kinds of ways to break those chains — working hard at this studies, becoming a monk and a priest, begging bread for the monastery, fasting and praying — but in it all he found no freedom, not even when he earned a doctor's degree in Bible study. Not until he finally learned the real nature of righteousness — that it is not the achievement of man but the gracious declaration of God for the sake of what Jesus accomplished — did Luther find the freedom for which he yearned. Luther himself stated that before this discovery he had looked on Jesus as a taskmaster ready to strike him down in his sin, rather than as the Savior who had become man to set him free.

How were the chains broken that had held Luther as a slave? What brought about his freedom? Luther tells us himself:

> I began to understand that the "righteousness of God" is that through which the righteous lives by the gift of God, that is, through faith . . . .
> As intensely as I had formerly hated the expression "righteousness of God" I now loved and praised it as the sweetest of concepts (Ewald M. Plass, ed., *What Luther Says* [St. Louis: Concordia Publishing House, 1959], III, 1226).

Do you enjoy this freedom? Jesus offers it to you in all its abundance. What He said to those Jews who believed in Him, He says to you, "If the Son makes you free, you will be free indeed." By the inspiration of the Holy Spirit the apostle Paul gave the assurance that Martin Luther always cherished, "We hold that a man is justified by faith apart from works of law" (Rom. 3:28), and again, "In Christ God was reconciling the world to Himself, not counting their trespasses against them, and entrusting to us the message of reconciliation. . . .He made Him to be sin who knew no sin, so that in Him we might become the righteousness of God" (2 Cor. 5:19, 21).

This is the heart of the Reformation, the heart of Lutheranism — freedom from the guilt and fear and worry of sin because by faith the righteousness of God is ours through the substitutionary sacrifice of Jesus Christ. We can now say with Paul, "Therefore, since we are justified by faith, we have peace with God through our Lord Jesus Christ" (Rom. 5:1). And we can sing with Martin Luther in the first congregational hymn that he wrote:

> God said to His beloved son: "It's time to have compassion.
> Then go, bright jewel of my crown, And bring to all salvation;
> From sin and sorrow set them free; Slay bitter death for them that they
> May live with you forever" (*LW* 353:5).

Truth

How does this freedom become and remain ours? Jesus adds the concept of truth to freedom. He says, "If you continue in My Word . . . you will know the truth, and the truth will make you free" (John 8:31-32). Other words for *continue* would be *abide, remain,* or *be at home.* To be at home in the truth means to be so firmly established in faith in Jesus Christ, who calls Himself "the Truth" (John 14:6), that no matter what assaults the devil may use, we will respond by singing and saying:

> I know my faith is founded On Jesus Christ, my God and Lord;
> And this my faith confessing, Unmoved I stand on His sure Word.
> Man's reason cannot fathom The truth of God profound;
> Who trusts its subtle wisdom Relies on shifting ground.
> God's Word is all-sufficient, It makes divinely sure,
> And trusting in its wisdom, My faith shall rest secure" (*LW* 354:1).

To keep us steadfast in this truth, God has given us His Word — the Word of truth. Faithful study of the Word of God is the basis of every true reformation in the church. Consider any reformation in Biblical history — those in the days of Samuel, Jehoshaphat, Josiah, or Nehemiah, or that in the Book of Acts. Freedom for God's people through reformation always came from getting back into the Word. This Word of truth is the means of grace by which the Holy Spirit accomplishes His blessed work in people's hearts.

Luther believed that and acted accordingly. Listen to these statements from his writings:

> Whenever a man reads the Word of God, the Holy Spirit is speaking to him (Plass, III, 1461).
> The Word should be heard and read above all else. It is the vehicle of the Holy Spirit (Ibid., III, 1462).
> Such is the power of the Word if it is seriously contemplated, heard, and used that it is never without fruit. It always awakens new understanding, pleasure, and devotion and purifies the heart and thoughts (Ibid., III, 1467).
> I have never drawn a sword but have only struck by word of mouth and the Gospel. . . .I have let God carry on, and I have let the Word work (Ibid., III, 1469).

Would that the value and potential blessing of God's truth could be impressed on all of us as we celebrate the Reformation! All Scripture is inspired by God. It is alive. It has God's breath in it. Its one central purpose and objective is to give us the truth of God that is in Christ Jesus. He is the Lord and Savior and Host in this house of the Word. As we meet Him personally in the Word and recognize Him as our perfect Substitute and Savior, we will have gained the freedom He longs to give us.

It is unfortunate that many Lutherans — and many Christians generally — have not heeded the Savior's suggestion to continue in the Word. The result is that they are not really as much at home in the truth as Jesus wants them to be. In the midst of all the sinister forces of confusion and evil around us — some even under the guise of religion, which makes slaves of its constituents — we have the truth that can make and keep us free. What better way could there be for us to celebrate the Reformation than to cherish Him who is the Truth and to grasp anew the blessings that are ours in Him. In gratitude we can determine to become so at home in the Word of Truth that we will eagerly meet the challenge Jesus gives us in the Great Commission to learn and to teach all that He has commanded us.

Disciples

When we know the truth, says Jesus, we will be His disciples indeed.

Disciple—this is the third member of our trilogy. We want to add it to *freedom* and *truth*. The word *disciple* occurs more than 250 times in the New Testament, but only in the first five books — Matthew, Mark, Luke, John, and Acts.

What is so special and unique about the word *disciple*, and what can it add to our Reformation celebration? Jesus gives us an indication when He says, "A disciple is not above his teacher, but everyone when he is fully taught will be like his teacher" (Luke 6:40). We could also say it this way: A disciple is not above Jesus, but every disciple who is fully developed will be like Jesus.

What better way can we as disciples of Christ celebrate the Reformation than to let all people see and hear our gratitude and joy in being what we are? We are "little Christs," free in the forgiveness of all our sins in Jesus Christ and dedicated to the will and work of God. We live as Jesus, who said to His disciples, "My food is to do the will of Him who sent Me, and to accomplish His work" (John 4:34).

May these three words of Jesus — freedom, truth, and disciples — help to make our life a continual Reformation celebration. We are free in Christ through the truth, justified by faith, having peace with God, standing in the grace of Christ, rejoicing in the hope of the glory of God (Rom. 5:1-2), walking in the footsteps of Christ wherever they may lead (1 Peter 2:21), and saying courageously and confidently:

> Jesus, I my cross have taken, All to leave and follow Thee;
> Destitute, despised, foresaken, Thou from hence my all shalt be.
> Perish every fond ambition, All I've sought or hoped or known;
> Yet how rich is my condition! God and Heaven are still mine own.
>
> (*TLH* 423:1)

A Savior Who Hears Our Pleas

TWENTY-THIRD SUNDAY AFTER PENTECOST
MARK 10:46-52

Rudolph F. Norden

Today's Gospel reading finds Jesus on the outskirts of Jericho with His sights steadfastly fixed on Jerusalem some 15 miles away. He is accompanied by a festive company of pilgrims who not only want to celebrate the Passover with Him but also hope to proclaim Him the Messiah-King in the Holy City. Little did they realize that in a week's time the glory road would become a trail of tears.

Jesus, of course, knew what the result would be, for He had predicted: "Behold, we are going up to Jerusalem; and the Son of Man will be delivered to the chief priests and the scribes, and they will condemn Him to death and deliver Him to the Gentiles; and they will mock Him, and spit upon Him, and scourge Him, and kill Him" (Mark 10:33-34).

Jesus was going to give His life for the life of the world. He would bear the sins of the whole world. All the millions of people who constitute the human race, past, present, and future, are the objects of His redeeming love. Yet He is not too busy or too preoccupied to give attention to individuals — to Zacchaeus in Jericho and to blind Bartimaeus outside the city. He ever seeks to help and heal persons in their individual needs. His ears are open to their cries and His heart is ready to show compassion. That is true of Jesus today in His relation to us here and now.

An Appeal to Jesus for Help

St. Mark reports that when Jesus *left* Jericho, He encountered a needy man sitting by the roadside. The other gospel writers, Matthew and Luke, likewise report this (or a similar) incident. Their accounts complement, rather than contradict, one another. Luke states that Jesus gave sight to a blind beggar as He *approached* Jericho. And Matthew seems to combine the two events by saying that Jesus healed *two* blind beggars. It was very common in those days to find incapacitated persons along roads leading in and out of a city. Mark's gospel focuses our attention on Bartimaeus, whose name identifies him as the *bar*, or son, of Timaeus.

The Petitioner's Need

Bartimaeus bore a heavy affliction: He was blind and consequently poor, for sightless persons in those days were rarely given the opportunity to be trained for useful work. Blindness and poverty constitute double distress. Blindness deprived the individual of the ability to see — to see the faces of dear ones, read a book, or behold God's wonderful works in nature.

The resulting poverty was likewise a load of grief to bear. Poverty not only deprives, it also demands. A well-known painter tells in his autobiography of a time when he was a starving artist in an unheated garret studio. He said, "The trouble with poverty is that it takes up so much of your time." Bartimaeus would agree. He had no time for amusements; he had to spend all his time by the roadside begging.

God has anticipated your need and mine by giving us eyes to see and hands to earn. He has, in Martin Luther's words, "given me eyes, ears, and all my members." Along with sight God gives us many other associated gifts to fill our many needs. The whole world is opened to us through our vision.

The Statement of His Plea

When told that Jesus of Nazareth was passing by — He whose fame as a teacher and healer had spread throughout the land — Bartimaeus immediately stated his case. His brief but fervent prayer was, "Have mercy on me!" (Mark 10:47). After Jesus responded to him, he made the specific request: "Let me receive my sight" (v. 51). The two short prayers are an outright appeal to our Lord's compassion. No personal merits are pleaded; no rash promises are made; no flattery is uttered as a possible inducement for Jesus to help. He casts himself unconditionally on the Savior's loving concern.

"Have mercy on us!" is the cry of Christians as they make their needs and requests known to Jesus. These needs, if not physical as in the case of Bartimaeus, are certainly spiritual — the need for forgiveness, for strengthening of faith, for the overcoming of doubts. We do well to follow the blind man's example and introduce our plea with "Lord, have mercy on us!" From ancient times the church assembled for worship has sung the Agnus Dei: "O Christ, the Lamb of God, who takes away the sin of the world, have mercy on us."

In laying his plea before Jesus, Bartimaeus was both hindered and helped by members of the traveling group. At first some sought to deter him by "telling him to be silent" (v.48). The implication was, Do not trouble the Master with your personal problem; He has His mind on bigger things in Jerusalem. But the beggar was not discouraged. He cried out all the more when he learned that Jesus of Nazareth was so near. Then, after Jesus had summoned him, there were others present who sought to help him by saying: "Take heart; rise, He is calling you" (v. 49).

To this day some people around us discourage us from making our plea to God in prayer. They say, "God is too busy running the universe; He has no interest in little you." Or they say, "It is useless to pray. Your situation is hopeless and beyond cure. What right have you to expect a miracle?" Thank God, others will tell us, "Jesus has invited all who labor and are heavy laden to come to Him. Take heart! State your plea to Him, confident that He is your dearest Friend." Here we must ask ourselves: How is it with us? Do we hinder or help others in coming to Jesus with their prayers?

In His Compassion Jesus Hears and Helps

Our Lord dealt with Bartimaeus in a very personal way — in a relationship of One on one. Having considered the need and request of the supplicant, we turn our attention now to Jesus, the Helper and Savior.

Who Is This Jesus?

Our Lord is called "Jesus of Nazareth" (v. 47). The unimposing Galilean city is His home town; it has become a part of His name, also in the superscription of the cross.

More than being a man from Nazareth, Jesus is all the things that Bartimaeus declared Him to be in his request. The names and title given Him describe His divine person and office. He is "Jesus, Son of David" (v. 47), a confession of faith that the blind man made twice. "Son of David" points to Jesus as the promised Messiah, who is both the descendant of David according to the flesh and the very Son of God born of a virgin. Isaiah prophesied of Him, referring to His teaching and healing ministry: "The Lord has anointed Me to bring good tidings to the afflicted; He has sent Me to bind up the brokenhearted, to proclaim liberty to the captives, and the opening of the prison to those who are bound; to proclaim the year of the Lord's favor" (Is. 6:1-2).

A third name or title ascribed to Jesus by the blind man is "Master" (Mark 10:51 — *Rabbouni* in the language then spoken), the same respectful title by which Mary Magdalene addressed Christ at the empty tomb. St. John, who reports this Easter incident, explains in that connection that *Rabbouni* means "Teacher." Jesus was truly the Teacher come from God, the divine Prophet who by word and deed revealed Himself as the Son of God. He came to proclaim the Gospel of the forgiveness of sins thanks to His reconciling life, death, and resurrection.

For Jesus to be our Healer and Helper, we need to believe in Him not only as the Man from Nazareth but also as the divine Messiah, our Lord and Master, as Bartimaeus did.

Jesus' Healing Act

The first step in our Lord's healing of Bartimaeus was His refusal to take one more step on His journey to Jerusalem until He had helped this man. Having heard the cry for mercy, "Jesus stopped" (v. 49). This was necessary, Jesus thought. He could certainly have spoken a word of healing as He kept walking. But that was not Jesus' way. He wanted to give this man His full attention as He ministered to him.

In order to perform His healing ministry, Jesus said, "Call him" (v. 49). He wanted the petitioner to be brought into His presence. The man's reaction was as immediate as it was energetic: "Throwing off his mantle, he sprang up and came to Jesus" (v. 50).

Jesus' question, "What do you want Me to do for you?" (v. 51), may at first seem superfluous. But it invited him to express his desire in specific words, helped him focus on his own need and on Jesus' power to heal, and let bystanders know that the plea was not for alms but for the far more precious gift of eyesight.

The meditations and desires of our hearts, although perfectly clear to our Savior, take on an added dimension for ourselves and for others when we put them into words. It is in words that the Lord speaks to us of His mercy, and He invites us to put into words our desire for that mercy. A Bible commentator has well stated,

> It is the will of God that we should in everything make our requests known to Him in prayer and supplication; not to inform or move Him, but to qualify [make ready] ourselves for the mercy. The waterman in a boat, who with his hook takes hold of the shore, does not thereby pull the shore to the boat, but the boat to the shore. So in prayer we do not draw the mercy to ourselves, but ourselves to the mercy.

Words help us to do this.

With preliminaries out of the way, Jesus proceeds with the healing act. How does He perform it? In Matthew's account we read that He "in pity touched their eyes" (Matt. 20:34). Mark omits this outward act but quotes these words of Jesus: "Go your way; your faith has made you well" (Mark

10:52). The effect was immediate. Thanks to the power of Jesus' word, the blind man was able to see.

Jesus commends those who in faith come to Him for help and healing. The supplicant had clearly expressed his faith in Jesus as the Messiah, mighty in word and deed and given to mercy. In this faith he had addressed Him in prayer, and now the promise held true for him: "Whatever you ask in prayer, you will receive, if you have faith" (Matt. 21:22). Faith in Christ as the Savior from sin and Giver of eternal life is an unspeakably great force in our lives. It has the power to save and to make whole, not because of any virtue or vigor in itself but because it is reliance on Christ and His Word.

Jesus Christ, although no longer with us in His physical presence, is still our Healer in a fulsome sense. It is not for us to set limitations on the promise and power of our almighty, loving Savior. He can do miracles today if He so desires. He can perform wonders through surgery and the healing arts of medicine. Who is to say that the power of God was not involved when one Bob Eden, who was born blind, did recover his eyesight at age 51 through skillful surgery? Who is to say that our Lord, either directly or working through the skills of medicine and research, cannot cure the so-called "incurable" diseases? Let us not sell short the power of Jesus Christ to heal us as total persons through prayer and our faithful use of the Word and the Sacraments.

The Response to Jesus' Healing Act

There can be no repayment for any gift God has given us, but there can and should be a response on the part of the recipient. So it was on the Jericho road after blind Bartimaeus had received his sight.

Words of Thanks and Praise

The short, crisp account in Mark makes no direct mention of a verbal thanksgiving, although such a response is certainly implied. We read in a parallel account: "Immediately he received his sight and followed Him, glorifying God; and all the people, when they saw it, gave praise to God" (Luke 18:43).

We sing in a hymn: "I thank Thee that my soul is healed by what Thy lips revealed." A line in a German hymn covers all aspects of healing: "*Dein Wort macht Leib and Seel' gesund* (Your Word heals body and soul)." Our response to God's grace and every blessing is the giving of thanks with gladsome voices. The Old Testament Reading for this Sunday (Jer. 31:7-9) brings us the Lord's bidding: "Sing aloud with gladness for Jacob, and raise shouts for the chief of the nations; proclaim, give praise, and say, 'The Lord has saved His people, the remnant of Israel.'" The keynote of joyful thanksgiving is sounded also in today's Psalm (126) and in the Introit that includes the Gloria Patri: "Glory be to the Father and to the Son and to the Holy Spirit." These words express our response to God's mercies to us in Christ.

Discipleship as a Response

Of the now-sighted Bartimaeus it is said that he became a disciple. He "followed Him on the way" — the way that led from Jericho to Jerusalem. On arriving in the Holy City, he undoubtedly was a member of that happy throng that hailed Jesus as the King come to His church, the daughter of Zion.

Discipleship, of course, involves more than following a procession and waving banners. It means to assume gladly the discipline of living under Jesus, believing in Him as the Savior, serving Him, and doing His works of mercy. Jesus spoke clearly on both the joys and the sacrifices involved in true discipleship. When He accepted someone for discipleship or said directly, "Follow Me," He let it be known that coming after Him was not a primrose path but often a hard road. He said: "If any man would come after Me, let him deny himself and take up his cross and follow Me" (Mark 8:34).

Was Bartimaeus equal to this challenge? We can be sure that he was — that he understood discipleship to be more than joining a festival-bound company of pilgrims. It meant entering the Master's training school and service as a disciple ready and willing to walk in His footsteps.

We, too, have become Christ's disciples. He has called us by the Gospel and filled us with His Spirit. Blessed with so many divine gifts, "sight, riches, healing of the mind," we are willing to follow Him. Christ first loved us; in response we love Him and serve Him as His disciples. This is a Christianity of the road, not of the balcony or easy chair. Drawn by the love of the Savior, spectators become disciples.

The last words written by Martin Luther in his final illness were: "We are beggars, this is true." What is more, we were by nature "wretched, pitiable, poor, blind, and naked" (Rev. 3:17). But God had mercy on us, ordained His Son to save us, and through the Gospel continues to send the Holy Spirit to build our faith in Him. In Jesus Christ we have a Savior who hears our pleas for mercy and helps us. To Him be all glory and honor!

Buildings that Last

THIRD-LAST SUNDAY IN THE CHURCH YEAR
MARK 13:1-13

Waldemar F. Hischke

When we put up some kind of building, we want that building to last. We hope it will stand and be useful for many years to come. Whether that building is a new home, a school for our children, or a church building like the one we are worshiping in, we certainly don't want it to be falling apart and coming down after only a few years.

In the Gospel this morning, Jesus talks about a building that is not going to last. He foretells that the temple in Jerusalem is going to be utterly destroyed. That brings to mind the various "buildings" that we work on in our lives. We have the "building" of our job. We work at "building" our children into useful and maturing Christians. Our whole life may be compared to the constructing of a building. The question is: Are these various buildings in our lives going to last? Or are we spending our time and energy on something that's going to come crashing down, almost before it's completed? Today's topic is

Buildings That Last

Some Buildings Don't Last

The temple church in Jerusalem at the time of our story was a very impressive building. It was constructed largely of white marble. Some tremendously huge blocks of stone had been used in its construction. A lot of money had been poured into that building, and the people were justifiably proud of their church. It was the kind of place where you would certainly take visitors from out of town when you were showing them the sights. That was where Jesus and His disciples worshiped when they were in Jerusalem.

On this occasion, "As He [Jesus] came out of the temple, one of His disciples said to Him, 'Look, Teacher, what wonderful stones and what wonderful buildings!'" (Mark 13:1). The disciples had been there many times before, but the great temple complex always impressed them whenever they saw it.

Now listen to the Lord's reply. What He says must have been a shock to His disciples. "Do you see all these great buildings? There will not be left here one stone upon another, that will not be thrown down" (v. 2). That's what happened not many years later, after Jesus had returned to heaven. The Roman armies came and besieged Jerusalem, destroying and killing the people. And because the great temple was a symbol of national unity, the Romans purposely burned it down. They even methodically wrecked the ruins until there was not one stone left on another, just as Jesus had predicted.

Jesus was not telling His disciples that the temple church was no good. Jesus Himself worshiped there. Nor was He saying that it's wrong to put a lot of money into a church building in order to make it look impressive. What the Lord *was* telling them was that we should not put too much importance on things that are only temporary.

Later in this same teaching session with the disciples Jesus predicts that the temple is not the only thing that is going to be destroyed. The whole world, He says, is one day going to be brought to an end. Therefore, the person who builds his life only around earthly things is one day going to find out that it has all been for nothing. He has wasted his whole life.

And how many people there are like that — including, in some ways, you and me! Perhaps you remember John DeLorean. He was building very expensive sports cars in Northern Ireland. Then, because he needed money to keep his plant operating, he allegedly got involved in illegal drugs. He was arrested. His life's work has come crashing down around him. What a waste!

But even if you build your life around something altogether within the law, unless what you do somehow reaches beyond the limits of what is earthly, the Lord says, all that you have built is eventually going to be destroyed. Like the temple in Jerusalem, it may be a nice thing for a time, but it is just not going to last.

Life in Jesus Is a Building That Lasts

If we want to build something that lasts, it has to be connected in some way with Jesus Christ. Remember what Jesus told the people of His day? "Destroy this temple," referring to Himself "and in three days I will raise it up" (John 2:19). Men might kill Jesus, and they did by crucifying Him. But He did not remain in the grave. His tomb was empty again on the third day.

Through His death and resurrection Christ was building the Kingdom, which will go on forever. He is the living King of people — forgiven and saved people — who are going on to heaven after they die. His Kingdom, according to today's Epistle, "cannot be shaken" (Heb. 12:28). It will still be there after this world is gone. We are part of this everlasting Kingdom through faith in Jesus Christ as our Savior. So if we want to build something in our lives that will last, what we build must be founded on Christ. It must be tied together in some way with the Lord.

But what does this mean in its principal application? Let's think of some specific examples of buildings that last. Take parents who are raising a child, for example. The raising of that child is one of the "buildings" on which they are working. As a parent, naturally you are going to be concerned about your child's health and physical welfare. Naturally you will want to provide your child with things — perhaps many more things than you had when you were young. So far, however, what you are building in your child is still missing what endures.

If a child grows up to be rich and famous, it won't mean a thing — it's a building that will not last — unless you bring Christ into the picture. There is nothing more important that you can do for your child than to lead him or her to know Jesus Christ. To provide the opportunity for your child to know Him and trust in Him with personal faith is first and foremost. Then it is also important to build Christian character into your child and to instill Christian values and attitudes. Even though your child should remain dirt poor all through life, never own a home, and drive only an old wreck of a car, nevertheless, you have built something that lasts if your offspring lives his or her life for and with the Lord. That is a building that will last eternally.

But think also of your own life. The words of the Lord in our text are a precise description of the lives of so many people: "There will not be left here one stone upon another, that will not be thrown down." People often work so hard at piling up their stones, working at various goals in their lives. They put so much of their time into it and spend so much energy on it. And what they are building may look ever so nice, but unless what they are building is tied together with Jesus Christ that building will eventually fall into ruins at the end of time. Not one stone will be left on another.

Not everyone, of course, is engaged in full-time church work. Yet if you can somehow reflect Christ to the people around you at your job — whether it is as a ditchdigger or as an executive — then you are building for eternity. Not everyone has the opportunity to meet other people day in and day out. And you don't particularly have to. If you simply make it your goal to live for Jesus in everything you do — in faith accepting the salvation He earned for you and following His will as outlined in His Word — then as you keep putting one stone on another in your life, they *are* going to stay in place. They are going to be cemented together with your love for Christ that results from His unfailing love for you. And that's also a building that is going to last.

Some of you may remember when this building in which we are worshiping was built. You may have been here for the dedication. It's a good, solid building. It should last for many years to come. But eventually this building will also come down. Let what you are building with your life be a building that lasts. Build with Jesus. Build on Him. Build around Him as your Savior and Lord, and you will be building for eternity.

Not Superman, but Jesus

SECOND-LAST SUNDAY IN THE CHURCH YEAR
MARK 13:24-31

Oscar A. Gerken

"Look! Up in the sky! It's a bird! It's a plane! It's Superman! Faster than a speeding bullet, more powerful than a locomotive, able to leap tall buildings in a single bound . . ." You may be smiling as you hear these words, for we are all familiar with them as the introduction of a radio/television program about the heroic exploits of a mild-mannered newspaper reporter who quickly changes into the man who can perform courageous rescues of people in distress.

As the current church year draws to a close, today's Gospel focuses our attention on the coming of one who is far greater than Superman. "Look! Up in the sky! It's not Superman, but Jesus Christ Himself!"

Jesus Describes His Second Coming

The initial words of today's Gospel are Jesus' description of His

second coming. He begins by saying, "In those days, after that tribulation..."
(Mark 13:24). "That tribulation" refers to the troublesome events that will
precede the final days. Our Lord has been speaking at great length with His
disciples about the tribulation that would serve as a sign of His return, and
now He describes in detail the events that will take place at His second
coming.

"In those days," says Jesus, "the sun will be darkened, and the moon
will not give its light, and the stars will be falling from heaven, and the
powers in the heavens will be shaken" (vv. 24-25). The word *shaken* really
means "dislocated." The sainted Dr. R. C. H. Lenski wrote about these
words of Jesus:

> All that holds the heavenly bodies in their orbits and enables sun, moon,
> and stars to light the earth, shall give way. Thus the sun's light will be
> extinguished, the moon's radiance will disappear in the same instant, and
> the stars will come tumbling from their places. Let no man try to imagine
> this cataclysm! It is utterly beyond human conception" (R. C. H. Lenski,
> *The Interpretation of St. Mark's and St. Luke's Gospels* [Columbus, OH:
> Lutheran Book Concern, 1934], p. 361).

To say that the events accompanying Christ's return are "utterly
beyond human conception" is really an understatement. According to
divine witness, every heavenly body — sun, moon, and stars — will be dislocated, and nothing will function properly. Everything will go to pieces.
The stage is set for Our Lord's dramatic arrival.

"And then they will see the Son of Man coming in clouds with great
power and glory" (Mark 13:26). The apostle John, in his vision of the
future, describes Christ's return in this way: "Behold, He is coming with
the clouds, and every eye will see Him" (Rev. 1:7). The psalmist may well
have been looking ahead to this event when he referred to the clouds as
God's "chariot" (Ps. 104:3).

The return of Jesus will be "with great power and glory." What a contrast between His first and second comings! He who came quietly and
humbly — born in a smelly stable, despised and rejected by those who
should have welcomed their Savior — will come with glory and majesty
and might to fulfill the promises of His eternal Kingdom of Glory.

The importance of this awesome event for you and for me is found in
Jesus' declaration that "He will send out the angels, and gather His elect
from the four winds, from the ends of the earth to the ends of heaven"
(v. 27). *We* are "His elect!" We are the ones God has chosen to be His
children in what has been described as "the most massive adoption proceeding in all history." St. Paul speaks of this adoption proceeding in this
way: "When the time had fully come, God sent forth His Son, born of
woman, born under the Law, to redeem those who were under the Law, so
that we might receive adoption as sons" (Gal. 4:4-5).

Actually, it all started in eternity, even before God created the world.
At the beginning of his letter to the Ephesian Christians, the apostle Paul
points out that God chose us in Christ "before the foundation of the world"

(Eph. 1:4). The key to this election proceeding is that we have been chosen "in Christ." We are God's elect, His adopted sons and daughters, *not* because of anything we have done, but solely because of the cleansing from sin that we receive *in Jesus Christ*, the Lamb of God who takes away our sin.

Remember when you were a child, and sides were being chosen for a ball game, and you knew you wouldn't be chosen because your athletic ability was so limited? Then the captain of one team chose you anyway because he liked you! Our election by God is something like that. As St. Paul puts it, "While we were yet sinners, Christ died for us" (Rom. 5:8). By the grace of God we who trust in Jesus as our Savior are the children of God, who will be gathered together by His holy angels when He comes in glory and majesty.

Jesus Tells Us to Be Prepared
for His Second Coming

In the second half of today's Gospel, Christ tells us why He alerts us to His second coming — so that we might be prepared for it. To emphasize the importance of being prepared, He uses an illustration from nature: "From the fig tree learn its lesson: as soon as its branch becomes tender and puts forth its leaves, you know that summer is near. So also, when you see these things taking place, you know that He is near. at the very gates" (Mark 13:28-29).

A few weeks ago, I looked at the elm tree in my back yard and noticed that the leaves were beginning to turn various bright colors. One by one, the leaves began to fall off the tree. Now the branches are completely bare, but in a few months there will be buds and leaves on that elm tree again, and the tree will again provide shade and beauty for our enjoyment. That's the normal progression in nature.

It strikes me as significant that Jesus cites an example from nature that is neither frightening nor to be dreaded. Rather, we welcome the promise of a tree in full foliage, and Jesus wants us to view His coming in the same manner — as something promised rather than threatened. We normally speak of the Lord's return to judge the world as a day of doom, and many of our hymns about Judgment Day reflect this type of thinking. While it is true that unbelievers have every reason to fear Christ's return to judge, we who know Jesus as our Savior and count on His payment for sin as our way into heaven do not have to be any more afraid of His second coming than a child needs to be afraid of the coming of Christmas.

Jesus is speaking in today's Gospel to His people — to all who believe in Him for forgiveness and life — not to unbelievers. Therefore, He tells us of the good thing that will happen to us, the elect of God. We will, says Jesus, be gathered by the angels from all parts of heaven and earth. The inclusiveness of this terminology is reassuring for us as we try to cope with the problems of life. The only requirement for inclusion in this never-ending celebration that begins when Jesus comes again is that we look to

Him as the Rescuer who has already made us eligible for eternal life by His death and resurrection.

Not all people feel this way, and Jesus takes note of the situation: "Truly, I say to you, this generation will not pass away before all these things take place" (v. 30). "This generation" refers to all who are opposed to God, for the term *generation* is often used in the Scriptures to refer to the evil and ungodly (cf. Deut. 32:5, 20; Matt. 12:39, 45; Luke 9:41; Acts 2:40). To Andrew and Peter and Nathanael and the rest of the Twelve — and also to us believers of the 20th century — our loving Lord is saying, "There will always be evil people who oppose Me, and they will not be subdued or eliminated until the day when I return, as I have said I would."

Jesus continues with a promise: "Heaven and earth will pass away, but My words will not pass away" (Mark 13:31). Similar language is used by Peter in writing about that day: "The day of the Lord will come like a thief, and then the heavens will pass away with a loud noise, and the elements will be dissolved with fire, and the earth and the works that are upon it will be burned up" (2 Peter 3:10). And John tells us in his apocalyptic letter, "I saw a new heaven and a new earth, for the first heaven and the first earth had passed away, and the sea was no more" (Rev. 21:1).

I envy those flamboyant preachers who can tell us with certainty exactly what is going to happen to this present creation, for I must confess that I don't know whether God will cause the heavens to "pass away" by destroying and replacing this present universe or by cleansing and transforming everything He has created. Frankly, I don't think it makes that much difference, and Jesus therefore has not revealed all the details to us. What is important is the comforting truth that we can look forward to a life of perfect bliss — a life that will never end, that will be filled with supreme happiness — when Jesus comes again.

About 15 years ago I visited a hospitalized member of my congregation who was dying of cancer. Although the doctor hadn't told him that his illness was terminal, Gus seemed to sense that it was. Gus Birk was a wealthy man, who was regarded as one of the leading citizens of our community, but he was a humble man. He didn't abuse his power and prestige. He attended Bible class and worship services regularly and was a faithful worker in the congregational program.

We had a good relationship with each other, and therefore it didn't surprise me when Gus looked up at me from his hospital bed and said with characteristic bluntness, "Pastor, I'm not going to make it, am I?" He knew I would tell him the truth. I hesitated briefly before answering, "Well, Gus, the answer is both yes and no. No, you probably won't leave this hospital alive, but yes, you'll make it to heaven, and that's what really counts. You'll probably be with the Lord very soon, and that's your hope and joy." I'll never forget the grin on Gus Birk's face as he responded, "Pastor, I know that, but thank you for telling me again."

Gus Birk could smile even though he knew that he would die soon because he believed the words of Jesus. These words, which, according to

Jesus' promise, "will not pass away," center around the wonderful promise that He is the Way by which we can come to the Father (John 14:6), that those who believe in Him will never die (John 11:26), that all who believe in Him will not perish, but enjoy everlasting life (John 3:16). These are the words that Jesus wants us to think about and remember in these closing days of the church year.

I don't know about you, but I can hardly wait to hear someone say, "Look! Up in the sky! It's Jesus!"

"Amen! Come, Lord Jesus!" (Rev. 22:20).

What Kind of a Kingdom Does Jesus Have?

LAST SUNDAY IN THE CHURCH YEAR
SUNDAY OF THE FULFILLMENT
JOHN 18:33-37

Gerhard Aho

He certainly didn't look like a king. He had no royal garb, no army, no trappings of worldly authority. Yet His enemies said that He had called Himself "the King of the Jews." Now Pilate was curious. "Are you the King of the Jews?" he asked (John 18:33). Pilate couldn't imagine how this helpless-looking man could possibly be a threat to the only kingly power that mattered in the world of that time, the power of Caesar in Rome.

Jesus did not deny that He was a king. He admitted it. But where was His kingdom? When we pray in the Lord's Prayer, "For Thine is the Kingdom, and the power, and the glory, forever and ever," we're saying that God the Father has a kingdom. Jesus is saying that He too has a kingdom, the same one God the Father has.

In the Old Testament Reading for today, Daniel refers to Jesus as "one like a Son of Man," and goes on to say that "to Him was given dominion and glory and kingdom" (Dan. 7:13-14). The apostle John in the Epistle also implies that Jesus has a kingdom when he designates Christ as "the ruler of kings on earth" (Rev. 1:5).

What Kind of a Kingdom Does Jesus Have?

A Kingdom Not of This World

Jesus said to Pilate: "My kingship is not of this world" (John 18:36). The answer puzzled the Roman governor, who couldn't understand how a kingdom could be anything but "of this world." The kingdom Pilate knew best, the Roman empire, had power to collect taxes and build roads and put down rebellions and wage wars. A kingdom worth talking about had to have that kind of power.

We tend to think the same way. We look down on governments that seem unable to protect their citizens from violence to persons or property, and we respect governments that make it possible for people to live in peace and security. We expect a kingdom or government worthy of the name to be stable and strong enough to maintain order, to defend itself against enemies, and to provide conditions in which people can feel reasonably secure. In short, we expect a kingdom to have authority and to exercise it.

That's why Jesus' reference to a kingship not of this world can sound as strange to us as it did to Pilate. Shouldn't Jesus' kingdom possess at least some of the qualities we associate with a kingdom? At the very least, shouldn't this kingdom afford protection to its citizens?

When we hear of Christians being persecuted, harassed, and imprisoned on account of their faith, we may wonder if Christ's kingdom is anything more thatn a theological concept or a heavenly hope. Why doesn't Jesus deliver His followers? Why doesn't He close the lions' mouths?

We're not being persecuted by governmental authorities. Yet haven't we been hurt by gossip, tormented by failure, or disappointed in a son or a daughter? Don't we as citizens of Christ's kingdom have the right to expect protection from such suffering? Or is this kingdom a fantasy, after all?

The kingdom of which Christ is King simply will not conform to our earthly expectations. Jesus never promised that we will escape either harassment by unbelievers or the trouble that inevitably accompanies earthly existence. On the contrary, He tells us through His apostle Peter: "Do not be surprised at the fiery ordeal which comes upon you . . . as though something strange were happening to you" (1 Peter 4:12). And Paul, writing to the Philippians, makes clear that it will be our privilege to suffer: "It has been granted to you that for the sake of Christ you should not only believe in Him but also suffer for His sake" (Phil. 1:29). We can count on neither physical weapons nor a heavenly police force to deliver us from suffering. Christ didn't say He would send armed servants to fight for us . He said, "My kingship is not of this world."

That doesn't mean Christ's kingdom is only a figment of the imagination. The Kingdom is real, and it's here. Jesus said: "The kingdom of God is in the midst of you" (Luke 17:21). Christ's kingdom is not coextensive with national boundaries or particular forms of government. It's not found just in the United States or England or Nigeria, nor is it restricted to nations that have a democratic form of government. The Kingdom is to be found wherever there are men and women and children who acknowledge Jesus Christ as their Savior and Lord. In that sense it's a worldwide kingdom.

It's also a kingdom with a special kind of power. When Pilate gave permission for Jesus to be executed outside Jerusalem for disturbing the peace, all standards of worldly power dictated that the event should have been forgotten. Yet in a few years His story and His kingdom spread throughout the Mediterranean world. In the 2,000 years since, His kingdom has been the most revolutionary force the world has known. And so it is still today, all the armaments of earthly kingdoms notwithstanding.

Earthly kingdoms are limited as to how much of us they can control. They may tax our purses, manage our time, and dictate our actions, but they cannot command our wills. They may discipline us outwardlhy, but they cannot control us inwardly. We can still think what we want to think and believe what we want to believe. But Jesus will have none of that. We who live under Him know that it's precisely at the center of our selves that He desired to rule.

Totalitarianism has made us wary of surrendering our autonomy to any one person. But we never have to be fearful about letting Jesus rule. He doesn't command; He invites us to place our hearts and minds and wills at His disposal. His claim to rulership is not naked power but gracious love. It is by the power of His love that He wishes to be the King of our life.

It's hard to believe that we are important in a world in which economic and political power structures so dominate people's lives. In and of ourselves, quite apart from any wealth, power, skill, or intelligence we may have, are we of any value?

To Jesus, we have infinite worth. He loved us all the way to the cross. In our baptism His love has worked to bring us into His kingdom. The kingdoms and powers of this world may not think that we have much value, but Christ does. He is the King who came down into the created world — down to us — and rose up again in His resurrection, pulling us up with Him.

And He is not like this world's rulers, who hide away in well-protected palaces or government offices. He is at our side, ready to hear us and to help us always.

The story is told of a young king who made a tour through his kingdom. In one of the villages he saw a beautiful peasant girl. Back in the palace he could not forget her. He had fallen in love with her. What should he do — go back to the village and ask her to be his wife, to become the queen? He didn't dare do that. He thought to himself, "She'll be shocked, overcome with awe, perhaps fear." But he didn't want her awe or fear. He wanted her love. So he disguised himself, returned as a peasant, and won her love. Only then did he tell her that he was king.

Jesus came as one of us — and won our love. He's not only our Ruler but our Friend. How different Christ's rule is from that of worldly political leaders! His kingdom truly is not of this world.

A Kingdom of Truth

Such a kingdom — in but not of the world — made no sense to Pilate. In a patronizing, mocking tone he asked, "So You are a King?" Jesus responded with another statement that Pilate was just as incapable of grasping. "For this I was born, and for this I have come into the world, to bear witness to the truth" (John 18:37). Jesus' words provide additional insight into the kind of kingdom He has.

One of the refreshing qualities of Christ's kingdom is that it deals with truth. Christ never spoke or acted untruthfully. The words He spoke are absolutely and eternally true, and His deeds always supported His words. That is why He can promise: "If you continue in My Word... you will know the truth" (John 8:31-32).

What is this truth? It is, first of all, the truth about ourselves. To be truthful with regard to ourselves is often difficult. We don't always see ourselves as other see us. It takes love and tact for another person to point out our faults in a way that does not hurt or anger us.

It's not easy to face the truth about ourselves, even when Jesus speaks it. He tells us bluntly: "From within, out of the heart of man, come evil thoughts, fornication, theft, murder, adultery, coveting, wickedness, deceit, licentiousness, envy, slander, pride, foolishness" (Mark 7:21-22). It's hard to face up to the truth that our hearts are sinful and desperately wicked. In His parables of the lost sheep and the prodigal son Jesus reminds us of our sin — that we have wandered away from God and have been indifferent to Him.

We may rationalize our sin and make excuses for it by saying, "I'm no worse than anyone else," or "I'm not responsible for something I can't help doing." But Jesus doesn't let us off the hook so easily. He keeps boring in with the truth. He wants us to see that we deserve not only the suffering and trouble we experience in this life but also eternal punishment. He wants to convince us that in each of us there is evil so pervasive and destructive and condemning that its therapy required nothing less than His death on a cross.

But this is also the truth: Jesus died for us. Having given us the painful truth about ourselves, Jesus then consoles us with the truth that He suffered the punishment of sin for us. Listen to the words of Christ's apostles: "He Himself bore our sins in His body on the tree" (1 Peter 2:24). "There is therefore now no condemnation for those who are in Christ Jesus" (Rom. 8:1). This is amazing truth. Christ is saying that God has forgiven us.

This forgiveness is complete. God doesn't forgive only some sins. He doesn't wipe out only a few debts from our debit book and leave others. He destroys the entire book. When Christ died, God set aside "the bond which stood against us with its legal demands... nailing it to the cross" (Col. 2:14). It's impossible that some sins would yet be unforgiven. Either all are forgiven or none.

To use another image, we who believe in Christ are completely cleansed. A cloth is either clean or it is soiled. If it has only one dirt spot, it is not clean. In cleanliness there are no degrees. Neither is there in forgiveness. We, the members of Christ's kingdom, are clean, white as snow.

God's forgiveness is complete also in the sense that in God's heart there is no longer any wrath toward us. He forgives "Generously and without reproaching" (James 1:5). Not one speck of anger does He have toward us on account of our sins. He regards us with complete approval. We can live under the light of His love.

And God forgives freely, not grudgingly. He doesn't say to us: "Well, then, I suppose I'll have to forgive you on account of Christ's death. But it surely was shameful that you sinned. You ought not to have done that." No! God's heart burns with a desire to forgive. The yearning father embraces and kisses His prodigal son.

It isn't harder for God to forgive some sins than others, nor is He less willing to forgive some sinners than others. He willingly receives every sinner—even you and me! All kinds of sins and all kinds of sinners He enfolds in His forgiving arms.

We who believe this Gospel truth have God as our Father and Christ as our King. Think of what that means. No threat by any worldly kingdom, no power on earth—or above it or beneath it—nothing in life or in death can now defeat or destroy us. When our conscience accuses us, this Kingdom truth encourages: "Take heart . . . your sins are forgiven" (Matt. 9:2). When our way turns dark and hope grows dim, this Kingdom truth supports: "My power is made perfect in weakness" (2 Cor. 12:9). When we are depressed and fearful, this Kingdom truth calms us: "Peace I leave with you; My peace I give to you; not as the world gives to I give to you" (John 14:27). There are no lies or half-truths here. Christ's kingdom is a kingdom of truth.

No, Christ didn't look like a King when He stood before Pilate. How could He, with a kingdom so unworldly in its power and so truthful in its message? Yet we know Him to be a King, for He lives within us and His Word of truth sustains us.

One day we shall actually see Him as the "Ruler of kings on earth." To us, to Pilate, and to all who have lived or ever will live in this world He will really look like a King, for on that last great day He will appear with a heavenly radiance and a divine glory. Then we shall see that His is indeed an everlasting dominion and that His kingdom shall not be destroyed.

INDEX OF SCRIPTURE TEXTS